Communication as Action

PHILLIP K. TOMPKINS, *Purdue University*

Communication as Action

An Introduction to Rhetoric and Communication

Wadsworth Publishing Company
Belmont, California
A Division of Wadsworth, Inc.

Communications Editor: Rebecca Hayden
Production Editor: Sally Schuman
Designer: Adriane Bosworth
Copy Editor: Jonas Weisel
Interior Illustrations: Inno Graphics
Chapter Opening Illustrations: D. J. Simison/Dow, Clement & Simison
Cover: D. J. Simison/Dow, Clement & Simison
Photo Research: Lindsay Kefauver

Printed in the United States of America
2 3 4 5 6 7 8 9 10 — 87

ISBN 0-534-01157-8

Library of Congress Cataloging in Publication Data

Tompkins, Phillip K.
  Communication as action.

  Includes bibliographies and index.
  1. Communication.   2. Rhetoric.   I. Title.
P90.T64   001.51   82-2649
ISBN 0-534-01157-8   AACR2

In memory of
J. Richard McNally
and H. Bruce Kendall,
gentlemen, scholars,
colleagues, friends

P R E F A C E

Although I have read many prefaces, I had to go back to the dictionary to find out what the word means. "A saying beforehand," "a prayer of thanksgiving," "a preliminary statement by the author or editor of a book, setting forth its purposes and scope, expressing acknowledgment of assistance from others, etc." are several of the definitions I found in the dictionary.

For the reader, a *pre-face* could be the small part of the book to be read before facing the rest of it. Let me tell you, the reader, what you face in the rest of this book. Perhaps the best way of beginning is to relate how the book came into existence.

The book grew out of lectures I gave in a course, "RCO 100," at the State University of New York at Albany. The course was offered for freshmen (although many sophomores, juniors, and seniors elected it) and had two objectives: first, to give students an introduction to rhetoric and communication in all its scenes or settings; second, to prepare students for applied courses in public speaking and interpersonal and group communication, as well as for advanced courses in rhetorical and communication theory. The course enrolled between 200 and 500 students per semester for nearly ten years.

The organization of the book is as follows. There are three main parts, each of which contains three chapters. Part One is called Foundations of Rhetoric and Communication. Chapter 1 sets the stage by examining the word *human*, the fundamental element in all the succeeding observations. This particular definition was inspired by Kenneth Burke. The reader is challenged to accept it, reject it, or modify it; in any case he or she should hold some definition before trying to understand human communication. Chapters 2 and 3, which give an account of the history of rhetoric and define basic terms, offer additional foundation for our study. Part Two moves on to the Micro-Communication Settings of dyad, triad, and small groups. In chapter 4 we look at approaches to dyadic, or two-person, communication; these ideas are enlarged in chapters 5 and 6 with discussions of three-person and group communication. Part Three makes the transition to Macro-Communication Settings. Chapter 7 explores the interactions within and between organizations, those yet broader and more structured groups. This chapter includes two case studies from my own research: Kent State University and NASA's Marshall Space Flight Center. From such management and hierarchy we turn, in chapter 8, to the communication of social movements, groups formed to seek reform or revolution. Finally, chapter 9 examines that realm engendered in our modern world — mass communication.

Enough of summary. How should the book be read? It can be read as the text in an introductory course on rhetoric and communication. Because of the practical instruction in these chapters and the exercises at the end of all the chapters, the book can also be used for the same kind of course in which students meet periodically in smaller groups for graded practice in public speaking or interpersonal and group communication. Moreover, it can be used as a text for courses in any communication area, including organizational communication, particularly when the instructor wishes the student to see the ramifications of human communication on both smaller and larger structures.

This book has been structured so that each chapter is tied to each other in numerous ways by a number of basic concepts. Although the subjects of some of the chapters have previously been developed in isolation, I have sought to relate them to each other in conceptual ways. In that connection I acknowledge with humility that this book owes much to Kenneth Burke and Talcott Parsons, two of the truly great thinkers of the twentieth century (as well as to thinkers of earlier ages such as Aristotle and Cicero).

I wish to thank Jesse G. Delia, Roger L. Garrett, Gerry Philipsen, Barbara G. Rosenthal, and Kenneth Williams for reviewing the manuscript of this book and providing numerous valuable suggestions.

At last, my secular "prayer of thanksgiving" to Elaine V. B. Tompkins, who suggested much, typed all, and without whom there would be no examples about Emily.

Phillip K. Tompkins

BRIEF CONTENTS

C O N T E N T S

Communication as Action

One

Foundations of Rhetoric and Communication

CHAPTER

1

A Definition of Human

Good Lord, what is man!

Sketch: inscribed to C. J. Fox
Robert Burns

*Man is an embodied paradox, a
bundle of contradictions.*

Lacon
Charles Caleb Colton

Why begin a book about communication with a definition of the word *human*? The answer is this: Logically speaking, a definition of what constitutes a human should be prior to observations about human behavior. Because we are humans, we generally speak of communication with an implicit definition of the word *human*. This chapter proposes to make such a definition explicit. That way you and I can communicate about communication with a minimum of hidden assumptions. An adequate definition should give order to the observations we make about human communication.

Burke's Human

The following definition comes from one of the original thinkers of the twentieth century, Kenneth Burke. Burke is a rhetorical theorist, a literary and social critic, a novelist, and a poet. He offered this definition "in the hope of either persuading the reader that it fits the bill, or of prompting him [or her] to decide what should be added, or subtracted, or in some way modified."[1] That is my hope also.

Let me quote the entire definition and then discuss it line by line.

[Hu]man is
the symbol-using (symbol-making, symbol-misusing)
    animal
inventor of the negative (or moralized by the negative)
separated from his [or her] natural condition by instruments
    of his [or her] own making
goaded by the spirit of hierarchy (or moved by the sense of
    order)
and rotten with perfection.[2]

The Symbol-Using Animal

[Hu]man is the symbol-using (symbol-making,
symbol-misusing) animal

This opening phrase of Burke's definition should contain no surprises. On second thought, perhaps there may be surprise, if not outright disagreement. Certain scientists have recently claimed that chimpanzees are capable of learning human languages. However, let's postpone our discussion of the chimps for the moment.

Burke recalls watching a wren that had succeeded in getting a brood of babies out of the nest — except for one stubborn and backward baby wren that refused to leave and continued to demand that food be brought to it.[3] Then came a moment of genius. A parent approached the nest with a morsel of food; instead of putting the food in the baby's mouth, the parent wren kept some distance between them. As the fledgling in the nest kept stretching its neck to reach the food, the parent wren suddenly clamped its beak shut on the youngster's lower mandible and jerked the baby out of the nest.

This incident has at least two implications. The first is that without language, or a symbol system, the parent wren cannot communicate its act of genius to other worried bird parents. Among wrens there is no Dr. Spock. With the use of symbols, Burke says, the wren might well have written a thesis on "The Use of the Principle of Leverage as an Improved Method for Unnesting Birds or Debirding a Nest." In fact, the brilliant bird observed by Burke probably never remembered the technique; without symbols by which to conceptualize, capture, and "store" the incident in its memory, this instance no doubt remained a fortunate accident.

The second implication is a happier observation from the wren's perspective. Without the human aptitude for symbol using and symbol making, the wrens are spared the effect of symbol misusing. Wrens have not been known to engage in demagoguery, that is, the practice of exploiting common prejudices and false claims. Nor can their expectations be built up to the point where they will inevitably be let down. I am thinking about such "human" acts as campaign promises, which will not be kept, and television commercials, which promise a life with pleasure and without pain.

Burke fears that he cannot emphasize enough the sheer symbolicity of modern life. My grandparents and great grandparents spent much more of their time than I have in manipulating *things* (plows, scythes, rakes, tools, and the like). Instead, I manipulate symbols (as, for example, when I write this book and deliver lectures).

Here's another personal example. At fifteen months my daughter Emily was already in the process of learning about the world. She was learning animals, from aardvark to zebra, in an alphabet book. Moreover, she was learning to connect the animals' names — not with flesh and blood and fur and feathers — but with pictorial symbols of them. She was, and will continue to be, in the process of learning symbolizing.

Most of our learning takes place in this way; we approach the study of the continents and oceans, chemical compounds, or the history of Europe via human-made names. The learning of the academic disciplines, at least the crucial first step, is the learning of the language of each discipline. The languages of chemistry, physics, and sociology are designed to focus on certain details in reality and ignore the rest. Burke calls this function of language the "terministic screen."

For example, suppose we assemble an economist, a psychologist, and a sociologist in the college cafeteria and ask each to give explanations of food choices made by a customer. Suppose further that the customer we observe happens to select custard rather than either cake or pie. The economist might explain that, because custard is less "labor intensive" and therefore cheaper than the other desserts, it was the only dessert the customer could afford. The psychologist might explain the choice by means of the customer's history; for instance, he or she might say that the customer's "past reinforcement schedule" provides the answer. The sociologist might explain the choice by pointing to the "ethno-social background" of the customer and showing how different classes of people favor different desserts. Affected by the terms and focus of his or her discipline, each of the specialists might describe the situation in different, even contradictory, ways. Thus, the terministic screen of vocabulary causes each to focus on elements and interpretations of the situation to the exclusion of others.

Figure 1-1 In scientific studies some chimpanzees, such as Lana shown here at the Yerkes Primate Center, have been taught to manipulate a computer to convey short sentences. Doubt remains, though, as to the extent of their ability to learn human language and to acquire humankind's symbol-using capabilities. (United Press International)

"Language referring to the realm of the nonverbal," says Burke, "is necessarily talk about things in terms of what they are not—and in this sense we start out beset by a paradox."[4] A school of thought called general semantics makes this point over and over again: A word is *not* the thing it represents.

What about those chimpanzees that seem to be acquiring human languages? Perhaps they can learn by rote the connection between words and things; perhaps they can even learn from their trainers crude groupings of words that some observers will accept as primitive sentences. For instance, the chimpanzee in Figure 1–1 has learned to group words using a simple computer. Far more difficult to imagine is these same animals producing grammars, logics, and rhetorics. That chimpanzees will ever develop languages *about* language—which is what grammars, logics, and rhetorics are—seems inconceivable to me.

Burke notes parenthetically that humans are also symbol-misusing animals. Burke is well known in Germany as well as in this country for his analysis of the symbolism of Hitler and the Nazis. By analyzing Hitler's book, *Mein Kampf*, Burke was able to be prophetic about its implications before the full facts of the holocaust were known. His analysis was based on a close reading of Hitler's misuse of symbols and Hitler's demagogic race hatred.[5]

Burke, however, means more than demogoguery with his phrase about misusing. He includes "psychogenic illnesses" under this heading because they have symbolic origins. The thought of eating human flesh is loathsome and nauseating to me and probably to you, but cannibals suffer no such "illnesses." Our symbol-using and misusing characteristic also makes us capable of deceiving others and even ourselves. Other definitions of human, for example, deceive us by flattery—as in "Man the rational animal."

The Inventor of the Negative

. . . inventor of the negative (or moralized by the negative)

Burke "hit" on this idea while reading a book, *Creative Evolution*, by the philosopher Henri Bergson. Reading the chapter "The Idea of Nothing," Burke was jolted into the realization that there are no negatives in nature. Everything in nature is positive. The concept of the negative was invented by humans; the "invention" of the negative was made possible by the "invention" of language, or symbols.

Let me try to illustrate the sheer symbolicity of the negative by having you concentrate on this book you are reading. If you grant me the assumption that the book is a positive reality, let me remind you that you could spend the rest of your life saying what this positive thing is *not*. It is not a joint of marijuana, it is not the *New York Times*, it is not *Leaves of Grass*, it is not an aardvark, and so on.

One of Bergson's main points is that the negative plays an important role in unfulfilled expectations. Again, to use this book as an example, you might say, "This book is *not* what I expected it to be." Yet the book cannot be a nothing (except by slang); the book has a positive existence.

Bergson's main emphasis, therefore, is on the *propositional negative*, that is, the negative of idea. An example would be "It is not." As a student of rhetoric and communication, Burke stressed in a highly original way the *hortatory negative*, that is, the negative of admonition or warning. An example would be "Thou shalt not." The difference is important for this reason. Bergson argues persuasively that we cannot have an "idea of nothing"; Burke argues just as persuasively that we can have an "idea of no" or an "idea of don't." Even infants get the idea. My daughter got the idea quite early. One of the first ideas she seemed to acquire was the hortatory negative as evidenced by the shaking of her head when she heard her parents say no. She even learned to shake her head in anticipation of the word while contemplating digging dirt from flowerpots in the living room.

Having invented the negative, humans became moralized by it. The Ten Commandments provide the prime example. The Ten Commandments are, of course, expressed in "thou shalt nots." They are meant to guide people in making moral choices. Most of our laws are expressed in negatives, telling us what we should not do. Our negativistic laws provide us with a kind of secular, nonreligious morality.

Human language made possible the invention of the negative, which, in turn, was used to codify our "no-nos." Thus, the negative moralized us, making possible both moral and immoral options. Other possibilities were also opened up: *innocence* and *guilt* (or not guilty and guilty), terms with more than one meaning.[6]

The negative also permits other marvels of human communication. One is the double negative, which miraculously produces a positive — as when I say, "I was not unimpressed with your work." A philosopher gave a lecture in which he announced that, despite widespread use of double negatives in the world's languages, no instance had been found of two positives constituting a negative. To this claim one member of the audience responded, "Yeah, Yeah." The response was said to have a negative effect on the philosophy professor.[7]

The previous example opens the way to still another marvel of human communication: irony. The two positive words, Yeah, Yeah, constituted a negative example only by paralinguistic cues, or cues beyond language itself (voice inflection, for example), which make clear that the speaker intends the opposite of the literal meaning of the words. I can say to a class of students, "This is a great class," in such a way that they get the idea that I am disappointed in them. Children come late to this trick of language; I did not use it with my young daughter because children before the age of seven are usually confused by such remarks and often "correct" an ironic statement in the belief that the speaker wishes to be taken literally. Even college students, I have been told, assigned to read Swift's "A Modest Proposal," often think that the author truly wished the Irish to forestall famine by eating their own children.

Before moving to the next phrase, we should consider whether the negative distinguishes humans from other animals. Some of my students have argued that animals do seem to grasp the hortatory negative, if not the propositional negative. If Fido defecates on the living room rug, he will learn that a negative (perhaps a sharp and painful blow) will follow. That, argued my students, means the dog has learned the negative. I do not know exactly what Burke's reply to the students would be, but I think it would go something like this: "No, Fido has learned a positive thing. If he does A, it will be followed by B. That B is unpleasant is not the same as grasping a hortatory negative. The example is troublesome, however, because Fido cannot be consulted on the matter."

The Maker of Technology

> *... separated from his [or her] natural condition by instruments of his [or her] own making*

This phrase seems to be simple enough; it asserts that technological inventions create a "second nature" for us. In so doing, they alter our needs and drives; what satisfied our grandparents will not satisfy us. "Invention is the mother of necessity."[8]

Consider the 1977 power failure in New York City. Some people rioted and looted. Others suffered from the heat and high humidity because they had accepted air conditioning as "natural" but were simultaneously fearful of walking in the "unnatural" and terrifying darkness of the city's streets. Living in a rural area of upstate New York, I found their behavior odd though understandable. I had no air conditioning in my home and found it quite natural to walk the dark, unlighted roads near my home.

In February 1975 a fierce storm knocked out the heat, water, and electricity in our home. We found it unnatural to huddle in front of the fireplace in sleeping bags, to cook with a campstove, and to read by the light of lanterns and flashlights. It was also odd not to have television announcers advising us of our unnatural condition.

Consider also the ways in which we have ravaged our environment with instruments of our own making in order to provide each of us with the amount of electricity needed to make life "natural." We have built power plants fueled by fossil and nuclear energy and have spoiled the environment

Figure 1-2 The stacks in the background of this photograph are the cooling towers of the Three Mile Island nuclear power plant near Harrisburg, Pennsylvania. Although these sophisticated instruments of our technology can generate vast amounts of electricity, they also separate us from nature by producing lethal by-products and by holding the potential to annihilate us in an accident. (Lionel J-M Delevingue/Stock, Boston)

with their by-products (see Figure 1–2). Electrical grids and power lines distract us from beautiful vistas. In the process of building electrical transformers, a company dumped the chemical PCB into the Hudson River with deleterious effects on fish and, quite logically, on fishermen.

Consider also the product of Henry Ford's genius — the mass production of the Model T automobile. This machine and its imitations made it necessary to build a vast network of interstate highways. As the machine was "perfected," it consumed greater and greater quantities of fuel per mile and traveled more and more miles per hour. However, American society soon learned that an imperfect state of nature contains too little oil by which to power machines. We have since become dependent on oil companies and foreign countries in a way that is frightening to many Americans. Ford may not have intended all of this, any more than he intended to change our courtship customs by moving the process from the parlor to the front (and sometimes the back) seat of the automobile. The consequences are nonetheless real to us.

It takes a student of technology to show us how much artificiality has been engineered into modern life. The following quotation from Herbert A. Simon, Nobel Prize winner in economics, is revealing.

> The world we live in today is much more a man-made, or artificial, world than it is a natural world. Almost every element in our environment shows evidence of man's artifice. The temperature in which we spend most of our hours is kept artificially at 70 degrees; the humidity is added to or taken from the air we breathe; and the impurities we inhale are largely produced (and filtered) by man.

> Moreover, for most of us — the white-collared ones — the significant part of the environment consists mostly of strings of artifacts called "symbols" that we receive through eyes and ears in the form of written and spoken language and that we pour out into the environment — as I am now doing — by mouth or hand. The laws that govern these strings of symbols, the laws that govern the occasions on which we emit and receive them, the determinants of their content are all consequences of our collective artifice.

> One may object that I exaggerate the artificiality of our world. Man must obey the law of gravity as surely as does a stone; and he is a living organism who depends, for his food and in many other ways, on the world of biological phenomena. I shall plead guilty to overstatement, while protesting that the exaggeration is slight. To say that an astronaut, or even an airline pilot, is obeying the law of gravity, hence is a perfectly natural phenomenon, is true; but its truth calls for some sophistication in what we mean by "obeying" a natural law. Aristotle did not think it natural for heavy things to rise or light ones to fall (*Physics*, Book IV); but presumably we have a deeper understanding of "natural" than he did.

> So, too, we must be careful about equating "biological" with "natural." A forest may be a phenomenon of nature; a farm certainly is not. The very species upon which man depends for his food — his corn and his cattle — are artifacts of his ingenuity. A plowed field is no more part of nature than an asphalted street — and no less.[9]

But what of Jane Goodall's discovery that chimpanzees use tools?[10] Although Burke wrote his definition before this discovery, he anticipated it and was not embarrassed by it, as were some anthropologists who had defined humans as the "tool-using or tool-making animal." Burke grasped the close connection between symbolicity and tool-using. Imagine trying to run a factory owned, say, by IBM without mathematics, computer languages, and other jargons. Notice also the "reflexive," or turning back upon itself, nature of both man's symbolicity and tool-making ability. As mentioned above, people can and have created languages about languages (for example, grammars, rhetorics, and linguistic systems); similarly, people can and have created tools with which to create tools.

Let me illustrate. I have seen films of Goodall's chimps using saliva-moistened sticks to draw ants out of their holes. I did not see the chimps create what we humans call a knife in order to fashion these ant-catchers with the efficiency of mass production.

Language can be thought of as a tool, an instrumentality, but it is more than that. Language is also expressive; a comment about the weather sometimes serves only to express the inner state of the speaker. "Language is a species of action, symbolic action — and its nature is such that it can be used as a tool."[11]

The Organizer

> *... goaded by the spirit of hierarchy (or moved by the sense of order)*

Here Burke is claiming that it is our nature to organize ourselves in a hierarchy. Organization charts, which portray the hierarchy, have a top and a bottom, and people occupy positions at both extremes and the several points between. Management experts talk about organizations as pyramids. "Top management" is in control; "middle management" also has control, but the mass of employees — the workers — do mainly what they are told to do.

Consider the word *order*. In one of its senses, it denotes a message from someone "up" requiring action from someone "down." Rarely, if ever, do people at the bottom order about people at the top. Exceptions to this generalization would include the relationship between kidnapers and victims, or between terrorists and hostages.

There is a "hierarchical rat race" in which many of us participate in order to "get ahead." Illustrating this in my classes, I sometimes use an ironical tone to remind my students that they are solely interested in the pursuit of knowledge for its own sake and that they are not in my classroom to learn how to clamber up the backs of their fellows in the struggle to the top. The parents of my students, I continue, have no ambitions for them at the university greater than the pure acquisition of knowledge. When I say these things, the students usually respond to the irony with widespread but somewhat nervous laughter.

Our larger society is also ordered into a hierarchy of classes. Those at the top dress, talk, and behave differently from those at the bottom. They are mysterious to the mass of us, and we are mysterious to them in the same way. The king and the peasants are mysterious to each other.

In a provocative, perhaps controversial, observation Burke argues that our placement in this social hierarchy at birth creates a secular analogy to the religious concept of "original sin." The sin takes the form of guilt. Those born "up" experience guilt for not being "down," and for enjoying privileges they have earned only by their "choice" of parents. Those born "down" are guilty of not being "up," partly out of the fear that they are not so worthy as the "ups." Often the "downs" are ambitious and enter the rat race to move up.

Humans also exhibit the tendency to order things into hierarchies. We establish priorities. (Recently the bureaucrats have invented a ghastly new verb to cover this process: "to prioritize.") Everything must be on its own rung in the ladder, and there must be a rung in the ladder for all things.

Rotten with Perfection

> *. . . and rotten with perfection*

This phrase is not so easy to explain. Burke refers to it as his "wry codicil," or humorous supplement. The principle of perfection is central, says Burke, to the very nature of language. This is illustrated by the mere desire to call things by their "proper" names.

Television commercials often portray perfect solutions to our mundane problems; they also promise a perfect life if only we would buy their products. We are shocked by divorces granted to people we thought to have perfect marriages.

Consider the centerfold in *Playboy* magazine. Can we explain this phenomenon as the monthly repeated pursuit of the perfection of the female form? Not content with the natural attractiveness of the women photographed, Hugh Heffner perfects them with body makeup, air brush, and torturous poses.

For the other sex, body-building is a similar pursuit of perfection. Mr. Universe may have bigger pectorals and triceps than Michelangelo's David, but art lovers often find the statue closer to their view of the "perfect" form. Indeed, in pursuit of perfection, humans often destroy natural beauty.

Perhaps Kenneth Burke is guilty of striving for perfection in his definition in the same way that a physicist seeks a perfect theory of subatomic particles.

Why, then, would Burke use the word *rotten* in connection with perfection? The reason is that he wants to be able to use the term ironically, as when we speak of a "perfect fool" or a "perfect villain." The concept is thereby widened. I have mentioned Burke's famous analysis of Hitler's *Mein Kampf*. Hitler's version of the Jew was the perfection of the archenemy. Hitler created the Jew as a perfect scapegoat for German catharsis, or release of feelings. Hitler invited Germans to project their guilt and troublesome traits upon the enemy and negate them in the holocaust. This human need to purge guilt by creating the perfect enemy for victimage troubles Burke a great deal. Humans have, in his view, a strong need to perfect victims by which to off-load and destroy our guilt.

Jeb Stuart Magruder of Watergate infamy has provided us in his autobiography with a good example of this phrase. The scene is this: After Richard Nixon was elected president in 1968, Magruder was invited to the San Clemente estate for interviews with members of Nixon's staff about the possibility of Magruder's joining the White House staff. After hours of interviews, Magruder joined Nixon's chief of staff, H. R. (Bob) Haldeman, and his assistant, Larry Higby. As the three left Haldeman's office for a reception in the president-elect's home, they discovered that Haldeman's golf cart was not waiting outside. Haldeman gave Higby a "brutal chewing out." Magruder thought that the tirade might have been calculated for its impact on him, that is, to warn him about how it would be on the White House staff. As Magruder put it:

> However, as I thought about it, I decided that Bob might have been genuinely angry about the missing golf cart. That might not make much sense in the ordinary world, where we take for granted a certain amount of inconvenience in our lives — that some days the car won't start or the furnace won't work. But the White House or San Clemente is not the ordinary world. In just a few hours at San Clemente I had been struck by the sheer *perfection* of life there. The flower gardens were perfectly trimmed, the communications system was perfectly tuned, limousines and helicopters awaited Haldeman's pleasure. After you have been spoiled like that for a while, something as minor as a missing golf cart can seem a major affront.[12]

One more illustration of "rotten with perfection" may help. Apart from one's belief or nonbelief in religion, consider — at the symbolic level — the words *God, Devil, Heaven,* and *Hell.* Here we have perfection in both directions.[13] God is the perfect audience for our praise and lamentation; the Devil provides the perfect butt for invective. Heaven and Hell, respectively, are perfect places for each to reside — one up, the other down.

To summarize, language gives us the chance to think abstractly about good and bad or right and wrong. Our behavior often falls short of these perfect thoughts, and the reflective, thoughtful person thereby has another reason to feel guilty. To put it another way, language makes it easy to be hard on ourselves.

The Composite Human

To repeat,

> [*Hu*]*man is*
> *the symbol-using (symbol-making, symbol-misusing)*
>   *animal*
> *inventor of the negative (or moralized by the negative)*
> *separated from his* [*or her*] *natural condition by instruments*
>   *of his* [*or her*] *own making*
> *goaded by the spirit of hierarchy (or moved by the sense of*
>   *order)*
> *and rotten with perfection.*

Some students have found this to be a rather gloomy vision of humanity. Perhaps it is. Perhaps young people think humans are perfectible to a degree that older people do not. No matter what, we know that humanity has reached the position where thermonuclear holocaust is a real possibility. Burke has no perfect solutions for our problems, but there is a note of optimism in this remark: "The best I can do is state my belief that things might be improved somewhat if enough people began thinking along the lines of this definition; my belief that, if such an approach could be perfected by many kinds of critics and educators and self-admonishers in general, things might be a little less ominous than otherwise."[14]

My purpose in presenting this definition arises from the same motive. I consider it to be the best definition I have seen for the contemporary human situation. I remain open-minded, however, and would appreciate your responses to it. A form is provided in the back of the book for you to use in communication with me. Please use it.

Implications for the Study of Rhetoric and Communication

As the symbol-using and symbol-misusing animal, we can expect each person to exhibit an all-pervasive symbolicity. If you doubt this claim, keep a log of your daily activities. When the radio alarm clock rings, begin jotting down the commercial appeals beamed at you and try to remember the symbolic fantasies of your dreams. Record the time spent reading the newspaper, watching the "Today" show, and talking to friends at breakfast and while walking to class. Estimate the number of words (at approximately 180 per minute) you try to get down in abbreviated form in your notes while listening to lectures. Record the symbols used in thinking if you spend an appreciable amount of time alone. Record the amorous advances made by others to you and by you to others. Do these suggest that modern life is symbolic action?

More importantly, note how symbolic exchanges encourage both cooperation and strife and how they create friends and enemies. Can you think of examples of your own symbol-using actions that others would regard as symbol-misusing? Do these tell you that rhetoric and communication work toward both good and bad ends?

From your recording of daily actions, notice how often you use and hear others use the propositional and the hortatory negative. In regard to the latter, how many signs did you see that urged you not to smoke, trespass, loiter, litter, and so on? Let me introduce another application of the negative not considered by Burke. Let's call it the *rhetorical negative*.

The rhetorical negative takes the perspective of the audience, the potential persuadee. How many times during the day did a source have a design on you? By that I mean, how many times did you receive an appeal to act in a certain way? If we analyzed such appeals closely, most of us would be struck by their high number. Appeals for the purchase of a new car, deodorant, toothpaste, shampoo, clothing, and tools seem to dominate a typical day. We would also be struck by requests to borrow things, to vote for candidates, and to help someone with homework. Learning to say no to rhetorical appeals is probably a precondition of sanity in modern life. If we constantly gave our assent to others, we would not be living our own individual lives.

It is interesting to contemplate the development of the skill of saying no. There is a period in the child's life — a particularly exasperating one to parents — in which the child says no to nearly every request. Parents refuse to take this no for an answer and try to invent new techniques to move the child out of this stage. Later the parents find it necessary to reverse the process and encourage the child's use of the rhetorical negative. Teenagers are encouraged by parents to say no to commercials as well as to their peers. In the not so distant past, the girl who couldn't say no to a sexual request acquired a tarnished reputation.

Another implication for rhetoric and communication flows from the phrase "separated from his [or her] natural condition by instruments of his [or her] own making." With our highly specialized division of labor, which is partly a function of new technology, I no longer raise all of my crops. I make few of the repairs on my house, water well, and automobile. Instead of meeting my needs through sheer physical action, I must resort to the symbolic action of persuasion and negotiation.

Technology seems to have made other changes in human communication. On a recent trip to Ireland I looked forward to hearing the Irish practice their justly famous gift for conversation. During a trip eight years prior to my most recent visit I had found the stereotype to have a firm foundation. Imagine my disappointment when a pubkeeper switched on the television at 6:00 P.M. or so. All conversation was silenced as the color cartoon — experiences of Tarzan — commanded our attention. Tarzan was followed by the news, livestock reports, and a program on local history. Television has altered Irish as well as American conversation.

If we are goaded by a spirit of hierarchy or moved by a sense of order, what are the implications for rhetoric and communication? It is a given rule in communication theory that status differences between parties to communication invariably lead to difficulties in communication. One must learn the rules of deference and patience in dealing with "ups" and "downs." The ambitious among us may decide to cheat on exams and be reluctant to reveal our true positions on matters. For example, one study of communication within organizations revealed that the most ambitious subordinates tell superiors little about their problems.[15] That is thought to be the case because the ambitious wish to appear to have things under control and do not want superiors to know of problems that might look bad.

Consider how communication would work (or fail to work) if there were no hierarchy of authority. Who would give the orders necessary to sustain life? Who would receive them? Without order we would have either to negotiate or to resort to physical force in all matters. If I could not expect you to stop for the red light, how should I respond? I could stop. I could try to negotiate with you via my CB radio. I might, however, buy a Sherman tank and totally disregard your intentions and interests. The absence of order would make for a kind of terrifying tyranny.

Without an understanding and acceptance of order, the process of verbal communication itself would be extremely difficult. To be coherent our utterances need to follow the rules of syntax, that is, the rules of order in the English language. There is flexibility in those rules, but not anarchy. Constructing sentences without any rules of order or syntax would result mainly in unintelligible gibberish. In addition, paragraphs, papers, and speeches must also follow rules of order for effective communication. Ancient and modern treatises in rhetoric and communication have taught effective ordering of messages. Perhaps the human need for order as it relates to communication is one of the best studied human motivations in rhetoric and communication.

The implications of being "rotten with perfection" have partly been made explicit in the preceding section. We spoke about the human need to "perfect" our enemies, the better to make them perfect victims. Consider our need to invent God terms and Devil terms, the more perfectly to label others.

"Pig" became a Devil term for police in the 1960s. "Communism" was such a term for dangerous thought in the 1950s. "Liberation," as it refers to various ideas of freedom, is currently a God term to some and a Devil term to others.

Consider, however, the work of a poet who attempts to create perfect symbolism or the perfect poem. Human life is enriched by such striving.

There are many other implications that flow from this phrase. Let me close with this one. Suppose we follow the advice of the "Define-your-terms-school-of-communication." From this perspective, every term of a message should be defined. That would include the words to define the terms. The "perfect" message would be never-ending, and life would be so boring!

Finally, the definition provides us with a definition of the audience we are trying to reach as communicators. Rhetoricians have long urged communicators to begin by analyzing the audience to be persuaded. This definition, or another that you may want to present in its place, is rather abstract because it tries to include *all* humans. As such it is perhaps the beginning of the first step. Emphasizing as it does symbolic action, it rejects B. F. Skinner's behaviorist position that all behavior is the result of genetics and environmental conditioning. Our definition assumes that humans do both "good" things and "bad" things and that we are susceptible to the use and misuse of symbols. Nonetheless we do choose. We do act, rather than merely react.

Looking Ahead

Before plunging into our subject, I will take a moment here to outline the chapters that follow.

Chapter 2, "Rhetoric: Old and New," takes to heart the advice given by Colin Cherry in *On Human Communication*:

> Real understanding of any scientific subject must include some knowledge of its historical growth; we cannot comprehend and accept modern concepts and theories without knowing something of their origins — *of how we have got where we are*. Neglect of this maxim can lead to that unfortunate state of mind which regards the science of the day as finality.[16]

Rhetoric was the first academic discipline to be established in ancient Greece. Knowing what was taught and practiced in those days and how it changed over the years is essential to understanding how communication is taught and practiced today in both democratic and totalitarian societies. The chapter concludes with a discussion of why the "new" rhetorics of today are generating so much interest. It also sets up the distinction implied by the title of the book — that it is more profitable to conceive of communication as *action* than as *motion* — and advances the thesis of the book: *A social system is the sum total of rhetorical – communicative acts within it (and comprising it)*.

Chapter 3, "Communication Concepts," defines some basic terms such as: *chunks, communication, meaning, symbol, signal, intention, feedback, redundancy, effectiveness,* and *efficiency*. The chapter places them in the historical context developed in chapter 2. Communication as action is also compared to "games" and "plays," two recent developments.

Chapter 4, "Interpersonal Communication: Several Dyadic Approaches," examines how two people talk and listen to each other. Some of the sections, such as "Getting to Know You" and "On Breaking Up," are self-explanatory. Five approaches to dyadic (two-person) communication are presented and illustrated: (1) the "action-interaction" approach (inspired by Talcott Parsons) carries forward the action theme of the book and explains how action becomes transformed into *inter*action; (2) the "constructivism" approach holds that when we interact with another, each "constructs" the other and acts accordingly; (3) the "self-disclosure" approach discusses how we reveal ourselves to others and looks at the often unanalyzed assumption that to "tell the truth, the whole truth, and nothing but the truth" is the best policy in all interpersonal communication as well as on the witness stand; (4) the "relational communication" approach stresses the point that a message conveyed from one person to another is about their relationship as well as about the objects of their remarks; and (5) the "argumentative approach" acknowledges that even lovers argue, some better than others. It looks into the reasons why this is so and introduces two important concepts, *presumption* and *burden of proof*, which reappear in later chapters.

Chapter 5, "Triadic Communication," enlarges the dyad to a triad, or three-person group. The chapter closely examines the group's special nature, the transformation of strength into weakness and weakness into strength. Methods of predicting winning coalitions in triads are presented, as well as a "dramatistic" interpretation of these phenomena.

Chapter 6, "Group Communication," as might be reasonably expected, concentrates on groups larger than three but smaller than twenty. The concepts of presumption and burden of proof are again considered while discussing problem solving, and they are compared to the results of a method (called "interaction process analysis") that is used to observe group communication patterns. In addition, an individual's contributions to a group are considered as functions needed by the group. Various approaches to group leadership are considered, and my own functional view of the subject is offered.

Chapter 7, "Organizational Communication," is a topic of increasing interest to students of communication. Just as individuals perform functions for groups, and groups perform functions for organizations, so do organizations perform functions for societies. Organizations are divided into groups for specialization and the division of labor; it takes communication to bring them back together as an organization. How groups are integrated into an organization by means of communication is explained. This is followed by a discussion of how organizations interact with their environments. These two points — integration and interaction with the environment — are combined in an original model of internal– external organizational communication. The model is followed by a summary of theories of management. The chapter concludes with a discussion of two noteworthy organizations that I have studied.

Chapter 8, "Communication and Social Movements," tries to make distinctions between organizations, such as General Motors, and social movements, which attempt to bring about reforms and revolutions. The chapter also describes what a movement has to do in order to succeed, and why, therefore, many of them fail. The concepts of presumption and burden of proof figure again in this discussion. A "dramatistic" theory is presented as a means of conceiving the life cycle of movements.

Chapter 9, "Mass Communication," needs little introduction. While considering a variety of media, it concentrates on television. More particularly, it reviews what scientists and humanists think television is doing to our "heads."

Summary

This first chapter has provided a starting point for our discussion of rhetoric by introducing Kenneth Burke's definition of the word *human*. This definition will help us come to an agreement as to what we mean by human communication.

In Burke's definition a human is, first, a symbol-using animal. Much of our learning and communication takes place by the use and misuse of symbols. [Hu]man is also the inventory of the negative. Language makes possible the negative, which is used to codify our moral sanctions.

We are makers of technology, and in the modern world we are largely dependent upon our inventions. As part of this characteristic language is one of our tools. We are organizers and are moved by a sense of order. We establish hierarchies, categories, and priorities.

Finally, Burke says, [hu]man is "rotten with perfection"; that is, we try to find our own image of perfection in everything.

This definition has important implications for our exploration of communication. Much of our daily interaction is in the form of symbolic exchanges. Part of our learning to communicate is learning the negative. Separated from our natural condition by our own tools, we have moved from being manipulators of physical objects to being manipulators of symbols. Language, which adheres to our concern for order and hierarchy, has its own rules and hierarchy. Language helps us strive for perfection.

By looking closely at this definition here we have established the book's perspective on behavior as symbolic action. We have seen that as humans we do choose. We act, rather than merely react.

In chapter 2 we shall review a brief history of rhetoric.

Questions for Essays, Speeches, and Group Discussions

1. How well does Burke's definition "fit" the thing being defined? If you have reservations about it, or any of its phrases, how could it be improved?

2. Defend or attack this statement: The act of defining man, no matter what the definition, logically requires that the first phrase pertain to the symbol-using, symbol-making ability of man.

3. Implicit clues in the chapter point to the fact that the phrases of the definition are closely interrelated. Make these relationships explicit.

Additional Readings

Burke, Kenneth. *Dramatism and Development*. Barre, Mass.: Clark University Press, 1972.

Burke, Kenneth. "The Rhetoric of Hitler's 'Battle.'" *The Philosophy of Literary Form*. New York: Vintage Books, 1957.

Notes

1. Kenneth Burke, *Language as Symbolic Action* (Berkeley: University of California Press, 1968), p. 3. The phrases quoted in this chapter are taken from this book. Reprinted by permission.

2. Ibid., p. 16. Reprinted by permission.

3. Ibid., p. 4. Reprinted by permission.

4. Ibid., p. 5. Reprinted by permission.

5. Kenneth Burke, "The Rhetoric of Hitler's 'Battle,'" *The Philosophy of Literary Form* (New York: Vintage Books, 1957), pp. 164–89.

6. More about guilt later on, but I must point out that in our increasingly heterogeneous society different groups disobey traditional "thou shalt nots"; other groups gain identity and cohesiveness by generating new hortatory negatives, such as "Don't eat meat" or "Don't eat foods that contain preservatives." I think it was Auden who wrote, "Thou Shalt Not Commit Social Science."

7. Taylor Branch, "New Frontiers in American Philosophy," *New York Times Magazine,* 14 August 1977, p. 46.

8. Kenneth Burke, "Rhetoric, Poetics, and Philosophy," in *Rhetoric, Philosophy, and Literature*, ed. Don M. Burks (West Lafayette, Ind.: Purdue University Press, 1978), p. 22.

9. Herbert A. Simon, *The Sciences of the Artificial* (Cambridge, Mass.: MIT Press, 1969), p. 3. Reprinted by permission of The MIT Press, Cambridge, Massachusetts.

10. Jane van Lawick-Goodall, *In the Shadow of Man* (Boston: Houghton Mifflin Company, 1971), pp. 51–53.

11. Burke, *Language as Symbolic Action*, p. 15.

12. Jeb Stuart Magruder, *An American Life: One Man's Road to Watergate* (New York: Atheneum, 1974), p. 7. Italics in original.

13. For a more complete discussion of ultimate (God and Devil) terms see Richard M. Weaver, *Language Is Sermonic*, ed. Richard L. Johannesen et al. (Baton Rouge, Louisiana: Louisiana State University Press, 1970), pp. 87–112.

14. Burke, *Language as Symbolic Action*, p. 21.

15. William H. Read, "Upward Communication in Industrial Hierarchies," *Human Relations*, 15(1962): 3–15.

16. Colin Cherry, *On Human Communication*, 2nd ed. (Cambridge, Mass.: The MIT Press, 1966), p. 32. Italics added.

2

Rhetoric: Old and New

Still worse is the destruction of rhetoric. Rhetoric does not mean fustian, exaggeration, or grand and empty phrases. It means —it meant —the effective use of language, and the study of that use. Suddenly beloved of politicians and journalists, rhetoric is now used to mean something doubtful and not quite honest, instead of something desirable.

Strictly Speaking: Will America Be the Death of English?
Edwin Newman

Today students are often somewhat reluctant to admit to their parents that they are studying rhetoric. Everyone knows that rhetoric is trickery or empty mouthings designed to conceal and mislead. Most politicians practice this wicked art — at least the untrustworthy ones do — and they are found mainly in the "other" party.

The word *communication*, by contrast, seems to have nearly universal acceptance and approval — even to parents who pay tuition, room, and board for their offspring to study the subject in a college or university. It comes as a shock to many that the modern science of communication grew out of what we shall call the rhetorical tradition.

There is much evidence to indicate a renewed interest in rhetoric as a field of study. For instance, the book *Zen and the Art of Motorcycle Maintenance*[1] is a fictional odyssey of a man who in the pursuit of "quality" becomes a student of rhetoric at the University of Chicago. He studies the quarrels between the rhetoricians and the philosophers of ancient Greece and decides that the former have been unfairly treated by history. (That he has a nervous breakdown during his study should not be generalized as a threat to all students of rhetoric.) Dealing with deep philosophical issues about rhetoric, this book became widely popular among college students as well as the general public.

In this chapter we shall look at both old and new theories of rhetoric. We shall begin with the ancient worlds of Greece and Rome. Then we shall look at how ancient rhetorical theory has been transformed in modern times. Two contemporary figures, Wayne Booth and Kenneth Burke, will be considered as representatives of this age, and their ideas will allow us to state the thesis of this book.

Ancient Rhetorical Theory

Let us turn to ancient rhetorical theory. In the case of Greece we shall consider two major figures, Plato and Aristotle, and the relevance of their ideas to contemporary life. In the case of Rome we shall consider five major figures — Cato, Cicero, Augustus, Quintilian, and Saint Augustine — and how rhetoric was practiced differently during the periods of the Roman republic and the Roman empire.

Greek Rhetorical Thought

Rhetoric was the first academic discipline to be established in ancient Greece. The study of rhetoric came into existence because Greek citizens were required to defend themselves and prosecute others in court. Instead of district attorneys or defense lawyers, teachers of rhetoric (and ghost writers) assisted the citizens in the preparation of their cases and speeches, The Athenian assembly also developed into a deliberative body in which the citizens were responsible for establishing, attacking, and amending state policy. Given these responsibilities of citizenship, it is not surprising that the Greeks made rhetoric such an important educational subject. Most of this rhetorical education was in the hands of the sophists (professional rhetoricians and teachers). Rhetorical education was provided primarily through imitation of the teacher and by the learning of commonplaces, that is, general passages that could be used in many different speeches. Two prominent Greek thinkers, Plato and Aristotle, had different views of rhetoric.

Plato.   The sophists came under attack from the philosophers (dialecticians) in two dialogues written by Plato (427–347 B.C.), the *Gorgias* and the *Phaedrus*. Plato made his sharpest attack on rhetoric in the *Gorgias*, where he characterized rhetoric as mere flattery, or as a knack comparable to cookery. Rhetoric, he argued, had no subject matter, was concerned with mere appearance rather than substance, had no system, and offered no truth. In the *Phaedrus* Plato's attack on rhetoric was a bit gentler. He defined rhetoric as the enchantment of the soul with words, indicating that to practice rhetoric legitimately—not as it was commonly practiced and taught—one must know (1) the nature of the souls of people, (2) the kinds of arguments that can be used, and (3) the truth. This truth was to be determined dialectically through the use of question and answer. Thus, Plato suggested the outlines of a rhetorical theory but did not develop the theory in his dialogues.

The first reply to Plato's attack on rhetoric and the sophists came from the sophist Isocrates; however, because it was concerned with educational issues, Isocrates' reply was not completely convincing. "The theoretical refutation of Plato was to come from the friendlier but no less ruthless hand of Aristotle," a former student of Plato's.[2]

Aristotle.   Aristotle's refutation was that in lacking a discrete subject matter, rhetoric was similar to Plato's dialectic method. He argued further that defending both sides of a case—a part of rhetorical education then—can help a person find the truth. Those who speak the truth have an obligation to be persuasive. Finally, he argued that although rhetoric can be misused, that is true of all good things. Perhaps his strongest refutation was the development of a theory of rhetoric that went well beyond the suggestive outline of Plato.[3]

Aristotle's views on the subject reach us today in a book called simply *Rhetoric* (see Figure 2–1). He defined the subject "as the faculty of observing in any given case the available means of persuasion."[4] The key term in that definition is *persuasion*. The study of persuasion came early to and was important to the Greeks, because, as already noted, it was through the

Figure 2-1 Aristotle made an important contribution to rhetorical thought with his book *Rhetoric*. This work analyzes the means of persuasion and the corresponding responses from an audience. Many of the methods he described for use in the Athenian assembly are still relevant in contemporary rhetoric. (Editorial Photocolor Archives)

practice of persuasive discourse in the assembly, in the courts, and in ceremony that they made decisions and judgments. Note also that the emphasis is on the *observation* or discovery of persuasive appeals. Aristotle meant to analyze persuasion so that citizens could practice and criticize the art.

Another key word in the definition is *means*. During Aristotle's time the ends of rhetoric were fixed by the city-state Athens. The person practicing the art, the *rhetor*, took those highest cultural values for granted and exercised discretion only in selecting, arranging, and delivering the means to those ends. The tight-knit agreements among the Athenians about the ends of society constituted a kind of homogeneity, or uniformity, of values that is unknown to us; our culture is characterized by a heterogeneity, or diversity, of values. Therefore, Aristotle's rhetorical principles may not work for us in the same way they worked for the people of Athens in the third century B.C.

The view taken here is that a modern rhetoric has to take into account the heterogeneity of our society; a modern rhetoric would also have to take into account the many means of persuasion not in existence during Aristotle's time. These include not only film, radio, and television but also books, newspapers, and magazines. Nonetheless, those means analyzed by Aristotle are still applicable in our culture today.

Aristotle divided the means or modes of persuasion into two classes: inartistic and artistic. The *inartistic* modes, he felt, do not properly belong to rhetoric. They include such things as contracts, oaths, and torture. These inartistic modes do change behavior — in the case of torture, they can even eliminate behavior — and are unhappily in widespread practice today. However, they are not part of the art of those who would persuade rather than coerce.

The rhetor does not create these modes of persuasion but may use them in persuasive messages. The inartistic modes may be viewed as forerunners of the modern concept of evidence. For example, the rhetor may build an argument that uses the clauses of a contract, the words of an oath, or the confession of someone who was tortured. In this way they may serve as "evidence" for an argument, but the rhetor does not create them. By contrast, the artistic modes are within the province of rhetoric because the rhetor, or persuader, has some control over them; he or she creates them in the rhetorical situation.

According to Aristotle, the *artistic* modes of persuasion are divided into three kinds called ethos, pathos, and logos: "The first kind depends on the personal character of the speaker; the second on putting the audience into a certain frame of mind; the third on the proof, or apparent proof, provided by the words of the speech itself."[5] The first mode is called *ethos*; a persuader has "high" ethos and will be effective if the audience or receivers perceive the persuader to be a person of good sense, good character, and good will. The persuader might — if we had objective ways of measuring these things — conceivably be a person of bad sense, bad character, and bad will; however, if perceived during discourse as appearing otherwise, he or she would probably be persuasive. Aristotle throught this mode "may almost be called the most effective means of persuasion."[6]

Is this mode of persuasion relevant in modern society? Thirty years of scientific research in communication would suggest a positive answer. The modern and closely related concept of credibility is no doubt the most thoroughly researched variable in communication studies.[7] Politicians, for example, can lose effectiveness because of "credibility gaps," that is, instances when the public loses faith in them.

Another application of ethos in our time is the attorney's practice of proof by character in law. Character witnesses are called to give testimony about the trustworthiness of the defendant. Attorneys also try to bring in information about the defendant's character and life-style to suggest that the person is of good or bad character, depending upon whether the attorney is prosecuting or defending the defendant. Sometimes such information is ruled out of order by the judge and is stricken from the record. The attorney, however, hopes that the information will remain in the jurors' memories. Attorneys often tell their clients how to dress and act for the trial in order to help establish the appearance of the client's appropriate character for the jurors.

The second artistic mode of persuasion, *pathos*, is sometimes called emotional proof. Aristotle felt that persuasion was accomplished when a speaker stirred the emotions of hearers; moreover, he believed that the decisions made by a listener in a friendly mood are different from those made while in a hostile mood. Aristotle complained that other writers on rhetoric during his time directed too much — even the whole — of their efforts to the subject of pathos.

In our own time television commercials promise sex appeal, popularity, and good health. Consider again the courts: The prosecutor attempts to incite the jury to the emotional states of anger and indignation; the defense attempts to incite pity and sympathy.

The third (and to Aristotle, the most important) artistic mode or means of persuasion, *logos*, is sometimes called logical proof. It is not the same, however, as formal logic. Rather, it is best viewed as rationality or consistency. Aristotle distinguished between two forms of logos: enthymeme and example. Most students have encountered a logical syllogism; it has two premises and a conclusion. One might be

> All men are mortal.
> Socrates is a man.
> Therefore, Socrates is mortal.

The *enthymeme*, a rhetorical syllogism, usually contains fewer parts than a logical syllogism. Because of this fact logicians have tended to define the enthymeme as a "truncated," or incomplete, syllogism. They have missed the fact that the defining characteristic of this form is that it links premises (values or beliefs) held by the audience to conclusions and courses of action not already held by the audience. Whether or not the persuader leaves in or takes out parts of the syllogism is a matter of taste, not effectiveness.[8] The nature of the enthymeme will become clearer later in this discussion after we look at the most important enthymeme created in American history, the Declaration of Independence.

As a technique of logos the *example* can be thought of as a kind of rhetorical induction; that is, the persuader may reason from one example to another or from one example to a generalization. Later rhetorical theorists stressed the point that inductive conclusions should be based on numerous and representative examples because reliance on isolated examples tends to produce faulty conclusions. Rhetorical induction, or use of examples to prove a point, is prevalent today, and sampling theory has made us more critical of example as proof than at the time of Aristotle. Modern sampling theory has taught us to expect random selection of examples and a considerable number of such examples before allowing a generalization to be made. These rules help to ensure that the examples will not be isolated but rather will be numerous and representative. Aristotle did not demand such rigor; a few examples, or even a single one, could warrant a generalization in Aristotle's system.

To come to an understanding of the concepts in the preceding discussion we shall look closely at how the enthymeme and example work together in one of the most important rhetorical documents in America, the Declaration of Independence (see Figure 2–2). Historians have called the Declaration "the great oration,"[9] and we can safely assume that the document was intended to be persuasive. Who was its intended audience? What rhetorical strategies are embodied in it?

Figure 2-2   The leaders of the thirteen colonies gathered in 1776 to sign the Declaration of Independence, a statement of principle that has become one of this country's most well-known rhetorical documents. The authors, among them Thomas Jefferson, skillfully used the rhetorical devices enthymeme and example to justify the colonial rebellion before the world tribunal. (John Trumbull; *The Declaration of Independence*, 1786. © Yale University Art Gallery)

In a letter to Henry Lee, Thomas Jefferson wrote that when it became necessary to resort to arms against the British, "an appeal to the tribunal of the world was deemed proper for our justification. This was the object of the Declaration of Independence."[10]

The tribunal of the world, therefore, was the intended audience, and the purpose was the justification of the American resort to arms. Jefferson continued in the letter that he and his fellow writers had not sought to discover "new principles or new arguments" and that they had not aimed at "originality of principle or sentiment." All of the document's authority "rests then on the harmonizing sentiments of the day" placed before mankind "in terms so plain and firm as to command their assent, and to justify ourselves in the independent stand we are compelled to take."[11]

Thus, Jefferson began with the premises or values of his audience, the world tribunal, and tried to link them to a justificatory conclusion. That is the method of the enthymeme, and the Declaration has been condensed to the following set of propositions:

> Major Premise: All governments denying that men are created equal and that mankind therefore have unalienable rights to life, liberty and the pursuit of happiness, may be altered or abolished at the hands of the people, from whose consent alone can governments derive their just powers.
>
> Minor Premise: The history of his present majesty is a history of unremitting injuries and usurpations having in direct object the establishment of an absolute tyranny over the American states.
>
> Conclusion: All allegiance and subjection of these states to the kings of Great Britain and all others who may hereafter claim by, through, or under them, are therefore rejected, renounced, dissolved, and broken off.[12]

The document proclaims what Jefferson thought the world would accept as self-evident truths, the premise of the audience, and proceeds to link these truths by means of the king's abuses to the conclusion, that is, rebellion. Thus, the argument of the Declaration takes the form of the enthymeme. However, if the reader returns to this great document, he or she will discover that the bulk of it is devoted to the detailing of George III's abuses. The authors must have felt that the truths of the minor premise were not so self-evident as were those of the major premise. Therefore, a kind of proof, the example, was used to support the premise that the king had injured the American states.

Our aim to this point has been to show the relevance of Aristotle's means of persuasion rather than to give an exhaustive account of his treatise. There are other concepts relevant to modern life. For example, Aristotle's treatment of topics (a system for finding and generating arguments) began a tradition that has been continued in modern textbooks on public speaking and persuasion.[13] Furthermore, his three kinds of persuasive speaking are reflected in the three branches of the United States Government. *Deliberative persuasion*, the attempt to find future courses of action, is largely what occupies Congress. *Forensic persuasion*, the attempt to decide the legality of past actions, is largely what occupies the Supreme Court. *Epideictic persuasion*, the praise and blame of people and institutions, is the staple of many presidential ceremonies (for example, the State of the Union Address).

We can conclude that Aristotle's *Rhetoric* is relevant to modern life although it can no longer be taken as the definitive rhetorical text. The means of persuasion — ethos, pathos, logos — are still useful in understanding contemporary rhetoric. The enthymeme and example are embodied in perhaps the most important document of our short history, the Declaration of Independence. Other means of persuasion are at work in modern life, and in later pages it will be our job to examine them.

Roman Rhetorical Theory and Practice

Aristotle lived from 384 – 322 B.C., and there were many other rhetoricians in Greece after his time. To discuss them all would be impossible, and their contributions are far less important than those of Aristotle. Instead it is necessary to leap in time and geography to the Roman republic. The Romans manifested an interest in Greek culture, including rhetoric. The Romans were practical people and found Greek rhetorical thought fit well with their values and institutions. Although they did not come up with insights comparable to those of Aristotle, the Romans adapted the study of rhetoric to their own culture and concentrated on rhetorical education.

Cato. Resisting this trend of importing Greek thought and culture was a formidable character called Cato the Censor (234 – 149 B.C.). Cato wanted to preserve the purity of Roman culture and went as far as to write a treatise on rhetoric. His own definition of an orator was *vir bonus decendi peritus*, or a man of high character who can make a good speech.[14] Although Cato was unable to repel the Greek invasion of thought, his definition would have an important impact on later rhetorical thought.

Cicero. The greatest Roman rhetorician was Cicero (106 – 43 B.C.). His speeches were admired for their eloquence; even today they are read by students of rhetoric and the classics and by those learning the Latin language. Cicero gave speeches in all three of the main categories. As a member of the senate he engaged in deliberative rhetoric, and he was famous as a pleader in the courts (forensic rhetoric). Although most of his speaking was in these two categories, he also delivered ceremonial speeches (epideictic rhetoric). He overshadowed all other Roman orators. A quantitatively minded classicist estimated that of all Cicero's speeches, he was successful (in the persuasive sense) in more than 80 percent of the cases.[15] Ironically, he failed to save his own life because of his own unsuccessful oratory.

Cicero was devoted to the idea of the Roman republic in which a strong senate was independent of the executive branch. In the senate the great policy questions were debated.

Cicero viewed Marc Antony as the chief threat to the republic and attacked him in a series of orations in 44 and 43 B.C., known as the *Philippics*.[16] Some were delivered to the senate and some to meetings of the people.

They failed to unify the Romans against Antony. Antony was more persuasive. He and his two co-rulers were called Triumvirs, meaning "The Three Men." Antony demanded from his fellow Triumvirs, Lepidus and Octavian (who later assumed the name Augustus), Cicero's blood. Cicero's "head and hands, which spoke and wrote the Philippics, were cut off and nailed over the rostrum at Rome."[17]

Cicero was not only a great speaker, he was also a rhetorical theorist. He wrote philosophical treatises (for example, *On the State, On the Laws,* and *On the Ends of Good and Evil*) as well as his most important rhetorical treatises (*Brutus, On Invention, On Oratory,* and *The Orator*). His rhetorical works were produced only after long study of the subject had been coupled with his own experiences. However, his works were not highly original; like other Roman rhetoricians he imitated Greek theory.[18] Cicero's contributions were, nonetheless, several in number. He gave the first expression in the Latin language to major treatises on rhetoric. He emphasized the importance of having something to say as well as knowing how to say it. While other Roman rhetoricians were pedantic and narrow, Cicero raised rhetorical theory to a high humanism. He described the ideal orator as one trained in rhetoric, philosophy, law, and history — in short, a virtuous man trained in all areas of knowledge. Thus, he continued Cato's example of the idealistic concept of ethos. Finally, his rhetorical theory taught adaptability; the style or language of oratory should, for example, be adapted to the occasion.

"With the death of Cicero the great tradition of Roman oratory came to an end."[19] The lesson of this fact — namely that "oratory flourished most in the democracies and least under tyranny" — has been repeated many times in history.[20] Cicero and the republic expired at the same time. The empire under Augustus had no room for deliberative orators such as Cicero.

The Augustan period of the empire, which followed shortly after the assassination of Cicero, developed a different kind of rhetoric. The figures whom we shall consider from this period include the first emperor, Augustus; a teacher, Quintilian; and a preacher, Saint Augustine. Rhetoricians retained their dominant position in the Roman educational system during the empire. However, much of the rhetorical training centered on *declamations*, the practice of delivering speeches on various set topics. They were usually epideictic in nature, that is, in praise or blame or something. Students were encouraged to find original ways of saying the same old ideas. Declamations were thus valued for their esthetic worth, rather than for their persuasive or pragmatic worth. Rhetorical education under the empire emphasized esthetics in place of the pragmatic, functional emphasis of the republic. Forensic oratory continued with only slightly different circumstances. As indicated previously, deliberative oratory declined.

Augustus. Augustus (63 B.C.–A.D. 14) did not want political debate to flourish. His own oratory tended toward the announcement and justification of decisions he had arrived at as emperor. He developed new forms of persuasion to influence public opinion. Some of these new techniques, which we shall call "administrative rhetoric" rather than political or deliberative rhetoric, have been described by George Kennedy:

> To win men's minds without opening the door to dangers of public debate Augustus developed new techniques of verbal and visual persuasion which took over some of the functions and adapted some of the methods of traditional oratory. The orator becomes a standard form in imperial sculpture and the iconography borrows from the [rhetorical] rules of gesture and delivery. Coins, monuments, and buildings employ devices analogous to rhetorical commonplaces, as when Augustus adorned the doorway of his ostentatiously simple house, and sometimes his coins as well, with the laurel of the victor and civic crown of one who had saved the life of a Roman citizen. Something rather close to methods of rhetorical proof is inherent in the repetition of key ideas on coins or inscriptions, such as the claim that Augustus has reestablished the republic. There was an appeal to ethos when the emperor was shown on a frieze with shining honest face performing some good or pious task, and to pathos when the horrors of barbarian invasion are represented as repelled.[21]

Even the poets Horace and Virgil and the historian Livy were encouraged to devote their rhetorical and literary talents to works that would exalt Roman heroes and encourage patriotism. Augustus' own devoutness is portrayed in Figure 2–3. The administrative rhetoric was successful to some degree. The Roman world was once again unified. Pax Augustan, or the Peace of Augustus, reigned.

Quintilian. The greatest teacher of rhetoric in Rome was Quintilian (A.D. 35–95). Unlike Cicero, Quintilian was not a great orator. He was, however, a successful pleader in the courts and a professor of rhetoric; in fact, his views on rhetorical education most interest scholars today. After years of study, he set forth these views in twelve books, *Institutes of Oratory*. This work deals with the lifelong education of the orator. It is an important work in the theory

Figure 2-3 This marble bust is of Augustus. To solidify his power and unite the Roman world, he designed new forms of "administrative rhetoric," which justified his decisions and glorified Roman heroes rather than encouraging deliberation or argument. (Editorial Photocolor Archives)

of education; elementary school teachers can and do read it today (in translation) with profit. The rhetorical theory is not original. Quintilian summarizes what other theorists have said and then takes his own position. He quotes approvingly Cato's definition of a rhetor (a man of high character who can make a good speech) and thereby continues the Roman tradition of an idealistic concept of ethos.

Saint Augustine. One final Roman rhetorician should appear in our brief history—Saint Augustine (A.D. 354–430). Before he became a saint, Augustine was a student and teacher of rhetoric. Upon his conversion to Christianity, he denounced his own teachings and his subject matter because of their amorality and their aspirations to success rather than salvation. Upon reflection, Augustine saw the good uses to which rhetoric could be put (that is, to his own religious ends). He set to work on a treatise entitled *On*

Christian Doctrine, which has two main parts: how to understand the Scriptures and how to preach them to others. Thus, he lost his hostility to rhetorical theory and seems to have produced the first Christian rhetorical theory, which was largely Ciceronian.[22] This in part leads to Barrow's generalization that "By the fifth century ... Christian leaders were often the best educated men of the day. ... the Roman training in rhetoric found a new outlet in the sermon and the theological treatises, which were often published in installments eagerly awaited by their readers."[23]

In summary, Roman rhetoric was imitative of Greek rhetoric. The practice of rhetoric as oratory reached its classical apex during the republic and provided us with an important example of the close relationship between democracy and the unhampered practice of deliberative (or political) oratory. One does not exist without the other. Rome also provided us with other lessons. The administrative rhetoric of Augustus and the less subtle practices of later emperors, such as explicit coercion rather than persuasion, should make citizens of democracies sensitive to these practices — particularly when they are offered as a substitute for open debate. Our recent experience with the "imperial presidency" should keep Americans more alert in the future to the dangerous practice of avoiding open debate in the name of "executive privilege" or national security.

Another lesson of Rome is that when rhetoric shifts its concentration from persuasiveness to esthetics (both in theory and practice), there will be corresponding changes in the political system. The Roman preoccupation under the empire with declamations, the display of ability not directed toward persuasive ends, resulted in a trivial and vacuous rhetoric; the republic was transformed into a form of despotism.

Nonetheless, because rhetoricians dominated the Roman educational system, the study of rhetoric had an inestimable impact on literature and other arts, law, and even the spread of Christianity. All of those influences have had an indirect effect on anyone reading this book.

As mentioned earlier, Roman originality in rhetorical theory was meager. Their genius was in classification. For example, they provided us with the classification of rhetoric as it is still taught today: *invention*, the discovery and analysis of arguments and other modes of persuasion; *arrangement*, the possible ways of organizing a persuasive message; *style*, the use of language to achieve the desired effect; *memory*, the means for committing a speech to memory (a skill extremely important to the Romans); and *delivery*, the presentation (including nonverbal aspects such as gesture, posture, and voice) of the speech.

The Roman rhetoricians were exhaustive in their classification of verbal phenomena such as the parts of an argument, the parts of a speech, and the figures of speech that many modern readers might consider primarily literary in nature. In fact, B. F. Skinner, the foremost proponent of behaviorist psychology, "has reminded us that classical rhetoric might have been the forerunner of a science of verbal behavior. . . . Hundreds of technical terms were developed to describe linguistic features."[24]

Transformations of Rhetoric from Ancient to Modern Times

After the Roman period rhetoric was transformed many times. Each generation wished to redefine the subject and its relationship to other disciplines. Fortunately, many of the classical treatises on rhetoric were preserved and translated into modern languages. A number of thinkers who made contributions in other fields including the sciences, such as Francis Bacon and Joseph Priestley (the discoverer of oxygen), also lectured and wrote on rhetorical theory.

The English Parliament nurtured another golden age of deliberative oratory in the persons of Edmund Burke, Charles James Fox, and William Pitt (both father and son). Nonetheless, rhetorical theory lost its predominance in education and during certain periods was limited to such concerns as how to deliver a speech. Rhetoric lost its close connection with literature and law. In a sense these continuous redefinitions of the territory of rhetoric was a kind of academic politics, and Kenneth Burke has described it as such. To paraphrase Burke, esthetics sought to outlaw rhetoric, while the newly created social sciences of anthropology, psychology, and sociology came to the fore by taking over in their new terminologies the rich rhetorical elements being banned by esthetics.[25]

This change is important. If other disciplines outlaw rhetoric and/or take over its rich elements, they tend to elevate their subject so that they are studied for their own sake rather than for pragmatic results. Logic for its own sake has a limited bearing on how people think and maintain a democracy through argument and debate. Literature for its own sake can become as empty and superficial as the epideictic oratory of the Roman empire. The social scientific study of communication sometimes fails to instruct the people how to practice rhetoric and debate. Separating the elements of human communication into various different academic disciplines means that this complex process is unlikely to be studied adequately; some elements, such as the esthetics of communication or the logic of arguments, will be studied to the exclusion of other elements. Such practices limit the opportunities for examining the interrelationships of the complex elements making up the totality of human communication. Burke and other theorists have tried to counter these moves with a "reclamation" of the territory of rhetoric and an extension of that territory beyond the traditional bounds of rhetoric.[26]

Contemporary Rhetorical Theory

We cannot discuss in detail the work of all the modern critics and theorists who have attempted to "reclaim" rhetoric and place it once again in the mainstream of academic study, but we can cite several and concentrate on two. For example, Richard McKeon has emphasized the power of rhetorical theory in assisting discovery, even scientific discovery.[27] I. A. Richards (coauthor of *The Meaning of Meaning*, discussed in the following chapter) has called for a transformation of rhetoric away from the traditional study of persuasion to the study of misunderstanding and its causes in human communication.[28] Chaim Perelman, a Belgian rhetorician, has reestablished the close relationship between the study of rhetoric and the study of law.[29] Richard Weaver has investigated the contemporary relationship between rhetoric and ethics.[30]

Two Critic-Theorists

The two contemporary critic-theorists we shall examine in greater detail are Wayne Booth and Kenneth Burke. The reasons for selecting these two for special treatment are compelling ones. First, although neither of them made rhetorical theory his formal academic specialty, each has tried to counter the attempt by esthetics to ban rhetoric in the study of literature. Second, Burke has led rhetoric back to the rich territory of study that was invaded during the past half-century by the social sciences.

Wayne Booth.   Wayne Booth's academic career has been mainly spent as an English professor at the University of Chicago; his deepest interests have been in methods of teaching composition and in literary criticism. He has written extensively on the methods of teaching students how to write. With his background in esthetics, which has been historically antagonistic to rhetoric, it is significant that he has advocated the rhetorical approach to composition. In the next chapter we shall call such a person a "reluctant source," a source who speaks against his or her apparent interest. He discovered that rhetoric deals in principles of persuasion that, as the ancients knew well, could be applied to writing as well as to speaking. Even Booth's own advanced graduate students in literature wrote pretentious, dull, disorganized, and obscure papers until they discovered a "rhetorical stance, a stance which depends on discovering and maintaining a proper balance among three elements: the available arguments about the subject itself; the interests and peculiarities of the audience; and the voice, the implied character of the speaker."[31]

He has continued to practice rhetoric on his fellow English teachers, exhorting them to go back to the texts of Aristotle, Cicero, and Quintilian if they would teach their students how to write. In another address to his colleagues, he used the title "The Revival of Rhetoric." He argued that "we live in the most rhetorical age of all time."[32] He continued by saying that the warrior's sword is now the typewriter and that our nuclear deterrent is not discussed in terms of its strength or power but in terms of its "credibility."

Booth has demonstrated the value of rhetorical studies as well as preaching for them. His book *The Rhetoric of Fiction* was perhaps the single stiffest counterpunch delivered to rhetoric's antagonist, the esthetic approach to literary criticism. A brief summary of that book will make clearer the issues dividing esthetics and rhetoric, as well as the position on the controversy taken by Booth (and this writer).

Esthetics has proposed a set of rules that must not be violated in good literature; one such rule is the author must show, not tell. Simply speaking, this means that the reader should infer motives and values from what characters do rather than learn these things directly from a comment by the author. By quoting from great authors approved by esthetics, Booth shows that they have violated this rule frequently and that the "line between showing and telling is always to some degree an arbitrary one."[33] An example would be the French novelist Gustave Flaubert, who, in talking about novels, disallowed the commentary of "telling"; however, as a novelist Flaubert told the reader of his novel *Madame Bovary* that the main character (Emma) gives attention to another character (Charles) not for his sake, but for her own vanity.

Another rule of esthetics is that authors should be objective; that is, they should be impartial, not take sides and should not adopt a rhetorical stance toward the characters within a novel. Booth refutes this rule when he argues that "In practice, no author ever managed to create a work which shows complete impartiality." For example, Shakespeare certainly lacks impartiality in his treatment of Shylock in *The Merchant of Venice*. "Even among characters of equal moral, intellectual, or aesthetic worth," Booth continues, "all authors inevitably take sides. A given work will be 'about' a character or set of characters. It cannot possibly give equal emphasis to all, regardless of what its author believes about the desirability of fairness. *Hamlet* is not fair to Claudius. . . . *King Lear* is not just to the Duke of Cornwall; *Madame Bovary* [by Flaubert] is unfair to almost everyone but Emma; and *A Portrait of the Artist as a Young Man* [by James Joyce] positively maligns everyone but Stephen."[34]

Still another rule of esthetics is "True art ignores the audience." It is impossible to imagine a more antirhetorical rule of human communication. Literature has had as an ideal for some time the notion of "pure art." The ideal of "pure art" requires that the novelist write for himself or herself in order to express or to be rid of; the attitude toward the audience is let the reader be damned. The credo of such a novelist would be, "I write, let the reader learn to read." In this respect Booth examines the work of Shakespeare. None of the characters in the play *Macbeth* watches the chanting and dancing of the witches; only the theatre audience watches. In other words, this action is solely for the benefit of the theater audience. Examples from other great authors are presented by Booth in refutation of this rule. Indeed, the theme of Booth's book is best captured in a quotation from the novelist Henry James,[35] "The author makes his readers, just as he makes his characters." With *The Rhetoric of Fiction* Booth added much momentum to the conversion of critics from esthetics to rhetoric. As a result of Booth's work, the relationship between rhetorical and literary studies has moved closer to the position it held in ancient Greece and Rome.

Kenneth Burke.   The second contemporary critic-theorist we shall consider is Kenneth Burke, whose "Definition of Man" provided the basis of our first chapter. Born in 1897, Burke threw a counterpunch at esthetics as early as 1931 in a book with the revealing title *Counter-Statement*.[36] The ideas in that book ran counter to the prevailing political, economic, and literary trends of the times. In his counterattack against esthetics, Burke showed how poets and other artists used literary form to arouse and fulfill expectations. He has maintained an interest in rhetoric ever since.

In 1945 in a book called *A Grammar of Motives* Burke developed the theory for which he is probably most famous — "dramatism."[37] This book was written out of a dissatisfaction with the ways in which social scientists were explaining motivation by reducing people to mere biological bundles of drives or to caricatures such as "economic man" or the passive-reacting agent of behaviorism.

Burke emphasizes the point that humans act; hence, the term "dramatism." The metaphor that connects human behavior and dramatic behavior is hardly an original idea. Shakespeare has this to say in *As You Like It:*

All the world's a stage,
And all the men and women merely players;
They have their exits and their entrances;
And one man in his time plays many parts.
[act 2, scene 7, lines 139– 42]

We speak of "playing a role," "theaters of war," or that "the stage is set." The difference here is Burke's contention that the application of dramatistic terms to human motivation is "not merely 'metaphorical,' that people do literally 'act.' "[38]

The dramatistic terms Burke provides for the application to human action are called the *pentad*, meaning a group of five. The five terms of the pentad in this case are act, scene, agent, agency, and purpose.

1. *Act*. This term names what took place in thought or deed; it answers the question, *What* was done?

2. *Scene*. This term names the background of the act, the situation in which it took place; it answers the question, *Where* or *when* was it done?

3. *Agent*. This term names what person or kind of person performed the act; it answers the question, *Who* did it?

4. *Agency*. This term names what means or instruments the agent used; it answers the question, *How* was it done?

5. *Purpose*. This term names the motivation for the act. It answers the question, *Why* was it done?[39]

Notice that the terms bear a close relationship to the stock questions posed by the journalist in writing a story: who, what, where, when, why, and how. (When and where are combined under "Scene.") Burke's point is that a rounded statement about human motivation—that is, the action—will contain some kind of answer to each of the five questions. The relationships among terms are determined by principles of drama. For example, one such principle is that the nature of agents and acts must be consistent with the nature of the scene that embraces them.

Burke calls this need for consistency "ratios" between terms of the pentad. The scene-act ratio specifies that the act be consistent with the scene. "It depends upon the situation" as an answer to a question about how a person would act is the honest recognition of this ratio. Human beings are like actors playing many parts; an act appropriate in a dormitory room might well be inappropriate in the classroom, even though performed by the same agent. That branch of psychology called behaviorism would reduce all human action to a scene-act ratio; behaviorists believe that the scene or environment conditions the act (or response).

The scene-agent ratio specifies that these two elements must be consistent. How confusing it would be if theologians had placed Satan in Heaven and God in Hell; our dramatistic principle would be violated. How do we explain people who were raised in the worst of slums? Brutal environments have a brutalizing effect on people, producing brutes. This poses an almost insoluble problem for writers of realistic fiction. If the hero is too brutal on account of his or her environment, who can identify with him or her? Who can be sympathetic?

Consider, for example, Truman Capote's *In Cold Blood*, the account of a mass murder in Kansas. Capote called this a "nonfiction novel"; that is, he claimed that, although he used the form and techniques of the novel, every statement in it was true and based on his own research of the case. In my research of the case I found a very different set of facts. The most important difference was in the nature of one of the killers, Perry Smith. Capote's depiction of Smith presents a rather sensitive and poetic fellow who can criticize the grammar of reporters and who has been brutalized by his background. The facts I encountered about Smith—partly garnered by reading his dictated confession — showed to my satisfaction that he was an obscene, semiliterate, cold-blooded killer without redeeming virtues.[40] Did Capote unconsciously transform one set of facts into another in order to gain sympathy for Smith and for his rhetorical thesis against capital punishment?

An agent-act ratio requires that these two terms be consistent because the agent is author of her or his acts. Imagine that you and several others are trapped on a rooftop during a flash flood. At first glance, action in this case would seem to be dictated by a scene-act ratio. However, if one person acted heroically and another cowardly, we would have to admit the importance of the nature of the agents who committed the acts; the one would be a hero, the other a coward.

The agency-act ratio requires a consistency between instruments (means or method) and action. We can use an example from the long-term national debate on gun control laws. The proponents of such a law seem to argue the agency-act ratio; if people have guns, they will use them. Opponents of such legislation argue that people, not guns, kill (agent-act ratio); if people wish to kill, they will find the means of doing so.

Consider the case of Charles Whitman. In 1966 he carried a 6-mm rifle with four-power scope, a 35-mm rifle, a shotgun, carbines, and pistols with about seven hundred rounds of ammunition up to the observation deck of the tower that soars three hundred feet above the campus of the University of Texas; there he killed thirteen people and wounded thirty-one others. Apparently he wanted to kill, but with what other instruments could he have killed and wounded so many people from that tower?

There are ten possible ratios among the terms of the pentad. They can be used as a kind of checklist for determining how motivations are assigned in descriptions of human action, and we shall return to this technique in chapter 6. Before moving on, however, an illustration may help to explain how the ratios can aid in illuminating the motivations suggested in a description of a human action. Senator Edward Kennedy explained his behavior at Chappaquiddick in a famous speech to the voters of Massachusetts. David A. Ling has shown that a scene-act ratio figures prominently in Kennedy's explanation: poor lighting, a sharp turn, and the absence of a guard rail; these "situational elements" produced the tragic automobile accident, not any fault of the agent.[41]

In 1950 Burke published *A Rhetoric of Motives*. In this book Burke contrasts the "old" and the "new" rhetoric. The old rhetorics of Aristotle, Cicero, Quintilian, and others (Burke also regards Niccolo Machiavelli and Jeremy Bentham as rhetorical theorists) still have insights for us today, but Burke wished to increase the scope of modern rhetoric to account for the changes in the human environment that have taken place since antiquity. The differences between the old and new can be reduced to two key terms. The key term for the old rhetoric was *persuasion*; the key term for the new rhetoric is *identification*. The old rhetoric was deliberate and conscious: Here's how to plead your case in court, here's how to smear your opponent, here's how to turn an audience to your position, and so on. By contrast, the new rhetoric is far subtler (and, to this writer, far more dangerous because of that fact).

Burke is not saying that the "old" rhetoric is without application in modern life. It is not a question of the "old" versus the "new." Modern life is different, and Aristotle's work must be expanded in scope if we are to understand modern life. The definitive rhetoric of contemporary life, then, is an integration of the old and the new.

This can be illustrated by Burke's use of the key term of the new rhetoric, identification. However, before explaining Burke's use of identification, one should acknowledge the fact that other thinkers have had quite a bit to say about the concept. Freud, for example, discussed it at length. One of the clearest definitions of the term was offered by Herbert A. Simon. In addition to clarity, Simon's definition is consistent with Burke's notion: "We will say that *a person identifies himself with a group when, in making a decision, he evaluates the several alternatives of choice in terms of their consequences for the specified group*."[42] Thus, when a person sincerely justifies a decision or advocates a course of action with a remark such as "It's good for the country," "It's good for world peace," "It's good for business," "It's good for General Motors," that person is revealing his or her identification.

For Burke, identification can be deliberate, as with the old rhetoric, and it can be without deliberateness. Most rhetoric, old or new, is motivated by differences or divisions between people. If there were no differences, no one would be motivated to proclaim unity. If humans were identical, there would be no motivation for rhetoric and communication. Whatever was said would be redundant (a concept discussed in the next chapter).

Identification is a kind of compensation for the human condition of division. As Burke puts it, "A is not identical with his colleague, B. But insofar as their interests are joined, A is *identified* with B. Or he may *identify himself* with B even when their interests are not joined, if he assumes that they are, or is persuaded to believe so."[43] Those two sentences are dense and require some explanation and examples.

1. A and B are identified when their interests are joined.
   Example: A is a black college student, and B is a white bartender. They have pooled their money to buy a lottery ticket.

2. A identifies with B, even though their interests are not joined, because A assumes they are.
   Example: A is a premed student who has taken over the values of B, a prominent physician in her hometown.

3. A identifies with B, even though their interests are not joined, because A has been persuaded to believe so.
   Example: A, the leader of Somalia, is persuaded by B, the Soviet premier, to sign a Treaty of Friendship, while B is surreptitiously sending arms to A's archenemy, Ethiopia (C).

In case 1, different people achieve a kind of oneness in their orientation to the outcome of the lottery. Their identification probably came about as a result of casual conversation that led to a negotiation about pooling their resources. In case 2, the eminent physician did nothing consciously or deliberately to change the values of the student (although she may have been conscious of "setting a good example for young persons") and would be surprised to learn of her effect on the student. In case 3, a long-term campaign of persuasion brought about the pact, but A renounced it when confronted with the relationship between B and C.

The second case is worthy of amplification because it is somewhat foreign to classical theories of rhetoric. Aristotle does say that when you praise a person in an epideictic speech, you are urging others to imitate the life of the person praised, but that case differs from ours in that the eminent physician inspired imitation without the formal praise of an epideictic speech. This form of identification of the student with the physician involves *self-persuasion*. Similarly, a person may so aspire to membership in clubs, professions, and causes that he or she shapes his or her behavior to make it consistent with that of the people in the valued groups.

If one admits the notion of self-persuasion to be within the province of rhetoric and communication, important ramifications follow: In the terms of the old rhetoric, a person's self-concept of ethos and a person's intrapersonal or internal logos and pathos are important determinants of human action. A second party is not necessary for persuasion or rhetoric to function.

Burke returned to the concept of identification in a later work and gave it perhaps his clearest expression.[44] He spoke of at least three applications of identification. The first is the case of the rich politician who tells humble voters about his or her humble origins. This was a favored tactic of Lyndon B. Johnson and Richard M. Nixon. Jimmy Carter, as candidate for the presidency, liked to tell voters how he grew up in a house without electricity. In these cases, identification can be a means to an end (votes).

The second application is more complex and subtle. This kind involves the working of *antithesis*. In the old rhetorics, antithesis means the setting of one clause of a sentence against another to which it is opposed; for example, "we preach conservation, yet we practice waste." An example of identification by antithesis would be when two governments who normally would be foes join together against a common enemy. Thus, the United States and the USSR joined forces against Nazi Germany during World War II, but soon after the common enemy was defeated, the Allies opened a "Cold War" between themselves. It is almost a reflex for world leaders to discover an external threat to security at moments when they have significant internal problems. That provides the opportunity for another application of identification by antithesis. If internal criticism surfaces while there is a threat to security from an external source, the critic can be denounced for giving "aid and comfort to the enemy." During the pre-Watergate stage of the Nixon Administration, H. R. (Bob) Haldeman, Nixon's chief of staff, gave a rare television interview to Barbara Walters on the "Today" show. In it, he denounced critics of the Vietnamese War as traitors, presumably to gain a unity of support for Nixon. Thus, identification by antithesis can create a form of unity between disparate parties.

The third application of identification is also the most powerful because it goes unnoticed. Burke's prime example is "the word 'we,' as when the statement that 'we' are at war includes under the same head soldiers who are getting killed and speculators who hope to make a killing in war stocks."[45] Burke would make us more sensitive to the use of "we," "they," "us," "them," and so on and help us to make discriminations whenever appropriate in order to limit opportunities for subtly creating unity through such uses of identification.

The ironic implication of identification is that it does not exist without division. When A and B are identified, they are united against others, sometimes the world. Burke calls war "the disease of cooperation." Think about the countless number of cooperative acts that must precede the destructive acts of war. Before a bomb can be dropped, it must be manufactured. It requires a vehicle, an airplane that must be manufactured by the cooperative acts of designers, engineers, and workers. The crew for the bomber must be recruited and trained for the task. These elements must be brought together in a geographic sense, and they must be ready at a moment's notice to undertake the mission. Finally, all of this must be provided for by acts of Congress and the acquiescence of the public in paying taxes to finance the mission. Burke seems to be correct in suggesting that war is more understandable if we think of it, not as disagreement come to a head, but as a disease or a perversion of communion.

Identification and communion also provide humans with some of their highest moments. For many years I have been asking students and other people to describe to me their "peak experiences" in life.[46] The majority of the peak experiences described to me have at their core the concept of identification and communion. My respondents say that during these peak experiences they feel "at one" with others, sometimes with many others, and sometimes even with nature.

We shall return to Burke in later chapters to apply his pentad and to explore other sociological aspects of his rhetorical theory of symbolic action.

We must prepare for the conclusion of this chapter (and the thesis of this book) by examining more closely the notion of *action*. We shall do so by contrasting it with the concept of *motion*. The *Shorter Oxford English Dictionary* defines the two terms in the following way:

> Action: The process or condition of acting or doing.
> Motion: The process of moving; the condition of a body . . . when at each successive instant it occupies a different position in space.[47]

Rhetoric as Action

A behaviorist psychologist would not make a distinction between the two terms because human acts are responses (reactions) to the "conditioning" environment. Dramatism emphasizes the human act or action. In the terms of the pentad, an act must have a purpose; otherwise it is sheer motion. When you picked up this book and sat in your chair to read it, you were engaging in action. If the chair collapsed while you were reading and you fell to the floor, that would have been an accident, or sheer motion.

Billiard balls are not purposive, they cannot act. Hence they can be neither moral nor immoral. They are subject only to the laws of motion. Humans are subject to the laws of motion (as in the case of the collapsing chair), but they are also subject to the "laws" of morality. This has important implications for the study of rhetoric and communication; we cannot approach this subject as mere motion, as physicists approach their subject. Methods of inquiry imitative of physics will not be helpful. Rather, we must take into account the purposiveness of human communication. Thus, Burke repeats his antibehaviorist slogan: "Things move, persons act."[48]

You will notice that the word *purpose* appears frequently in this book. We shall discuss its close relation, *intentionality*, in the next chapter. In subsequent chapters we will speak of the *goals* and *objectives* of groups, organizations, and movements. These are similar terms and will be used to suggest that human behavior is action, whether it is individual or collective.

We can now state the thesis of this book: *A social system is the sum total of rhetorical or communicative acts within it.* It is a simple notion, but it is one that is often overlooked or forgotten. We fall into the habit of thinking that society is made up of government, bureaucracy, business organizations, labor unions, universities and colleges, mass media, and families; these are real, but they are not things, structures, or whatever other names we may choose to apply to them. Under closer inspection, what appear to be things are patterns of action, that is, communicative action. Our thesis is therefore somewhat misleading; although rhetorical or communicative acts do take place within a society, they also comprise the social system. The rest of the book will follow this thesis by examining some abstract notions about communication in chapter 2 and then examining communicative patterns of ever-increasing size: dyads, triads, groups, organizations, movements, and mass communication.

Summary

In this chapter we have found that the study of rhetoric has a long history stretching back to the ancient Greeks. In Athens rhetoric was an important educational subject taught mainly by the sophists. This study was attacked by Plato in two of his dialogues. Aristotle provided the major refutation of Plato's position with his development of a theory of rhetoric in his book *Rhetoric*. His theory centered mainly on the potential means of persuasion available to the rhetor in deliberative, forensic, and epideictic situations.

Greek rhetorical theory was later carried over to the Roman world, where it was also central to the educational system. The study and practice of rhetoric flourished in the time of the Roman republic. Although Roman rhetoricians such as Cicero were not highly original, they classified and considerably expanded the theory originated by the Greeks. During the Roman empire, rhetoric continued to maintain a dominant position in the educational system but mainly through the teaching and practice of declamations. However, because political debate no longer flourished, such speeches were primarily valued esthetically, not pragmatically. The Emperor Augustus developed a new form of persuasion to influence public opinion through his "administrative rhetoric." Centuries later, the primary outlet for rhetoric was sermons and theological treatises.

After the Roman period rhetoric was transformed and redefined many times; its relationship to other disciplines was altered, often in ways that limited the scope or domain of the study of rhetoric.

Some contemporary rhetorical theorists have sought to reclaim rhetoric and its rich territory of study. Wayne Booth, for example, has shown how the principles of rhetoric apply not just to speaking but to writing as well.

From the writings of Kenneth Burke we have seen how human behavior can be understood in terms of dramatism. Humans act; they do not merely react. Human action can be illustrated and analyzed by means of Burke's dramatistic terms of the pentad. The relationships among these terms are determined by principles of drama. In addition, Burke contrasts the "old" rhetoric, whose key term was persuasion, with the "new" rhetoric, whose key term is identification.

Finally, we have seen that dramatism emphasizes the human act or action as opposed to motion. This concept aids in understanding and accepting the thesis of this book: A social system is the sum total of rhetorical or communicative acts within it.

Questions for Essays, Speeches, and Group Discussions

1. Support or attack this thesis: Rhetoric is more important today than in the fourth century B.C. because of the modern media of communication.

2. Imagine that King George III gives you, one of his loyal subjects, the job of refuting the American Declaration of Independence. After completing your rebuttal, compare it with the actual response as described by Garry Wills in *Inventing America: Jefferson's Declaration of Independence* (Garden City, N.Y.: Doubleday & Co., Inc., 1978).

3. Prepare for class an analysis of three television commercials that employ the enthymeme. Assuming that the conclusion of each is "buy this product," what basic values and/or beliefs must the viewer have for the commercial to be effective? Are these values explicit or implicit?

Additional Readings

Bitzer, Lloyd F. "Aristotle's Enthymeme Revisited." *Quarterly Journal of Speech* 45(1959): 399–408.

Bryant, Donald C. "Rhetoric: Its Function and Its Scope." *Quarterly Journal of Speech* 39(1953): 401–424.

Burke, Kenneth. "Rhetoric—Old and New." *Journal of General Education* 5(1951): 203–209.

Hauser, Gerard A. "The Example in Aristotle's Rhetoric: Bifurcation or Contradiction?" *Philosophy and Rhetoric* 1(1968): 78–90.

Kennedy, George. *The Art of Persuasion in Greece*. Princeton, N.J.: Princeton University Press, 1963.

Kennedy, George. *The Art of Rhetoric in the Roman World: 300 B.C.–A.D. 300*. Princeton, N.J.: Princeton University Press, 1972.

Notes

1. Robert M. Pirsig, *Zen and the Art of Motorcycle Maintenance* (New York: William Morrow and Co., 1974).

2. George Kennedy, *The Art of Persuasion in Greece* (Princeton, N.J.: Princeton University Press, 1963), p. 18.

3. Plato continues to be attacked in both fiction and nonfiction. For the former, see Pirsig, *Zen and the Art of Motorcycle Maintenance*; Plato is attacked for being unfair to the Sophists. For the latter, see I. F. Stone, "I. F. Stone Breaks the Socrates Story," *New York Times Magazine*, 8 April 1979, pp. 22–23, 26, 34, 37, 66–68. Stone introduces evidence to support his charge that Plato hated democracy and that his "Apology," or defense of Socrates, is "a masterpiece of evasion" (p. 34).

4. Aristotle, *Rhetoric*, trans. W. Rhys Roberts (New York: Random House, 1954), p. 24.

5. Ibid., pp. 24–25.

6. Ibid., p. 25.

7. Jesse G. Delia, "A Constructivist Analysis of the Concept of Credibility," *Quarterly Journal of Speech* 62(1976): 361–75.

8. See Lloyd F. Bitzer, "Aristotle's Enthymeme Revisited," *Quarterly Journal of Speech* 45(1959): 399–408; and Patricia M. Cypher, "An Empirical Test of Contemporary Definitions of the Enthymeme: Believed Major Premises and Truncation of the Enthymeme" (Thesis, Wayne State University, 1968).

9. Charles A. Beard and Mary R. Beard, *The Rise of American Civilization* (New York: Macmillan Co., 1930), p. 239.

10. Thomas Jefferson, *The Writings of Thomas Jefferson*, ed. Paul Leicester Ford, 12 vols. (New York: G. P. Putnam's Sons, 1892–1899) 10: 343.

11. Ibid., p. 343.

12. W. Samuel Howell, *Poetics, Rhetoric, and Logic* (Ithaca, N.Y.: Cornell University Press, 1975), pp. 185–86. I am aware that my enthymemic analysis differs from Howell's, but his interpretation depends entirely on the tenuous assumption that the word "self-evident" is in Jefferson's handwriting. Howell himself acknowledges that a strong case has been made that Franklin added the word. More importantly, nothing Howell says about the argument is inconsistent with enthymeme theory.

13. John F. Wilson and Carroll C. Arnold, *Public Speaking as a Liberal Art* (Boston: Allyn and Bacon, 1969).

14. R. H. Barrow, *The Romans* (Baltimore: Penguin Books, 1958), p. 66.

15. J. E. Granrud, "Was Cicero Successful in the Art Oratorical?" *Classical Journal* 8(1912–1913): 234–43, as cited in George Kennedy, *The Art of Rhetoric in the Roman World: 300 B.C.–A.D. 300* (Princeton, N.J.: Princeton University Press, 1972), p. 276.

16. Cicero selected the name in order to make the comparison with the great Greek orator Demosthenes and his oratorical attack on Philip of Macedon.

17. Kennedy, *The Art of Rhetoric in the Roman World*, p. 275.

18. Ibid., p. xv.

19. M. L. Clarke, *Rhetoric at Rome: A Historical Survey* (New York: Barnes & Noble, 1963), p. 100.

20. Kennedy, *The Art of Rhetoric in the Roman World*, p. 23.

21. Ibid., p. 383.

22. Clarke, p. 151.

23. Barrow, p. 199.

24. Marie Hochmuth Nichols, "I. A. Richards and the 'New Rhetoric,'" *Quarterly Journal of Speech* 44(1958): 16.

25. Kenneth Burke, *A Rhetoric of Motives* (Cleveland: World Publishing Co., 1962), p. 521.

26. Ibid.

27. See Richard McKeon, *Introduction to Aristotle*, 2nd ed. (Chicago: University of Chicago Press, 1973), pp. 716– 22.

28. I. A. Richards, *The Philosophy of Rhetoric* (London: Oxford University Press, 1971).

29. Chaim Perelman, *The Idea of Justice and the Problem of Argument*, trans. John Petrie (London: Routledge and Kegan Paul, 1963).

30. Richard A. Weaver, *The Ethics of Rhetoric* (Chicago: Henry Regnery Co., 1953).

31. Wayne C. Booth, "The Rhetorical Stance," *College Composition and Communication* 14(1963): 141.

32. Wayne C. Booth, "The Revival of Rhetoric," *PMLA* 80(1965): 8.

33. Wayne C. Booth, *The Rhetoric of Fiction* (Chicago: University of Chicago Press, 1961), p. 20.

34. Ibid., p. 78.

35. Quoted by Booth in *The Rhetoric of Fiction*, p. 1.

36. Kenneth Burke, *Counter-Statement* (Berkeley: University of California Press, 1968). Originally published in 1931.

37. Kenneth Burke, *A Grammar of Motives* (Cleveland: World Publishing Co., 1962), pp. xvii– xxv.

38. Kenneth Burke, *Dramatism and Development* (Barre, Mass.: Barre Publishers, 1972), p. 12.

39. Burke, *A Grammar of Motives*, p. xvii.

40. Phillip K. Tompkins, "In Cold Fact," *Esquire*, June 1966, pp. 125, 127, 166– 71.

41. David A. Ling, "A Pentadic Analysis of Senator Edward Kennedy's Address to the People of Massachusetts, July 25, 1969," in *Methods of Rhetorical*

Criticism: A Twentieth-Century Perspective, ed. Robert L. Scott and Bernard L. Brock (New York: Harper & Row, Publishers), pp. 327–35.

42. Herbert A. Simon, *Administrative Behavior*, 2nd ed. (New York: Free Press, 1957), p. 205. Italics in original.

43. Burke, *A Rhetoric of Motives*, p. 544. Italics in original.

44. Burke, *Dramatism and Development*, p. 28.

45. Ibid.

46. See Abraham H. Maslow, *Toward a Psychology of Being* (New York: Van Nostrand Reinhold Company, 1968), pp. 71–114.

47. C. T. Onions, ed., *The Shorter Oxford English Dictionary on Historical Principles*, 3rd ed. (Oxford: Clarendon Press, 1965), pp. 19, 1287.

48. Burke, *Dramatism and Development*, p. 21.

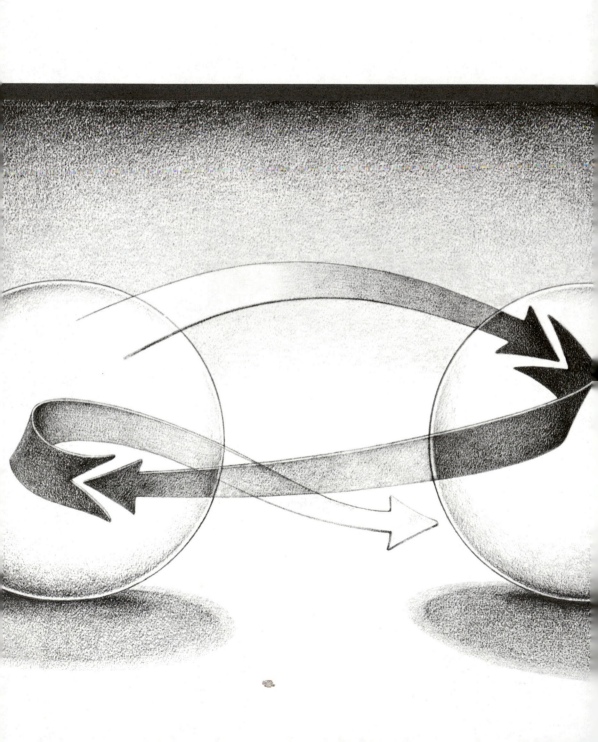

CHAPTER

3

Communication Concepts

Future historians who record what is being said and done today will find it difficult to avoid giving a prominent place to our preoccupation with communication.

"Communication, Truth, and Society"
Richard McKeon

The following chapter defines a number of terms for our discussion. Because it explains highly abstract notions, some readers may find it difficult. Nonetheless, comprehension of these terms is essential to an understanding of the theories in later chapters. After a brief discussion of communication as symbolic action, we shall define the concept of communication. Here we shall consider three elements — process, meaning, and intention — and describe two closely related models of communication that have been designed by theorists. A term that has been used popularly in recent years, feedback, will be presented as a control aid to communication. Having established the main theory of communication, we shall look at an alternative model, which incorporates the concepts of plays, games, and rules. Redundancy, which means superfluous or more than necessary, will be examined as another tool, like feedback, that can be valuable in communication. Finally, we shall look at two ways of evaluating communication: effectiveness and efficiency.

Communication scholars have not reached total agreement about how to define their subject. They have reached, however, substantial agreement about which elements should be avoided in such a definition. For years I have asked beginning students to define communication. Invariably a student will fall into the trap by saying "the sending and receiving of ideas." I then divide the students into pairs and ask one to play the role of a person blind from birth. The other is asked to "communicate" the idea of the colors of the rainbow or the spectrum to the handicapped person. What follows is much noise signifying little. There is considerable "cheating" as the communicators describe in sweeping gestures the arc of the rainbow.

My students readily admit that they find it difficult to perform the task. The more confident seem to employ a metaphoric approach; that is, they compare that which is known with that which is unknown by speaking, for instance, of "warm" and "cool" colors. However, even these participants are less than totally confident about their effectiveness. To quote from Colin Cherry, "In the country of the Blind the one-eyed man is not king — he is a gibbering idiot."[1]

The lesson to be learned from this demonstration is that "ideas" can neither be sent nor received. A close analysis of communication reveals that the only things sent (and received) are physical signals, light waves, and sound waves. As these signals impinge on the sensory organs of the receiver, that person attempts to impose order or "sense" upon them while taking into account the other person. It is a kind of guessing game or a kind of hypothesis making and testing. What, we ask implicitly, does the other person mean by these noises, these ink-marks, or these gestures?

Notice that both parties, source and receiver, are participating in *symbolic action*. Each party is active, seeking to achieve certain goals. The speaker wants to achieve the goal of understanding. He or she speaks language to achieve that goal. The listener is actively trying to make sense of the speaker's sounds and gestures. Language is a part of action.

Viewing human communication from this perspective of information processing has led one scholar to a rather startling thesis: "*A man, viewed as a behavior system, is quite simple*."[2] This thesis is at odds with what textbooks in the social sciences (and rhetoric and communication) claim. The prevailing assumption is that human behavior is incredibly complex. Perhaps conceit requires us to define ourselves as complex.

After surveying a number of studies dealing with solving puzzles, learning concepts, and memorizing and storing information, the Nobel laureate Herbert A. Simon concluded:

> The evidence is overwhelming that the system is basically serial in its operation: that it can process only a few symbols at a time and that the symbols being processed must be held in special, limited memory structures whose content can be changed rapidly. The most striking limits on subjects' capacities to employ efficient strategies arise from the very small capacity of the short-term memory structure (seven chunks) and from the relatively long time (five seconds) required to transfer a chunk of information from short-term to long-term memory.[3]

Some interpretation of that passage is in order. A "chunk" is the smallest familiar unit of a message. A nonsense syllable *AIQ* would contain three chunks, but the familiar word *RUN* would constitute one chunk even though it has the same number of letters. The results of these studies are persuasive in their support of the thesis that human behavior — if limited to the cognitive processes of information processing — is quite limited and simple; we can completely process very few symbols at one time.

If we are to cling to our (perhaps proud) assumption that human behavior is complex, we must reject the assumption that behavior is nothing more than information processing. That seems to be plausible in the case of human communication. For example, when A speaks to B, B must do more than process the verbal message. B must also process, simultaneously, A as a source, A's intentions toward B, and the context in which A speaks to B. These additional considerations may be trivial in laboratory experiments, but in the real world they are significant.

Consider this piece of behavior reported in the *New York Times*:

> Until very recently Tom McNamara worked as a part-time clerk at the law offices of Carter, Ledy and Millburne on Wall Street. He would work there nights and on Sundays.

> One Sunday Mr. McNamara hailed a cab near his home in Greenwich Village for his ride to work. The driver, who picked him up, was so enamored by the lack of traffic at that hour that he sped furiously downtown.

> Mr. McNamara was less than enchanted with the ride and decided to get out and get another taxi.

> "Okay, that's far enough," he told the driver, "pull over to the side."

On hearing this, the driver was certain that what Mr. McNamara had in mind was to hold him up. What he did was to drive toward the curb, slow down to 10 miles an hour, open his door and roll out of the moving cab. The vehicle, meanwhile, came to rest when it struck an immovable lamppost.[4]

To account for this act from an information-processing perspective, we would have to posit that the cabdriver misinterpreted the words of the message. From the perspective of this book, we would say that the cabdriver correctly processed the verbal message, or the command, but simultaneously construed bad intentions on the part of the passenger; this was partly true because the context of the exchange was New York City.

I cannot overemphasize that understanding language involves more than mastering vocabulary. Given our limited capacity to process symbols, we must learn how to infer beyond the information given and hence to engage in communication as an interpretive activity. Moreover, communication requires that we learn certain rules that shape our actions.

Definition of Communication

Communication will be defined as *the process of assigning meaning and intention to the acts of others*. It will be necessary to consider the implications of three of the terms: process, meaning, and intention. The first term will receive little space, but the second and third will require more attention.

Process

One of the early books on human communication theory was by David K. Berlo. He was one of the first writers to emphasize communication as a *process*; the title of his book, *The Process of Communication*, attests to this emphasis. Berlo explains the process in the following way.

> Communication theory reflects a process point of view. A communication theorist rejects the possibility that nature consists of events or ingredients that are separable from all other events. He argues that you cannot talk about *the* beginning or *the* end of communication or say that a particular idea came from one specific source, that communication occurs in only one way, and so on.[5]

Berlo goes on to say that in talking or writing about communication we cannot avoid arresting, or stopping, the process (as in a sports photograph), and we cannot avoid making a dynamic concept seem static. We can make this point clearer by reference to a more recent distinction between *state* descriptions and *process* descriptions. A circle can be described in two quite different ways:

1. A circle is the locus of all points equidistant from a given point.
2. To construct a circle, rotate a compass with one arm fixed until the other arm has returned to its starting point.[6]

The first is a state description; the second is a process description. If you carry out the instructions in the second case, you would produce the static artifact described in the first. Process descriptions help to avoid making the phenomenon static to the point of being misleading. One day it may be possible to describe communication by means of differential equations, but that seems to be in the distant future. Let us turn now from process to meaning.

Meaning

The Symbol-Referent-Reference Model.   The classic analysis of *meaning* was made by C. K. Ogden and I. A. Richards some years ago. They divided meaning into three essential elements: symbol, referent, and reference (thought). They expressed the relationships among the three elements in their "triangle of meaning" represented in Figure 3–1.[7] The symbol is the word *chair* in the example I have added to the diagram. The referent is the thing the symbols stand for, or refer to; in my example it is a physical object with a seat, legs, and back and is used to sit on. The reference is the idea of "chairness."

The importance of the triangle is to be found in the relationships between each pair of terms. Notice that the base of the triangle is a broken line. This indicates that the relationship between symbol and referent is an arbitrary or imputed one. The word for chair in French, for example, is *chaise*. This relationship is fixed by convention or rule. I have insisted in my classes that everyone use the word *aardvark* in place of chair to prove the point; we have communicated splendidly ever after.

The relationship between symbol and reference is causal or deterministic; that is, one phenomenon produces the other. The symbol "calls up" or evokes the thought of the referent it stands for. Ogden and Richards used the term *engram* to explain this relationship, but we shall use the word *memory*. The relationship between referent and reference is similarly deterministic or causal. One's unique thought of "chairness" is shaped by one's past experience with the things or referents having the properties of chairness.

Figure 3-1   The triangle of meaning (Adapted from Ogden and Richards, *The Meaning of Meaning*, p. 11.)

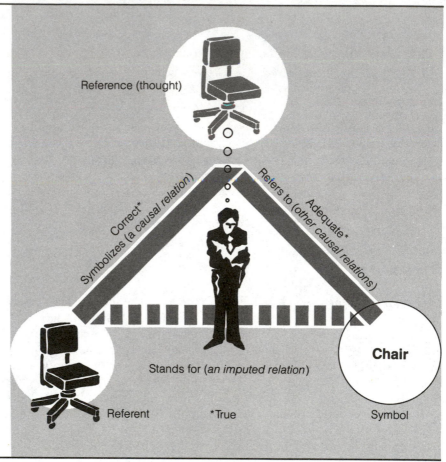

This model deals with the cognitive, or denotative, dimension of meaning, that is, the meaning of a term or symbol when it identifies something by naming it. There is, of course, an affective or connotative dimension of meaning, that is, the implied meanings of a word. Words and symbols evoke feelings as well as ideas. This dimension has been explored by Osgood and his associates. In the process of exploring meaning they developed a measuring device called the *semantic differential*. Although this device has since been used to measure attitudes, it was originally created to study the connotative meaning of words. Osgood and his associates discovered that three main factors best account for the connotative meaning of a word. The factors, in order of their importance, are evaluation, potency, and activity.[8]

The connotative meaning of a word is the intersection of three ranges, or continua: good–bad (evaluation), strong–weak (potency), and active–passive (activity). Let us take two examples. Although I have not measured the words with the semantic differential on a sample of our population, I would guess that people who have not had a rhetorical education would react to the word *rhetoric* as relatively bad, weak, and passive. *Communication*, I would predict, would be placed more toward the good, strong, and active poles of the continua. Someday a person may need a pair of dictionaries, one for the denotative (cognitive) and another for the connotative (affective) meanings of words.

A Meaning-Centered Model. Colin Cherry has adapted the Ogden and Richards triangle into the functional flow diagram of meaning shown in Figure 3–2.[9] This can be thought of as a kind of comprehensive meaning-centered model of the communication process. Cherry replaces the term *referent* with *designata* because some "things" referred to are often "non-existents" such as unicorn, phoenix, and Julius Caesar. A designatum may not always be a concrete thing. Meaning sometimes emerges from a complete utterance, as in "How do you do?" The word *good-bye* may refer to the act of parting and to events in the future.

Symbol is replaced by *signal* in Cherry's scheme because he wishes to reserve the former "for the Crown, the Cross, Uncle Sam, the olive branch, Father Time, and others . . . interpretable only in specified historical contexts."[10] Memories and external environment were added by Cherry because these two concepts interact in the selection of thought assigned to the signal or symbol. For example, an unabridged dictionary contains four hundred definitions of the word *run*. Most people can recall a large number of these; by adding a single word of context I can suggest a good number of these: hosiery, baseball, election, bull ——, track, banks, and so on. Thus, verbal context helps a person assign meaning (dredged up from memory) to a symbol. Physical context or environment also functions in this way. The nonverbal symbol of a hand clenched with the thumb extended will evoke one meaning on the highway and a different one in Yankee Stadium.

With the definition of communication adopted in this book, one could argue that people are free to assign meaning to any and all acts of another; that is, even silence and an absence of action can be interpreted as a message. Indeed, the authors of a textbook on interpersonal communication say that "We Cannot Not Communicate When We Are With Others."[11] There is some truth to this statement, but it does seem to reduce communication to sheer perception. Certainly people do assign meaning to the verbal and nonverbal behavior of others, but much of this may be closer to motion than action.

The forked arrow in Cherry's schema suggests another important concept, feedback, to which we shall return after we complete our survey of terms in the definition of communication.

Figure 3-2 The triangle of meaning as a functional flow diagram (Cherry, *On Human Communication*, p. 113.)

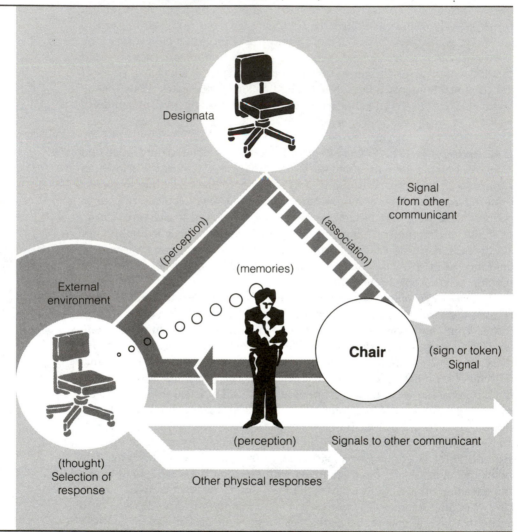

Intention

An *intention* can be viewed as the source's desired "end," or result, and whatever action is required to achieve it. When processing the meaning of a message, the receiver makes judgments about the intentions of the source. Those judgments may be correct or incorrect (as in the case of the cabdriver

Figure 3-3   The effect of environmental pressure on perception of intentionality. The biased source is strongly affected by environmental pressures to express a given opinion. The unbiased source is apparently unaffected by such pressures, and the reluctant source contradicts the pressures.

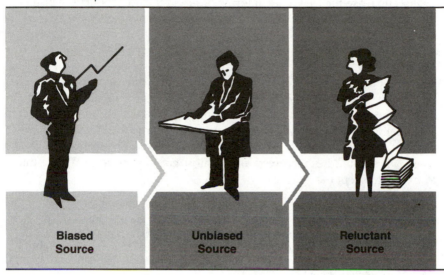

Biased
Source

Unbiased
Source

Reluctant
Source

described earlier). Many elements may be considered by the receiver when judging the source's intentions: past actions of the source, the situation in which the communication occurs, the verbal context of the message, the nonverbal cues consciously or unconsciously exhibited by the source, and the receiver's perception of the environmental pressures on the source.

This last element, environmental pressures on the source, has been considered in a theory of intentionality in communication developed by Elaine Vanden Bout Tompkins. The theory is expressed in the spectrum, or continuum, in Figure 3–3. A biased source is one whose communication is apparently coerced by environmental pressures. The unbiased source is apparently unaffected by environmental pressures. The reluctant source (as in the "reluctant testimony" concept of the law in which a witness who testifies against himself, herself, or a loved one is assumed to be especially credible) is one whose communication apparently contradicts the environmental pressures. For example, we called Wayne Booth a reluctant source in chapter 2 in order to emphasize the credibility of his statements. The theory predicts that as we move from left to right on the continuum the source will become more credible (intentionality corresponds more or less to the "good will" constituent of ethos) and more persuasive.

As an example, suppose we receive three identical messages that argue that automobile airbags are unworkable and not worth the expense. Let the biased source be a General Motors executive. Typically, car manufacturers have been opposed to the addition of safety devices to cars because such devices increase the cars' cost in terms of research and production. Listeners to our messages would probably discern that the executive was coerced by the pressures around him or her and that the executive's interest dictated the stance. Let the unbiased source be a safety engineer who is employed in a university-based research center and who has nothing to gain or lose by his stance. Let the reluctant source be a consumer advocate, such as Ralph Nader (see Figure 3–4), who has in the past championed the development of air-bags. If the consumer advocate now claims that on the basis of new research he or she must reluctantly admit that airbags are unworkable and not worth the cost, such a source is speaking against the typical pressures he or she faces. Who would be perceived as the most credible source? Whose intentions would seem the nobler?

Figure 3-4   If Ralph Nader, a longtime vigorous advocate of automobile safety, were to reverse himself and admit that automobile airbags are unworkable and not worth the cost, he would then be a reluctant source and, thereby, a most credible witness (United Press International).

Feedback

It is now appropriate to return to the forked arrow in Cherry's model, the line that drops down from the "thought" point and turns back to the "other communicant" in the form of "signals" and "other physical responses." To be faithful to the process, we should draw another triangle representing the original source who now becomes the receiver. As a receiver, the original source will process these verbal and nonverbal messages in precisely the way described in the preceding section. Indeed, it is a distortion to talk about a source and a receiver as discrete roles in face-to-face communication because each person is simultaneously sending and receiving. It is difficult to specify in many interactions who began as the source and who began as the receiver. To the extent that feedback implies discrete source and receiver roles in such situations, it is a misleading concept.

Feedback became a popular concept with the advent of *cybernetics*, the scientific study of information. Information theory, a mathematical theory of communication, promised to teach us a great deal about human communication, but the promise has been unfulfilled. Cybernetics and information theory cannot cope with *meaning* in the human sense. These sciences did find, however, interesting analogies between the functioning of machines, on one hand, and human beings, on the other. Such analogies can have heuristic, or learning, value in that they allow us to see processes from different angles, but analogies can also mask real differences between the things or processes being compared.

Despite the shortcomings of the analogy, the concept of feedback has provided some insight into the process of human communication. Cybernetics has considered communication and control to be more or less synonymous.[12] The concept of *feedback* reflects that attitude and can be defined as the principle of self-regulation by means of monitoring responses to messages.

The classic example of machine feedback is the furnace thermostat. The furnace transmits heated air through channels called ducts into the living areas of the home; the thermostat feeds back the results of the transmission to the furnace. As the result of this feedback, the furnace either continues or discontinues its transmission.

Interestingly enough, the feedback system on machines must itself be controlled. For example, if the feedback provokes too great a correction, this overreaction must be corrected. This oscillation back and forth can create a destructive instability. Thus, in machines, feedback functions as a system of control and self-regulation.

Let us now consider a human feedback situation. Suppose the top executives of a business organization issue a directive that changes work procedures. Unless the executives monitor the response to the directive (that is, obtain feedback), they will have lost control of the organization. However, if it is an effective organization, the directive would not have been issued without having received many messages from the people who have to implement the changes. Which is the message and which is the feedback? The answer is that each message performs both functions. We shall therefore restrict the meaning of feedback to the function it performs (*control and self-regulation*) and not include the role played by a person.

The analogy between machine and human communication should be obvious. The source transmits messages and reads responses. If the responses indicate understanding and compliance, the source has been effective; that is, the source has been informative and persuasive. If the responses indicate either misunderstanding or noncompliance, the source has been ineffective and will have to alter subsequent messages in order to become effective. When monitoring and adapting to responses, both machines and humans are operating on the basis of actual performance. Machines and humans who have no access to feedback are operating on the basis of expected performance. In the absence of a feedback system we would have to set the furnace on the basis of the weather forecast and hope for the best. An unexpected change in the weather would result in an unexpected and ineffective performance. Similarly, the source who cannot read the responses to his or her performance or cannot make adjustments in subsequent acts (such as a speaker or writer who cannot view his or her audience) is operating on the basis of expected results.

If one uses a role perspective of feedback, rather than a functional perspective, the traditional notion of source influencing receiver is somewhat reversed. If the source adapts to responses, the receiver is in control. Henry David Thoreau realized the power of this control and committed to his journal the decision to discontinue giving his popular lectures because he feared that he might adapt his message to the audience. Thoreau's rhetorical ethic required him to speak the truth, as he knew it, rather than adapt his beliefs to be effective.

The power that the receiver has in controlling the source is the defense of the television industry to critics who indict the low quality of network programming and the high incidence of violence. Networks flourish by capturing audiences for the commercial messages of other companies that have something to sell. The larger the audience, the larger the revenues from advertisers. Feedback takes the form of ratings. In communication terms, the networks defend their performance by saying that they are controlled by the audience (ratings) and that they give the people what they want. In a sense that is a democratic ethic of communication, but the economic ethic is somewhat masked by the defense.

Television and other mass media illustrate another characteristic of feedback. Face-to-face communication permits instantaneous or concurrent feedback. The mass media, however, are mainly restricted to delayed feedback. Newspapers are published, and sometime later they receive letters to the editor and circulation figures. Magazines are one of the few products sold in our society for *less* than they cost to produce. They show a profit by demonstrating a wide circulation and thereby selling space for ads. Television depends on the periodic publication of the ratings. Even certain public speaking situations, such as a presidential address on foreign affairs or the reading of a scholarly paper, require that the source stick to a prepared text. In these situations the spontaneous adaptation of the "textual deviant" can be dangerous; in that case he or she would be responding to the visible audience in front of him or her when the real audience is unseen behind the television cameras. Feedback from the small visible audience may not at all reflect the responses of the larger invisible audience.

In cases in which the source makes use of feedback, the probability of communication effectiveness on the basis of actual performance is theoretically much higher than on the basis of expected performance. This is supported by empirical evidence; the now classic study of feedback was conducted by Harold J. Leavitt and Ronald A. Mueller. They asked a college instructor to communicate geometric patterns (for example, one looked like six numbered dominoes, without spots, each touching one another in an otherwise random configuration) to groups of students under four different feedback situations:

1. *Zero feedback*. The instructor was not visible to the class, and the students could ask no questions.
2. *Visual feedback*. The class could see the instructor, and he could see them; however, again no questions could be asked.
3. *Binary feedback*. The instructor was again visible, but in this case the class members could ask questions answerable by either yes or no.
4. *Free feedback*. Both parties were again visible, and a free exchange of questions, statements, and objections was permitted.

The student reproductions of the geometric patterns were compared to the originals to determine the degree of effectiveness under each condition. The results were predictable. The mean accuracy of communication increased markedly from zero feedback to free feedback. The participants had increasing confidence in the effectiveness of communication as it changed from zero feedback to free feedback (and the measure of confidence correlated highly, or often matched, with the actual accuracy of communication). The source, however, felt increasingly under psychological attack in the free conditions as opposed to the limited conditions. (In one of my classroom replications of the study the source—a student volunteer—said, "They're going to kill me.") Related to this finding was the finding that open feedback was noisier than restricted feedback. Another important cost in improving communication was time. The free feedback situation was the most time-consuming of the four, a point to which we will return at the end of this chapter. We can safely conclude that, despite the cost of time and psychological stress, free feedback does improve communication.[13]

Plays, Games, and Rules: The Speech Act Model

An alternative approach to the symbol-referent-reference theory of communication is gaining considerable support among scholars in the field. This approach is not inconsistent with most of this chapter, but it does challenge the theory of meaning presented earlier in this chapter. We refrained from introducing the newer theory at that point because more than meaning is involved (for example, a metaphor linking communication action and games, as well as the notion of rule-governed action). We present it now so that, if an exclusive choice must be made, the reader may choose between the two alternatives.

Advocates of the games approach to communication have challenged the idea that words get their meanings by standing for things. One such challenge is that words such as *and* and *but* do not stand for things; they have meaning only by expressing relationships among words that do stand for things. (We could reply that relationships are things, but it would be wiser to hear out the argument.) Another challenge is that both expressions "the morning star" and "the evening star" refer to the same planet; to have two names for the same referent refutes the referent theory of meaning. Still another challenge is that the reference (image or idea of a chair) evoked by a word is not enough to determine the use of a word. Perhaps the most telling challenge to the symbol-referent-reference theory is that it concentrates on linguistic forms — that is, words — rather than on the activity of speaking a language. That challenge has considerable appeal to this book's approach to rhetoric and communication as human action.

The alternative approach, which we shall call the "speech act model," is made by comparison of communication and games. This is not inconsistent with a dramatistic approach. Indeed, *play* is a synonym for *drama*; we *play* games, and *players* can be either actors in a play or the personnel of a football team. Both plays and drama require a conflict, and sportscasters speak of the drama of a World Series or Super Bowl. Drama is governed by principles; games are governed by rules. In developing the analogy, John B. Searle asked what would result if Martian social scientists came to earth and happened to see an American football game. If they were armed with the latest statistical techniques, they might come up with some observations having the force of scientific laws. One might be the "law of periodical clustering: at statistically regular intervals organisms in like colored shirts cluster together in a roughly circular fashion."[14] This and other laws would not allow the Martians to understand American football the way you and I do. They would have found regularities but would not have understood the game because of their ignorance of the invisible rules of the game.

Searle has distinguished between two kinds of rules: *constitutive rules* and *regulative rules*. The constitutive rules define the game. For instance, a touchdown is such and such. A checkmate is such and such, and so on. The constitutive rules make possible the playing of the game. They define such things as touchdown (in football), love (in tennis), and a trick (in bridge). Constitutive rules come in systems and are collected in the rule book. The rule book, however, also includes regulative rules, which is what one normally thinks of when the concept of rules is introduced. They are used to regulate the behavior of the players by stipulating what is illegal and what penalties are to be imposed. For example, when face masks were first introduced into professional football, an enterprising defensive back learned to grab the bars of the mask and vigorously fling the opposing player to the turf (no artificial surfaces in those days). The league quickly passed the "face mask rule" and thereafter imposed a penalty when such an act was detected. As defined by the constitutive rules, the game existed prior to this regulative rule. Similarly, people began to drive cars before there were traffic regulations, and people went to sea before there were the regulative rules of maritime law.

To these two categories of rules I would add a third: *prudential rules*. Students say that this category reminds them of an insurance company, but they do acknowledge that the category is an important part in games. These rules are not in the rule book; they are generated by astute observers of the game. They have a coaching function. They instruct the player on how to play the game effectively. "Run to daylight" was the main prudential rule of a successful football coach named Vince Lombardi. That rule is not in the book. Nor is the prudential rule in chess, "Never take a knight's pawn." Nor is the prudential rule in baseball, "Never walk the opposing pitcher." Although prudential rules are not in the book, they are like regulative rules in that they come after the constitutive rules have defined the game. To begin the shift in the metaphor from games to communication, the "old" rhetorics discussed in chapter 2 dealt with prudential rules at great length (for example, "Your speech must have a beginning, middle, and end."). The "new" rhetorics are less concerned about prudential rules and instead are more analytic.

To complete the analogy between games and communication, let us consider the statement made by an automobile passenger who is familiar with the road to the driver who is unfamiliar with the road.

"There is a large pothole on the next curve," she states.

The symbol-referent-reference theory would take that sentence at face value and assume that the driver would assign meaning by means of the triangular relationship. The speech act approach of Searle would challenge this. It would not focus on the linguistic elements of the message and their relationship to referent and reference; instead, it would consider the message-as-a-whole as an *act*, an act that constitutes a warning. The warning could be rewritten: Hit-that-pothole-with-your-wheels-cramped-for-the-curve-at-this-rate-of-speed-and-we'll-all-be-killed! In other words, the message as a speech *act* performs a function larger than a symbol-by-symbol referent-reference relationship. If the games approach or speech act theory is correct, it does not necessarily refute the triangular theory of meaning. The driver would be able to discern that the utterance was a meaningful warning only if he or she could make the connection between the words *pothole* and *curve* and the referents and references for such symbols, and if he or she knew the constitutive rules for a warning.

One is tempted to say that we could test this theory by asking the driver to tell us what the constitutive rules are for a warning. That would be unfair. Humans function continuously by means of rules they cannot express. Let me pose an easy question and a hard question to prove my point. First, here's the easy question. In the word *continuously* in the sentence above, which rule caused me to add *ly* to the stem. The hard question is, How do you spell the word, beginning with the letter *u*, that designates the stringed musical instrument associated with Hawaii and Arthur Godfrey. Granting that Arthur Godfrey is not much of a clue to my generation of readers, I submit that less than 1 percent of my readers will correctly spell the word because it violates a linguistic rule of English.[15] Write out the word, and only then look it up. What is the linguistic rule that is broken?

In short, there is a large class of messages or utterances called speech acts. If we are to make sense of them, we must transcend the symbol-referent-reference relationship and assign meaning to them not as a set of words but as a holistic communication act. This class of messages includes such acts as commands, questions, requests, and promises. For instance, if a receiver does not perceive a speech act as a warning, he or she may not survive — even if meaning has been correctly assigned to each word in the message.

Notice also that a speech act can be discerned only if the receiver (1) understands the constitutive rules, and (2) correctly infers the purpose, intention, or end of the source as manifested by the act. At this point I am not sure whether (1) and (2) are two different ways of saying the same thing. It makes no difference, however, to the definition of communication offered earlier in this chapter. That definition should be etched on your cortex, and I need not repeat it; recall that it calls for the assigning of both meaning and intention and can thus accommodate both approaches to meaning.

Redundancy

About one-half of the English language is redundant and superfluous. Let us suppose that you, as a professional linguist, have just come upon this "law" of language (it does seem to be a close approximation of the truth). Furthermore, let us suppose that you wish to send your generalization in the form of a telegram to several hundred professional colleagues around the world. You will be charged by the word, and, therefore, it is in your interest to remove as many words as possible.

Where to begin? *Superfluous* seems to be superfluous and can come out. At the same time you can remove *and*. With a slight loss of precision, *about* can come out. And so on. Thus, given the nature of the audience, you might communicate effectively with *Half English redundant*.

Most students regard redundancy as a dirty word, no doubt because of the blue penciled remarks ("Redundant!") written in the margins of their compositions by zealous English teachers. It is unfortunate that redundancy has taken on such negative connotations because it is an important concept. Moreover, it is impossible to draw the line between good taste and optimal redundancy.

For example, consider the simple, brief statement, "A girl is here." There are three indicators of the number of that sentence's subject. The article *a* indicates one; the singular noun *girl* indicates one; and the singular verb *is* indicates one. Is three too many? A well-known English professor melted his lectures down to a series of terse, redundancy-free prescriptions. He found that he had so little to say in his lectures that he recited each statement three times.[16]

Redundancy is adding more information than is ideally necessary to communicate a message. Why is it that so much of language is redundant? Why is it that we do not ordinarily speak and write in telegramese? There are two closely related explanations. One reason is that humans have a limited span of attention, so that we cannot attend to every utterance or word in a message. Another is that "noise" is a part of every communication system. Signals get garbled. The "noise" may be literal; someone other than the source may be talking; there may be static. It can also be subtler, as when the lecturer uses a phrase that makes the listener recall the previous evening or anticipate the upcoming weekend. It is for these reasons that the language has built-in redundancy. We need more clues than are ideally or logically necessary. We can, therefore, reconstruct the message even though "noise" has distorted much of that message. Colin Cherry has defined *zero redundancy* as being the case when "any errors in transmission and reception, owing to disturbances or noise, will cause the receiver to make an uncorrectable and unidentifiable mistake."[17] Not much could be garbled in the telegram described earlier (Half English redundant) without causing uncorrectable and unidentifiable mistakes on the part of the receivers. Redundancy helps decrease the number of such mistakes by decreasing uncertainty.

The advantage to understanding given by redundancy can be seen by considering two quite different studies. In the first, P. C. Wason took two popular essays by Bertrand Russell (A and B) and reduced them to two five-hundred-word abstracts (a and b); the abstracts included the essential "ideas" of the originals. Human subjects were exposed to one of the long essays and one of the abstracts. (The effect of order of presentations was controlled by giving some subjects A first and b second and others b first and A second and so on.)

The subjects were asked to underline important concepts as they read and take as much time as necessary for comprehension. They were asked to recall the main points at three different times after exposure. Wason found that recall of the longer essays was superior to recall of the abstracts. Of the twenty serious errors made by the subjects, fifteen were made after reading an abstract, and only five were made after reading the longer essay. The subjects underlined a higher percentage of words in the abstract than in the original, indicating that they realized the greater "density" in the abstracts. An additional finding was that the subjects took more time to read the longer essays than they did to read the abstracts. However, there was not a linear, or one-to-one, relationship between the number of words and the time used to read them. Instead, although the abstracts contained only 25 percent of the words in the originals, reading the abstracts took 50 percent of the time required to read the originals.[18]

Consider another study by Thomas L. Dahle. He tried to communicate basic information to three groups (college students, industrial workers, and the employees of a mail order catalogue company) via different media: bulletin boards, written messages, oral messages, and a combination of oral and written messages. The subjects were later tested on their comprehension of the messages. In order of most effective to least effective, the media in all three experiments were

1. Oral and written messages
2. Oral messages
3. Written messages
4. Bulletin boards

The most important differences were between oral messages and written, the former being significantly more effective than the latter.[19] That is so because the actions of another human being have a greater attention-demanding quality than does a written message. What is important to the concept of redundancy is that the combined oral and written messages were most effective.

Wason's study reveals the importance of what has been called *syntactic* and *semantic redundancy* (more rules and words than necessary), while Dahle has shown the importance of what we shall here call *media* or *channel redundancy*. Dahle found that it was most effective to present the material via two different media. We have given this interpretation to Dahle's study after conducting studies of organizations (to be discussed in chapter 7) in which redundant channels seemed to accompany organizational success while the absence of redundant channels accompanied organizational failure.

The principle of redundant channels or media seems to be intuited by many professional communicators. As I write this passage at the kitchen table, my daughter Emily is watching "Sesame Street." A basic technique of this show is the combination of oral and written messages. Letters are shown visually while being spoken by an unseen source. The same technique is used for numerals and words. This book is still another instance of the practice; your instructor no doubt comments in her or his lectures about the text, increasing redundancy while decreasing uncertainty.

It appears that the "natural" world has a kind of built-in redundancy, which makes science possible. The complexity of nature is "decodable" to scientists in the same way that redundancy makes the human messages "decodable" to communicators. As Herbert A. Simon has said, "It is a familiar proposition that the task of science is to make use of the world's redundancy to describe that world simply."[20]

Having presented a case for the advantageous nature of redundancy to human communication, I must make a qualification. There are limits to redundancy. For example, I would rather not listen to a professor give the same lecture three times. It is a rare book that I want to read more than once and a rare film or television show I want to see more than once. Communicators face the need to optimize, not eliminate, redundancy.

Effectiveness and Efficiency

The optimization of redundancy can best be addressed by the final concepts considered in this chapter: effectiveness and efficiency. This book has often employed the word *effectiveness* or one of its variants. Unfortunately, that is true of the field of rhetoric and communication. Theorists and researchers have devoted their attention almost exclusively to effectiveness and have largely ignored the equally important concept of efficiency.

Barnard compares effective and efficient in the following way:

> When a specific desired end is attained we shall say the action is "effective." When the unsought consequences of the action are more

important than the attainment of the desired end and are dissatisfactory, effective action, we shall say, is "inefficient." When the unsought consequences are unimportant or trivial, the action is "efficient." Moreover, it sometimes happens that the end sought is not attained, but the unsought consequences satisfy desires or motives not the "cause" of the action. We shall then regard such action as efficient but not effective. In retrospect the action in this case is justified not by the results sought but by those not sought. These observations are matters of common personal experience.[21]

An action is *effective* if it accomplishes its specific aim. (I ask you to lend me a clean shirt to wear to a rock concert, and you comply.) An action is *efficient* if it satisfies the motives of that aim, whether it is effective or not, and the process does not create offsetting dissatisfactions. (You refuse to lend me your shirt, but you borrow one from your roommate who is happy to lend it.) An action is inefficient if the motives are not satisfied. (The shirt you lend me is inappropriate to wear to the rock concert.) It is also inefficient if offsetting dissatisfactions are incurred, even if it is effective. (You lend me a shirt, but you remind me and all around us ever after about your great sacrifice.) We often find that we do not want what we strove mightily to get.

To return to redundancy, the distinction between effectiveness and efficiency may help us clarify the issue about optimal redundancy. Redundancy aids understanding (effectiveness), but too much redundancy can lead to inefficiency. A source could be effective by employing excessive redundancy, but the receiver could also be so bored as to avoid the source in the future. Indeed, sleep caused by the boredom of excessive redundancy could become part of the "noise" in the system. Certain television commercials have achieved this in me by their constant repetition.

Let me conclude with a generalization about feedback and redundancy. The theory and research surrounding feedback and redundancy suggest that these two principles can improve understanding (one kind of effectiveness), but there is a corresponding cost (inefficiency). That cost is time. As research, casual observation, and common sense indicate, it takes time to allow feedback; it takes time to employ an additional medium or channel, or to utilize repetition, restatement, and even illustration. If a message is crucial, it is wise to invest considerable time in it. There may be times, however, in which the investment of the additional time might preclude the generation of another and more important message. Studies indicate that foremen, supervisors, managers, and executives spend up to 90 percent of their time in communication—primarily speaking and listening. As cost accounting becomes more sophisticated, there will be additional pressures to make this communicative behavior more efficient as well as effective. People who make their living by working in organizations—and that is nearly everyone—are quick to quote the folk wisdom that "We never have time to give adequate directions or orders, but we always find time to do it over again when the job is screwed up." Truly sophisticated cost accounting in the future will have to take that phenomenon into account.

Summary

In this chapter we have considered human communication as a part of action — that is, symbolic action. This led to the definition of communication as the process of assigning meaning and intention to the acts of others. Three crucial terms of the definition are process, meaning, and intention. The term process emphasizes that communication is dynamic, not static. Meaning, in its denotative sense, was analyzed in terms of the symbol-referent-reference approach. We have also considered the importance of intention in acts of communication. When processing the meaning of a message, the receiver makes judgments about the symbols, referents, and references as well as about the intentions of the source.

We have discussed feedback not as a role played by a person (that is, implying discrete source or receiver roles) but in terms of the control and self-regulation function it performs. Use of immediate feedback to monitor and adapt responses allows humans to operate on the basis of actual results. Situations that inhibit access to feedback force humans to operate on the basis of expected results, thereby decreasing the probabilities of an effective and efficient performance. Although immediate, free feedback may increase the effectiveness and efficiency of communication, it exacts its costs in psychological stress and time.

The speech act model — plays, games, and rules — has been presented as an alternative to the symbol-referent-reference approach to communication. This alternative approach is made by comparing communication and games, stressing the activity of speaking a language rather than concentrating on linguistic forms, or words. According to this approach, communication, like games, has rules. Constitutive rules define the game, regulative rules stipulate the behavior of the players, and prudential rules instruct the player on how to play the game effectively.

The role and importance of redundancy in communication have also been discussed. Redundancy is adding more information than is ideally or logically necessary. It serves an important function in communication because it compensates for a human's limited span of attention and the inevitable noise that is a part of every communication system.

Finally, the distinction between effectiveness and efficiency as criteria for evaluating communication has been presented. Both feedback and redundancy may serve to increase the effectiveness of communication, but too much use of either one can lead to inefficiency. Both redundancy and feedback increase the cost of communication in terms of psychological stress and time. Communicators, therefore, should seek to optimize the use of redundancy and feedback to achieve effectiveness and efficiency.

Having agreed upon a common set of terms for our discussion, we shall proceed next to examine how communication takes place in a variety of contexts. In chapter 4 we shall begin with dyadic, or two-person, communication.

Questions for Essays, Speeches, and Group Discussions

1. Choose a "typical" communicative act, and write a process description of the event.

2. Using the "dramatistic pentad" as a checklist, determine what would be left out if we paid attention only to the information-processing dimension of human communication.

3. How does one spell the Hawaiian stringed instrument beginning with the letter u, and why is it so difficult to spell? (A clue is in a footnote.)

4. Eliminate all redundant words from the following message: "The current political situation is now reaching a potentially dangerous and threatening point in time."

5. Support or reject Tompkins's Law: "The cost of improving the effectiveness of communication is *time*."

Additional Readings

Barnlund, Dean C. "Toward a Meaning Centered Philosophy of Communication." *Journal of Communication* 11(1962): 197–211.

Cherry, Colin. *On Human Communication*. 2nd ed. Cambridge, Mass.: MIT Press, 1966.

Simon, Herbert A. "How Big is a Chunk?" *Science*, 8 February 1974, pp. 482–88.

Thomas, Lewis. *The Lives of a Cell: Notes of a Biology Watcher*. New York: Viking Press, 1974.

Notes

1. Colin Cherry, *On Human Communication*, 2nd ed. (Cambridge, Mass.: MIT Press, 1966), p. 19. Reprinted by permission of The MIT Press, Cambridge, Massachusetts.

2. Herbert A. Simon, *The Sciences of the Artificial* (Cambridge, Mass.: MIT Press, 1969), p. 52. Italics in original. Reprinted by permission of The MIT Press.

3. Ibid., p. 53. Reprinted by permission.

4. *New York Times*, 22 June 1972, p. M37. ©1972 by The New York Times Company. Reprinted by permission.

5. David K. Berlo, *The Process of Communication* (New York: Holt, Rinehart and Winston, 1960), p. 24.

6. The distinction and examples are taken from Simon, *Sciences of the Artificial*, p. 111. Reprinted by permission.

7. C. K. Ogden and I. A. Richards, *The Meaning of Meaning*, 2nd ed. rev. (New York: Harcourt Brace Jovanovich, 1927), p. 11. Reprinted by permission of Harcourt Brace Jovanovich, Inc. and Routledge & Kegan Paul Ltd.

8. C. E. Osgood, G. J. Suci, and P. H. Tannenbaum, *The Measurement of Meaning* (Urbana, Illinois: University of Illinois Press, 1957), pp. 31–75.

9. Cherry, *On Human Communication*, p. 113. Reprinted by permission.

10. Ibid., p. 7.

11. Bobby R. Patton and Kim Giffin, *Interpersonal Communication: Basic Text and Readings* (New York: Harper & Row, 1974), p. 122.

12. Norbert Wiener, *The Human Use of Human Beings: Cybernetics and Society* (Garden City, N.Y.: Doubleday Anchor Books, 1954), p. 16.

13. Harold J. Leavitt and Ronald A. Mueller, "Some Effects of Feedback on Communication," *Human Relations* 4(1951): 401–10.

14. John B. Searle, *Speech Acts: An Essay in the Philosophy of Language* (London: Cambridge University Press, 1969), p. 52.

15. Carl H. Weaver and Warren L. Strausbaugh, *Fundamentals of Speech Communication* (New York: American Book Company, 1964), pp. 81–86.

16. William Strunk Jr. and E. B. White, *The Elements of Style* (New York: Macmillan Co., 1959), p. viii.

17. Cherry, *On Human Communication*, p. 186.

18. P. C. Wason, "The Retention of Material Presented Through Precis," *Journal of Communication* 12(1962): 36–43.

19. Thomas L. Dahle, "An Objective and Comparative Study of Five Methods of Transmitting Information to Business and Industrial Employees," *Speech Monographs* 21(1954): 21–28.

20. Simon, *Sciences of the Artificial,* p. 111. Reprinted by permission.

21. Chester I. Barnard, *The Functions of the Executive* (Cambridge, Mass.: Harvard University Press, 1972), pp. 19–20.

PART

Two

Micro-Communication Settings

4

Interpersonal Communication: Several Dyadic Approaches

It takes two to speak the truth, —one to speak, and another to hear.

A Week on the Concord and Merrimack Rivers
Henry David Thoreau

Whatever view we hold, it must be shown
Why every lover has a wish to make
Some other kind of otherness his own:
Perhaps, in fact, we never are alone.

Collected Shorter Poems
W. H. Auden

One could guess that out of intrinsic interest many readers—particularly those who have not been assigned or required to read this book—might open it first to this chapter. The interest in interpersonal communication rose dramatically in the 1960s and 1970s. According to Gerald R. Miller, the topic became a "hot" educational, consultative, and research item during this period, and Miller has traced this relatively recent interest to several origins:

> Among [instructors] in speech communication, the realization that much everyday discourse occurs in small, face-to-face settings and consists of brief, punctuated exchanges between the communicators suddenly added import. Moreover, the "times" reinforced the shift in emphasis from public platform to private dialogue; encounter groups and sensitivity sessions stressed communicative purposes other than persuading and informing large, heterogeneous audiences, and students themselves began to demand answers about how to relate communicatively with their acquaintances, close friends, and romantic partners.[1]

Many of the concepts discussed in the first three chapters, nonetheless, apply directly to interpersonal communication. For example, ethos or credibility surely applies to interpersonal communication as well as to public speaking. A scholar at the University of Washington has shown how the Aristotelian concept of the enthymeme applies to the interaction of college roommates.[2] Interpersonal communication does, however, have features not encountered in public speaking situations, and therefore our explanations must take them into account. The expectation of turn-taking in interpersonal

Figure 4-1 A dyad is a group of two people in a face-to-face situation. The full cycle of dyadic communication starts when the dyad comes together, advances through one or more kinds of interpersonal communication, and ends if the dyad splits apart (Joseph Hirsch: *Two Men*, 1937. Oil on canvas, 18⅛ x 48¼ in. Collection, The Museum of Modern Art, New York. Abby Aldrich Rockefeller Fund).

communication, for example, requires more participation by both parties. Indeed, we might define interpersonal communication, in contrast to public speaking and mass communication, by emphasizing that the roles of "performer" and "audience" are less sharply drawn.

This chapter treats interpersonal communication as a *dyad*. A dyad is simply a group of two actors or agents in a face-to-face situation (see Figure 4–1). The chapter is organized in a cyclical manner. First, we shall consider how two strangers come to develop a dyad. This will require examining levels of knowing and looking at a number of strategies by which we come to know one another. Second, we shall consider five different approaches to interpersonal communication. The first two approaches (action-interaction and constructivism) are general positions; the final three (self-disclosure, relational communication, and the argumentative approach) deal with aspects of interpersonal communication. Third, to complete the cycle, we shall consider research on why dyads break up, which will also teach us something about why dyads do not break up.

Getting to Know You

Charles Berger and associates' article in a collection on interpersonal communication has the rather forbidding title "Interpersonal Epistemology and Interpersonal Communication."[3] Nonetheless, the authors' discussion lays out in a lucid fashion the conditions under which people "know" or "understand" another person, and some common communicative strategies used to gain knowledge about another person. The terminology advanced by Berger and associates will be employed in this discussion, even though the treatment and analysis will be somewhat different.

Levels of Knowledge

Suppose that you have been assigned a dormitory roommate who is a total stranger to you. All you know is the other person's name. At this point you could hazard some guesses about the other—for example, whether the person is male or female, his or her ethnic origin, and so on. Even with these factors, however, you might be fooled. Only after meeting the person could you pass on to a third party the first level of knowledge, which is called *description*. Such facts as tall or short, heavy or slender, black or red, male or female are characteristic of the descriptive level of knowledge.

The second level of knowing the other is *prediction*. Gerald R. Miller and M. Steinberg have advanced the notion that interpersonal communication is largely a prediction-making activity.[4] Focusing on the initial interactions of strangers, Charles R. Berger and R. J. Calabrese have made the reduction of uncertainty a central concept in the development of interpersonal relations.[5] How predictable are people? National opinion polls currently operate within a four-percentage-point margin of error in predicting elections from descriptive (or demographic) evidence and statements of intention. You are probably a better predictor of others' acts than you realize. Otherwise, you would either not be surprised by a friend's acts, or the concept of surprise would be meaningless.

To predict the acts of others we use *demographic information*, or social statistics about human populations. This tells us, for example, that Catholics are more likely than Jews to oppose abortions. We also make what we shall call *act-attitude-act* predictions with other people; that is, we infer from past acts of the individual an underlying attitude or value from which we predict future acts. For example, if I observed you demonstrating against the expansion of nuclear energy, I might infer from that act that you have a proenvironmentalist attitude. I could predict that you will be willing to sign a petition calling for a legislative ban on dumping industrial waste into the Ohio River. I might also predict another's act by knowing the situation or scene in which the person will find him or herself. For example, I have a friend who talks on elevators only when just the two of us are riding in the elevator. If a third person joins us, I can predict silence from my friend.

The third level of knowing is *explanation*. At this level we must know the other in such a way as to explain why he or she acted in this or that way. For example, in the elevator example just mentioned I predicted that my friend would fall silent when a stranger joined us in the elevator car, but I did not explain *why* he would do so. The ratios of the pentad (see chapter 2) suggest the various types of explanations that might be offered. For example, an agent-act ratio would cover those explanations involving the character, personality, and predispositions of the other person. A scene-act ratio would include those explanations that implied that the scene, situation, or environment influenced the act.

In a dyad, each can come to know the other at each of the three levels. Notice that the "getting to know you" stage of interpersonal communication produces ecstasy in lovers.

"I particularly like the Beatles, the Juilliard String Quartet, and Paul Hindemith," says she.

"So do I," says he breathlessly, "and what about oysters Rockefeller, frijoles, and yogurt popsicles?"

"Oh my, you've named my three favorite hors d'oeuvres," she answers, squeezing his left hand with both of hers.

Perhaps some relationships become stale when the two parties fail to grow or when the other's acts can be predicted with monotony and explained with precision. If so, the pressing need may be for certainty reduction. On the other hand, some relationships may fail because one or the other is unpredictable (or "unreliable"). Finally, our predictions and explanations are not always confirmed. Complete mutual understanding does not exist, and life would probably be boring without surprises.

Communicative Strategies of Knowing

The five common strategies to be discussed are interrogation, self-disclosure, deception detection, environmental structuring, and deviation testing.

Interrogation. After you and your new roommate have exchanged names, smiles, and handshakes, we would expect you to question each other. Each will ask the other to identify hometown, high school, intended major, and so on. Implicit rules will govern this process. For example, "appropriate" questions deserve an honest answer; answering a question earns the right to ask one; the questions will move in the direction from impersonal-descriptive to personal-explanatory; the questions will probably decrease in number over time.

Self-disclosure. As a strategy of communication, self-disclosure is usually thought to be a means of letting others come to know one's self. The intimacy of this form of communication is reflected in the aspects and expressions of the two women in Figure 4–2. In the Rogerian (named after psychologist Carl Rogers) school of psychotherapy, the therapist encourages the client to engage in self-disclosure in order that the client knows himself or herself better. We discuss it in this context as a means of learning about others because there are situations in which self-disclosure on one's part can encourge the other to reciprocate, to "open up." It does seem reasonable that in some situations self-disclosure does produce self-disclosure. However, again there are powerful rules governing its practice. Imagine the likely effect of hearing your roommate announce shortly after introduction that he practices pederasty, sexual relations with young boys. Imagine the effect on your interpersonal relationships if you were equally open with parents, fiance, and academic advisor. The unedited thoughts of a character in a novel, Molly Bloom, led to the banning of James Joyce's great novel *Ulysses*. Even if we grant that such a banning was an injustice and grant that honesty is the best policy in interpersonal communication, we must also acknowledge that many people do not want to hear our most private thoughts, problems, and desires. We shall have more to say about self-disclosure as one of the approaches to interpersonal communication.

Deception Detection.   Can you be trusted? That is an implicit question one asks in meeting others for the first time. Although some people answer the question strictly at an intuitive level, others have developed conscious devices by which to detect deception. For example, I once heard an academic dean dismiss a visiting candidate for the position of department chairman by saying that the person was too "agreeable." He meant "agreeable" in a sense different from the conventional usage. The dean went on to explain that he had "larded" his own conversation with contradictory statements, both of which were readily accepted by the candidate. In another academic search situation, candidates for a university presidency were invited to visit separately with campus constituencies having different interests — professors, stu-

Figure 4-2   The women in this painting appear to be sharing a close, personal kind of communication. Self-disclosure may be a way of helping others to come to know one's self and, in turn, of leading others to reveal aspects of their selves. Common social rules, however, prescribe its extent and appropriate use. (Isabel Bishop: *Two Girls*, 1935. The Metropolitan Museum of Art, Arthur H. Hearn Fund, 1936.)

dents, governance leaders, and administrators. Notes were taken of what the candidates had said to each group. One leading candidate was eliminated because he was thought to have compromised himself by making different and contradictory promises to the different groups. One of the better methods of detecting deception is to ask questions of a third party who has had more extensive relations with the other.

Environmental Structuring.   The preceding example concerning candidates for a university presidency was also an example of environmental structuring. The meetings with separate groups having different interests did not happen by chance.

A technique known as the "leaderless group discussion" has been used by organizations such as the State Department to select employees from those who have passed written examinations. The candidates are placed in a group and are assigned a topic previously unknown to them to discuss without benefit of appointed or elected leaders. Those who emerge as leaders or who stand out from the group are chosen. Some business firms use stressful interviews to determine how well people hold up under such conditions. Social situations are often structured in a way to "draw out" the new person, the stranger, or the candidate for inclusion in the group. Seating arrangements for dinner parties are also often determined by this purpose.

Deviation Testing.   Initial interactions between strangers are highly ritualistic. The rules governing such situations are rather powerful. Deviation from such rules reveals considerable information about both the person who violates the rule and the other(s) who observe the violation. In one experiment, for example, transcripts of the first two minutes of conversation between two strangers were judged by randomly selected third parties. Rule violators are perceived to be less attractive, less mentally healthy, and less predictable than those who follow the rules.[6] It may be the case that violations of the rules for initial interactions may lead to a termination of the conversation.

How people react to such rule violations is also informative; however, if they terminate the conversation, that is obviously the last piece of information one can learn from them directly. Sociologists who specialize in this field are called ethnomethodologists. As part of their experiments they sometimes purposely break social rules or norms so that they can study the reactions to these violations. In certain situations, for example, it may be appropriate for dinner guests to kiss the hostess goodnight as they leave the party. Imagine a guest who is a relative stranger getting up from his or her chair during a meal, walking to the hostess's chair and kissing her squarely on the mouth. The reaction to such an act might provide much useful information about rule violations. Imagine, too, your reaction to a perfect stranger who got on an elevator with you, invaded your private space by placing his or her nose two inches from yours, and began asking questions about your sex life. Again, the reaction may reveal something about our social rules and their violations.

These communicative strategies of coming to know the other are probably not exhaustive (we have not, for example, discussed the possibility of hiring a private detective to spy on the other), and we have seen that they overlap to some degree. It will be useful, however, to keep in mind these strategies and the levels of knowing as we consider the following approaches to dyadic communication.

Approaches to Interpersonal Communication

Action-Interaction Approach

Much nonsense has been written about interpersonal communication, especially in books written for popular consumption, but also regrettably in textbooks. We are advised to be open with others; our goal in interpersonal communication should be affection. Certainly openness and affection are important, even indispensable, elements of interpersonal communication, but this advice is indiscriminate and, therefore, unhelpful. This will become clearer after considering another action theorist, Talcott Parsons (1902– 1979).

Parsons's Definition of an Act. As befits an action theorist, Parsons decided that the basic unit of human behavior is the act. He defined the unit act in a way reminiscent of Burke's definition of action (in chapter 2).

> In this sense then, an "act" involves logically the following: (1) It implies an agent, an "actor." (2) For purposes of definition the act must have an "end," a future state of affairs toward which the process of action is oriented. (3) It must be initiated in a "situation" of which the trends of development differ in one or more important respects from the state of affairs to which the action is oriented, the end. This situation is in turn analyzable into two elements: those over which the actor has no control, that is which he cannot alter, or prevent from being altered, in conformity with his end, and those over which he has such control. The former may be termed the "conditions" of action, the latter the "means." Finally (4) there is inherent in the conception of this unit, in its analytical uses, a certain mode of relationship between these ele-

ments. That is, in the choice of alternative means to the end, in so far as the situation allows alternatives, there is a "normative orientation" of action.[7]

As you might have discerned from that passage, Parsons's style or language is difficult to understand. Before hastening to explain the ramifications of his definition, we should note again the similarity to Burke's pentad (discussed in chapter 2). This similarity is probably not coincidental. These two towering figures of twentieth-century thought were very much aware of each other and even gave credit to each other.[8]

The first important implication is that an act is always a process in time, which recalls David Berlo's discussion of process in chapter 3. The end, for example, exists in the future. It is a picture in the mind of the actor. The would-be doctor reading this book might have mental pictures in which he or she is handed a diploma or license, wears a white lab coat, and is respectfully addressed by others as "Dr. Cohen," "Dr. Smith," or "Dr. Cimaglia." The end is not yet in existence; it will not come into existence unless the actor does something; or, if it does already exist and the actor wants it to continue, it would not do so unless the actor does something.

Second, the fact that there is a range of choice in regard to both ends and means implies that there may be an error or mistake on the part of the actor. One cannot become a doctor by going to law school. As for ends, it would be a mistake to visualize handing in a term paper on T. S. Eliot's poetry to one's chemistry professor.

Third, the actor is not a passive respondent to stimuli, but he or she is also not totally free. The force of the actor's culture — as embodied in rules, norms and values — will strongly influence choices. Our culture specifies what ends and means are appropriate to action. Thus, it is appropriate to aspire to be a doctor; it is not appropriate to become one by stealing a diploma and a license and opening up a clinic.

Fourth, although Parsons regarded his definition as a scientific conceptualization of human action, he acknowledged that it includes a highly subjective factor. The things and events involved in action must be considered as they appear to the actor's point of view. These phenomena have a scientifically relevant subjective aspect. To understand an act, we must understand the meaning (see chapter 3) assigned to the phenomena by the actor.

Fifth, we should emphasize that the end as visualized by the actor — that is, the pictures in his or her head — is usually incomplete in detail. To use the previous example, the student can picture himself or herself handing in the term paper even though he or she is unable to see the details of the content. This fact is the theme of much popular literature; after years of hard work and self-deprivation, the apparently successful person finds the end unsatisfying or finds it depressing to be alone at the top.

Sixth, the actor may be an individual, a group, an organization, or even a total society. If you miss this point, you will miss much of the rest of this book. Thus, an understanding of this action scheme allows you to understand more than an individual. For example, two sovereign governments will have to interact with each other even though it appears that a discussion between their representatives is no more than interpersonal communication. Keep this in mind while reading the subsequent chapters. However, inasmuch as this chapter is devoted to interpersonal communication, or to dyads, we must now drop another actor into the situation.

With the other party in the situation, action becomes transformed into interaction. Ego the actor is joined by a second player, alter the actor. A new and different kind of action is now possible. The language, or system of symbols, that makes this possible was also analyzed by Parsons.[9] His analysis is consistent with our discussion in chapter 3. Symbolism has a cognitive, or thought-related, meaning and a cathectic, or emotion-related, meaning; as a result of society's conventions or rules, these meanings allow us to transcend "private" interpretations. Ego's expression of symbolic action also permits alter to impute intentions to him or her.

We have now set the scene for alter-ego interaction. Each is free to choose an end in the situation. This freedom is limited by the pressure of biological and psychological needs and the norms and rules of the social system. I ask for your patience in reading the following:

> The simplest case is that of the dyad: ego has alter as a significant object in his situation and alter has ego as an object in his own. In acting with respect to alter, ego must *predict* [italics added] how he will respond; in effect, his action is designed to produce a certain desired reaction in alter. And of course alter is presumably doing the same sort of thing with respect to ego. Interaction thus has the characteristic which Parsons has called double contingency. If the two are not well acquainted, we may expect that there will be many wrong *predictions* [italics added] at first, and many communication failures. But after a while, Parsons observes, they may get to be rather good at it. Their actions with respect to one another tend to become patterned and stabilized: when interacting, ego comes to play a specific sort of role in relation to himself. In some such manner, a child and his mother learn what to expect of one another and we have a miniature two-role social system, in which each role is complementary to the other.
>
> Presumably, if the relationship endures, each member of the system derives certain satisfactions and meets certain needs through his participation in it: to this extent, each develops a vested interest in the continuity and stability of the relationship. Where this is true, alter's conformity to role expectations will come to have reward value for ego, and his deviations will quickly be countered with negative sanctions of some sort. And alter, of course, would do the same for ego. The effect of this mutual sanctioning is to create a mechanism which operates to preserve the equilibrium of the miniature social system: minor distur-

bances set forces in motion which function to restore the *status quo ante*. In the course of time, moreover, the dyad is likely to develop its own private culture, consisting of shared bits of knowledge, techniques, symbols with special shared meanings, tools and other significant objects, normative standards and even goals. Culture, in this sense, thus represents the shared property of the members of the social system: the items which comprise it are all potentially teachable or transferable to some new member of the group.[10]

This long quotation also requires interpretation. As emphasized by italics, ego and alter engage in predicting the acts of the other. As expectations build up on both sides, the dyad stabilizes and takes on the characteristics of a tiny social system. As the relationship endures, each actor meets his or her needs, rewards the desired acts of the other, and punishes the undesired ones. As minor events tend to upset the equilibrium, the actors will attempt to restore it. The dyadic "culture" can now be taught to others.

This is not the life of every dyad. One could not function if every encounter became a long-term relationship. As promised earlier in this chapter, we need to find principles by which to categorize different kinds of dyads, which, in turn, require different kinds of participation. Parsons called these principles "pattern variables," or variables that affect the patterning of interaction.

Pattern Variables.   Each of the four pattern variables is, in fact, a dichotomous choice (or pair of opposites) to make about your relationship with others. The four pattern variables are: (1) affectivity-affective neutrality, (2) specificity-diffuseness, (3) performance-quality, and (4) universalism-particularism.[11]

1. *Affectivity-Affective neutrality*. Put as simply as possible, this attitudinal dichotomy, or division, asks whether feelings — positive or negative — should be an important part of the relationship between alter and ego. In the case of husband and wife the answer is clearly affirmative. Think of the negative consequences, however, if doctors and their patients allowed either hate or love to distract them. This dichotomy also implies a choice between a relationship that is an end in itself versus a means to an end. A social worker, if effective in helping his or her client, would be working to terminate the relationship; the desired end should be independence for the client. In general, task relationships tend toward affective neutrality; friendships and family relationships tend toward affectivity.

2. *Specificity-Diffuseness*. This is another attitudinal dichotomy; it refers to the scope or inclusiveness of the relationship. Marriage partners can again illustrate one side. When alter and ego marry, each vows to deal with a total personality; the relationship has *diffuseness*, or many different sides. When alter deals with the clerk in the record shop, on the

other hand, the relationship is highly specific. In the latter case most aspects of the actors' personalities are submerged in the interchange. A cliché among teachers is the remark, "The students are amazed to find out that we are people." One meaning of that cliché is that students see only one narrow dimension of teachers and are surprised to learn of other facets of their personalities. The child has a diffuse love for mother and specific affection for the person at the ice cream stand.

3. *Performance-Quality*. Parsons considered the actor in a situation to be one among the totality of objects to be considered before acting. This dichotomy allows alter to judge the objects — including ego — on either what it does or what it is, that is, on either its performance or its quality. Modern society tends to apply performance standards such as diplomas, degrees, licenses, and experience. Past societies tended to apply quality standards, including the patrilineal right of kings. Should the teacher deal with the student as student, or as the son of a famous celebrity? Should people be forced to retire at age sixty-five even if they are effective workers?

4. *Universalism-Particularism*. This is the second of the pair of pattern variables in which the actor must judge an object — again including other actors — according to specified criteria. For example, teachers quickly learn that they must judge their students by universal criteria rather than particular ones. A parent, however, is quite likely to judge sons and daughters by more particular criteria. Of course, a degree of particularism does creep into the teacher's judgment, and a degree of universalism is applied by a parent. Nonetheless, the dominant emphasis in each case is as we have described. The dilemma requires acknowledging fairness and justice, on one hand, and recognizing the uniqueness in individuals, on the other. Nepotism again intrudes when particular, rather than universal, standards are employed. "One should choose a doctor on the basis of his [or her] competence and not on the ground that he [or she] is friend, neighbor, or cousin."[12] This dichotomy seems also to imply a cognitive versus affective set of criteria in judging others. To illustrate, the teacher who chooses to employ universal criteria in evaluating students will emphasize learning, intellectual growth, and performance. The parent-child evaluation will emphasize particular criteria that are consistent with feelings for each other.

This set of pattern variables is offered here not as a theory of interpersonal communication but as a heuristic, or learning, device. It should allow you to describe, predict, and explain how certain persons will act in dyads. In general, family and friendship dyads display a pattern of affectivity, diffuseness, quality, and particularism. Business, vocational, and professional dyads tend to stress affective neutrality, specificity, performance, and universalism. Deviations from these patterns may bring about negative consequences. Using these pattern variables, you should also be able to evaluate research that studies, for example, self-disclosure in task-oriented dyads and tries to generalize to friendship and familial dyads. It should also make you sensitive to the ways in which dyads function differently from situation to situation. Thus, a doctor can ask you to undress, can touch you, and ask for intimate self-disclosure in one situation — his or her office — but is prohibited from acting in these ways in other situations — such as a wedding reception.

Constructivism Approach

This approach to interpersonal communication is a fairly recent development, but one which is gaining rapidly in acceptance. It has been advocated by Jesse G. Delia and his associates (colleagues and students) in the Department of Speech Communication at the University of Illinois.

Many social scientists divide the world into "us" and "them." Freudian psychology, for example, assumes that "they" are sex-starved neurotics. "We" psychoanalysts, on the other hand, are normal scientists capable of creating theories that explain "them." Constructivism erases this distinction by proclaiming that Everyman and Everywoman act as scientists. Each one, in fact, has to communicate with others; therefore, each is an amateur communication scientist or rhetorical theorist.

Basic Premises of Constructivism. Let's turn now to the four basic premises of the constructivist approach and to the constructivist view of the self and communicative competence.

1. The first premise is that "persons approach the world with an ordering attitude."[13] I assume that my readers are serious scholars. Even if you are young, you are beginning to take pride in building a personal library. As the number of books in that library increases, it becomes necessary for the sake of efficiency in information retrieval to order them. They can be ordered in many ways — by date of publication, color, size, publishing company, and so on — but the considered opinion of the world's great libraries is to order by subject matter.

Similarly, when we confront unfamiliar objects or events, we act as if we were scientists. We try to create order among the objects and events in order to understand them. Primitive people must make sense of their world and give order to both seen and unseen forces (we would call the latter "magic" or "religion"). In reading a number of studies of such persons, I was struck by the thought that the anthropologists who were trying to explain the actions of the "primitives" were acting in the same way as those being explained; that is, they were trying to explain seen phenomena and unseen phenomena (for example, rules) by means of science.

2. The second premise is that "persons order and understand events within a system of personal interpretive constructs or categories."[14] *Personal*

constructs (hence "constructivism") can be defined as individual classification and interpretation schemes by which we describe, predict, and explain the world. We construct the world, including other people, in which we act.

For example, suppose we ask a thousand persons selected at random to think of the most credible person they know and describe his or her three most important characteristics. Their answers would reveal the construct system employed by each person in perceiving and constructing communicative sources. We would expect the Aristotelian categories of good sense, good character, and good will to be mentioned by most of our respondents. However, constructivism would also expect us to find exceptions because construct systems are individual and idiosyncratic. Some respondents might choose such characteristics as chaste, religious, temperate, or even promiscuous. (Aristotle might reply that these respondents have revealed what they consider to be good character, a single component of ethos.)

3. The third premise is that "persons construct personally and socially meaningful understandings of events and persons in their world."[15] This premise is a combination of two main points made earlier in this book. The first is that one must act upon his or her symbolic interpretation of the situation. The second is that meaning is at the center of human action or communication. In short, this constructivist premise holds that we confront nature, including human nature, through symbolic perceptions; we create a world of meanings.

4. The fourth premise is that "a person's actions are based upon his personal interpretation of the persons, events, and situations facing him."[16] As a corollary of the third, this premise directs our attention away from the receiver's source, the receiver's situation, and the message received; rather, what is needed is an understanding of how the receiver interprets or constructs the message, source, and situation.

Thus, constructivism is consistent with the action orientation espoused in this book. Humans are not viewed as passive, mechanistic agents — that is, as billiard balls bumped about in a life of sheer motion — but as active, organismic agents acting upon their constructions of reality.

> This point [the fourth premise], of course, stands in marked contrast to the billiard-ball thinking of the passive-mechanist view in which persons and communications are naively assumed to produce direct influence. If we are to understand human conduct we must recognize that persons give *personal meaning* to situations and messages and these personal meanings form the basis of their actions. A noted language theorist of the first half of this century, Benjamin Lee Whorf, emphasized this characteristic of human action by recalling a number of examples from his earlier employment as a fire insurance adjuster. In one case, for example, Whorf reports that a fire was caused because lighted cigarette butts were tossed into "empty" gasoline drums. Since "empty" drums can't burn, no hazard was perceived. Unfortunately as

most of us realize, it is not gasoline, but gasoline fumes — fumes which remain in cans where gasoline was once stored — that burn. The point is that the person in this situation construed the gasoline drums as "empty" and as "safe" (he erected a personal symbolic interpretation) and acted toward them accordingly. Thus we always act toward situations on the basis of the symbolic meanings we give to them.[17]

This quotation does not deny that social norms and education teach us how to construct reality in standard ways. Otherwise the fire insurance adjuster would not be able to construct a "full" drum out of an obviously "empty" one.

Perspective Taking and Rhetorical Adaptation.   Before considering the constructivist view of the self and communicative competence, we should consider two additional concepts: perspective taking and rhetorical adaptation. The concept of *perspective taking* helps resolve an apparent dilemma for the constructivist approach. Some readers may have perceived that dilemma during the discussion of the four basic premises. If human interpretations are personal and if the constructs by which we erect meanings are individual, how can one person ever understand the other?

One answer is by perspective taking, or the processes by which a person infers the other's point of view in a situation. Because we have ends and intentions, we can imagine another's ends. When one has empathy for another, or when one tries to step into the other's shoes, one is engaged in perspective taking. It is true that we are still limited to our own construct systems during this process of perspective taking, but we can understand the other's categories in spite of their differences. For instance, it is relatively easy for a nonbeliever to realize how important religion is to the devout.

Constructivism considers the systematic practice of perspective taking to be the equivalent of the traditional concept of "audience analysis." This, of course, allows the communicator flexibility, or to practice what is called *rhetorical adaptation*. Thus, even the constructivist approach to dyads illustrates the application of traditional rhetorical theory to interpersonal communication. Rhetorical adaptation is the use of strategic choice in persuading the other.

Self-concept and Constructivism.   The constructivist view of *self* is consistent with the view of self put forward by George Herbert Mead, an American philosopher of human behavior.[18] The "constructivist view of persons also places great stress upon the self-concept as the central organizing feature of the perceptual field."[19] The self-concept is an organized totality of beliefs or inferences about oneself. These beliefs or inferences come from interaction with others. As we watch and hear others respond to us, we begin to form beliefs about ourselves. We use others as mirrors in which to see ourselves.

If others seek our advice, we infer that we possess judgment or wisdom. If others seem to seek us out just to be with us, we infer likeability or attractiveness on our part. In a sense, interpersonal communication creates self-discovery. Again, we are not passive reactors to others; we present ourself to others in an active way, hoping to see indications of wisdom or likeability reflected in the reactions of others. Thus, in interpersonal communication we are continuously looking to confirm or deny our self-conception.

One could read the foregoing paragraphs and assume that the self is plastic, malleable, and perhaps even capable of changing radically after each encounter with another. However, this is not true for most of us. The self-concept is given some stability by discriminating among the others who react to us. The anonymous stranger we meet in one brief encounter is likely to have neither an important nor a lasting effect on the self-concept. Rather, each of us has a select group of *significant others*, or valued acquaintances. They may be parents, teachers, or friends. These significant others have an important influence on our self-concept. In facing a difficult choice, we find ourselves wondering what a certain significant other would do in the situation or would advise us to do. After an accomplishment we enjoy imagining how our significant others would react to the good news. These significant others and the *generalized other*, which is society as a whole, help us become what we are.

The categories or beliefs making up the self-concept are rich in complexity. Different aspects of the self are presented to different others and groups of others.

> While one's generalized feeling of worth and value as a person is of unquestioned importance, thinking of the self in this simplified way leads to too restricted an understanding of persons. Just as the diamond is multifaceted, so is the self multi-dimensional. Thus, in communication, we are not bound to a narrow range of ways of behaving and presenting ourselves; instead, we have a diversity of "facets," any one of which might be "turned toward" a particular social situation. Hence, most of us have great flexibility in the ways that we can deal with situations.[20]

Communicative Competence. *Communicative competence* is a concept defined differently by different scholars in linguistics and communication. The constructivists' meaning of the concept can be best approached by explaining what it is *not*. By age four or five, most children in our culture have mastered the English language. This is not equivalent to saying that the child is a competent communicator. This early mastery of language is employed by the child in egocentric speech, or speech that fails to take others into account. Two children of that age might well engage in "duologue," two independent monologues.

Prior to achieving communicative competence children do not adapt to the perspective of the listener. Communicative competence involves (1) adaptation of sentences and vocabulary to the perspective of the listener; (2) adaptation to the situation and the role of the listener; and (3) strategic adaptation throughout sustained interaction. An example of the first would be the child who addresses an even younger child with short sentences and simple words. An example of the second would be the child who knows when to use the appropriate title or mode of address for adults in the situation. An example of the third would be the child who has reasons that are adapted to the perspective of the parent to support a request for, say, a cookie. The young son of a colleague showed he was entering this third level of communicative competence in the following way.

Young Matthew had a slight articulation problem. He substituted "yuh" for "luh," as in "Please turn on the yight." His parents corrected him on these occasions by saying, "Watch my mouth," and then by repeating the word *light* several times before asking Matthew to repeat the word. One day Matthew came in from playing in the yard and asked for cookies and milk. His mother denied the request with the explanation that it was too close to time for the evening meal. "No," she replied to each of his requests.

"Watch my mouth," Matthew finally said. Very deliberately, he formed the word *yes*. Matthew showed that he was developing communicative competence.

We should not assume, however, that communicative competence, or the strategic adaptation of messages to the perspective of others, arrives fully developed at a particular age. We must battle the egocentric tendency throughout our life and strive to improve our ability to describe, predict, and explain the perspective of others. Making our growth even more difficult, this need to adapt our messages must be balanced by our ethical responsibilities. As noted previously, although Henry David Thoreau was an effective speaker, he decided at one point in his life to stop giving speeches and lectures. His reason was that he feared adapting to the audience and compromising his beliefs.

Self-disclosure Approach

This is not an approach to interpersonal communication in the same sense as action-interaction and constructivism; that is, it is not a general position on interpersonal communication. Rather it is an aspect of dyadic communication. It is included among the approaches discussed in this chapter because it is intrinsically interesting to most people and because it is a thoroughly researched variable. As we look at some of the generalizations prompted by that research, keep in mind the pattern variables of interaction discussed earlier in this chapter. Also keep in mind our discussion of self-disclosure as a strategy by which to know another.

Self-disclosure is the communication of favorable or unfavorable information about the source, which the receiver would not be likely to receive otherwise. It is usually measured by asking a person what he or she has disclosed in the past, and this question is sometimes combined with questions about one's willingness to disclose in the future. In general, "situational variables may outweigh individual differences in disposition to disclose."[21] We should expect this from our discussion earlier in the chapter of the effect of pattern variables on interaction.

Another generalization is that females have higher disclosure scores than males. A number of studies indicate this; some studies indicate no differences between males and females, but no studies indicate that males disclose more than females. There is no completely satisfactory explanation for this finding.

The relationship between self-disclosure and mental health has been studied, but the results are somewhat confusing. After reviewing the research in this area, Cozby hypothesized:

> Persons with positive mental health (given that they can be identified) are characterized by high disclosure to a few significant others and medium disclosure to others in the social environment. Individuals who are poorly adjusted (again assuming a suitable identification can be made) are characterized by either high or low disclosure to virtually everyone in the social environment. Future research should help to clarify this rather confused aspect of self-disclosure.[22]

Self-disclosure seems to be related to the "stages" of the development of a relation, and some degree of reciprocity seems to be involved. Relationships, for example, proceed from nonintimate to intimate topics of exchange. A study of Korean female university students concludes that "there is a linear inverse association between stage of relationship and the generation of non-intimate reciprocal self-disclosures."[23] The psychological jargon of this quotation can be translated in the following way: As the relationships progressed, the persons generated fewer nonintimate disclosures. The same study found a "curvilinear association between the stage of relationship and the generation of intimate reciprocal self-disclosures."[24] This means that the exchange of self-disclosure between two strangers increased until it reached a peak; at its peak the relationship became an advanced relationship (best friends, lovers, spouses), and the level of self-disclosure diminished. In these real-life relationships, approximately 47 percent of the self-disclosures were reciprocated at each stage of the relationship.

The fact that the Korean study was done with real-life relationships is somewhat reassuring because many people are suspicious of laboratory studies. Subjects in studies with strangers might be more likely to disclose because there is no possibility of future interaction with the other person. This is known as the "stranger on the train" phenomenon.

There also appears to be a relationship between liking and self-disclosure; such a finding supports common sense. Do we like people with whom we reciprocally disclose, or do we reciprocally disclose with people we like? Probably both are true. In one study, subjects had a ten-minute "getting acquainted" period and then indicated their liking for each other. Then each person chose information to disclose to each other person on ten "trials" or interactions. On the first trial the most information was disclosed to the most liked other, and the least information was disclosed to the least liked other. After the ten trials, a final liking score was obtained; analysis showed that subjects most liked others who had disclosed most to them.[25]

Cozby suggested that the relationship between liking and self-disclosure is also curvilinear. In a curvilinear relationship as the scores, or number values, of one variable increase, the scores of the second variable also increase up to a point, and then the pattern reverses. As scores of the first variable continue to increase, the scores on the second variable begin and continue to decrease. Curvilinear means that two variables behave in the way that age and motor skills relate. The infant (low age) and the senile person (high age) will probably both be low in motor skills; during the age period between these extremes the person will have high motor skills. Thus, the person who discloses little or nothing will not be liked; it is impossible to get to know such a person. A high discloser, however, will probably not be liked because we would construe or construct such a person as lacking in discretion and truthworthiness. The person who discloses in moderate amounts may invite us to reciprocate and thereby develop a mutual feeling of liking.[26]

We see, therefore, that there are limits to the value of self-disclosure. There is a limit to the degree to which it can facilitate liking and the development of a relationship. There is also a limit to its reciprocation and its strategic use in getting to know the other. In fact, Cozby concluded that there are two forces at work in this area — a force that encourages self-disclosure and a force that discourages it. The first force has been studied much more extensively than the second. Self-disclosure has been "closely associated with the encounter group movement which emphasizes the need to relate, communicate, and be honest and open with others."[27] One writer on the subject classifies people who withhold information as "hermits, prudes, paranoids, or rascals."[28] We should be wary of those who wish to impose on us a tyranny of self-disclosure. As the pattern variables of interaction and the research surveyed suggest, we ought to cultivate the arts of self-concealment (which is not synonymous with lying and deception) as well as self-disclosure. Knowing when to speak and when to remain silent is the reasonable middle ground between the extremes.

Relational Communication Approach

This approach, which also deals with only one aspect of dyadic communication, was inspired by an anthropologist, Gregory Bateson, who with his associates at the Mental Research Institute are known as the Palo Alto Group. Although their work has focused on "disturbed" communication — the problems of psychiatric patients — they have produced insights useful to "normal" communication. Perhaps the best way to consider this approach is by "some tentative axioms" put forward by representatives of the group.

1. "*One cannot* not *communicate*."[29] All behavior, according to this group, has message value. Suppose I ask, "Do you still love me?" Suppose further that you remain silent and motionless. Surely that is a message that I would be stupid not to get. In that situation, speech or silence and action or inaction would constitute messages. In short, one cannot not communicate.

Some experts have questioned such a global definition of communication. Although advocates of this approach say that communication need not be intentional, their examples (a man closing his eyes on an airplane to signal that he does not want to talk) all assume clear ends or intentions. Otherwise their examples would not make sense. Nonetheless, this axiom does remind us that others are free to construe and construct any of our behaviors, intentional or not, in such a way as to understand us.

2. "Every communication has a content and a relationship aspect such that the latter classifies the former and is therefore a metacommunication."[30] This axiom reveals why the approach has received the label "relational communication." The claim is that in addition to content, or information, a message also conveys the nature of the dyad's relationship. The content is called the "report"; the relational aspect is called the "command." In teaching the student writer, the instructor says, "Find a rhetorical stance." The message has a report, but the command defines the teacher-student relationship. The word *metacommunication* simply means a message *about* a message. In our example, the message about the message would be "This is what to do with the report." The command is about the relationship of the two actors, hence the "relational" approach to interpersonal communication. This notion of report-command is similar to the speech act approach to meaning discussed in chapter 3.

3. "The nature of a relationship is contingent upon the punctuation of the communicational sequences between the communicants."[31] Here again we have a stress on the relational aspect of interpersonal communication. As members of the Palo Alto Group put it:

> Disagreement about how to punctuate the sequence of events is at the root of countless relationship struggles. Suppose a couple have a marital problem to which he contributes passive withdrawal, while her 50

percent is nagging criticism. In explaining their frustrations, the husband will state that withdrawal is his only *defense against* her nagging, while she will label this explanation a gross and willful distortion of what "really" happens in their marriage: namely, that she is critical of him *because of* his passivity. Stripped of all ephemeral and fortuitous elements, their fights consist in a monotonous exchange of the messages "I withdraw because you nag" and "I nag because you withdraw."[32]

Note that neither of the actors in the dyad is wrong; each is right. On the one hand, he is "punctuating," or ordering, the sequences of their communication in this way:

She nags, I withdraw.

On the other hand, she punctuates the sequence as:

He withdraws, I nag.

The couple's problem is (1) the inability to engage in metacommunication, that is, the inability to communicate about their communication; and (2) the mistaken belief that there is a beginning to such a sequence. Perhaps the couple has only the first problem. If they could communicate about communication, they might come to see that there is no gross and willful distortion of reality and that there is no beginning in such communication sequences. This problem, by the way, may be a main cause of the quarrel between stimulus-response behaviorists and action theorists. What the first group sees as a response, the other group sees as a stimulus.

4. "All communicational interchanges are either symmetrical or complementary, depending on whether they are based on equality or difference."[33] To say that all exchanges are either symmetrical or complementary is another way of stressing the relational character of interpersonal communication. In a complementary relationship one asserts control, and the other accepts; only by examining the pair of messages can one understand what is happening in the relationship.

In a complementary exchange, alter produces a one-up (↑) message followed by ego's one-down (↓) reply. As an example, alter offers advice, and ego accepts it; or, alter commands ego, and ego obeys. In another example, alter asks for information (↓), which is supplied in an answer by ego (↑). Note that only the exchange, not a single remark, may be regarded as complementary. The one-up and one-down exchange (↑↓) or the one-down and one-up exchange (↓↑) implies an inequality in the relationship. One of the two actors is in control of the relationship.

A symmetrical exchange or relationship involves an equality between parties. One behavior produces a like behavior. If one actor in the dyad boasts, the other actor boasts. Thus, a symmetrical exchange can be competitive. Still another symmetrical exchange could be alter confessing an inadequacy, which is met by ego's similar confession. Each exchange is a comment on the equality of the relationship.

An elaborate coding scheme has been worked out, however, for analyzing real-life conversations.[34] This will permit an empirical test of the ideas of the relational approach.

The Argumentative Approach

This is also an analysis of one aspect of interpersonal communication rather than a general position. People in dyads argue, and some do it better than others. In fact, some marriage counselors have found that verbal conflict between husbands and wives is constructive and highly desirable.

Rules for Fair Fighting. Let us consider some of the findings of the Institute of Group Psychotherapy in California about dyadic arguments. For years this institute has been helping married couples learn the rules or principles of fair fighting. As indicated above, they spend much of their time teaching people that arguing, if done fairly, is highly desirable for the dyad. Many people camouflage their hostilities out of the belief that people who love each other do not have such feelings. The reader of this book knows better. Recall the dichotomous pattern variables of affectivity-affective neutrality. Some members of dyads have no feelings for each other, while others have strong feelings that can be either positive or negative. An occasional indication of hatred in a marriage is probably preferable to affective neutrality, or an attitude of "I couldn't care less how you feel about this."

Other couples have a different kind of problem. They may argue much of the time but without a knowledge of the rules that make for fair play and for productive and disirable conflict (see Figure 4–3). Let's consider a snatch of dialogue from such an argument:

> Mr. and Mrs. Bill Miller have a dinner date with one of Bill's out-of-town business associates and the associate's wife. Mrs. Miller is coming in from the suburbs and has agreed to meet Bill in front of his office building. The Millers have been married for 12 years and have three children. They are somewhat bored with each other by now, but they rarely fight. Tonight happens to be different. Bill Miller is anxious to make a good impression on the visiting fireman from out of town. His wife arrives 20 minutes late. Bill is furious. He hails a taxi and the fun begins:
>
> He: Why were you late?
>
> She: I tried my best.
>
> He: Yeah? You and who else? Your mother is never on time either.
>
> She: That's got nothing to do with it.

He: The hell it doesn't. You're just as sloppy as she is.

She: (*getting louder*): You don't say! Who's picking whose dirty underwear off the floor every morning?

He: (*sarcastic but controlled*): I happen to go to work. What have *you* got to do all day?

She: (*shouting*): I'm trying to get along on the money you don't make, that's what.

He: (*turning away from her*): Why should I knock myself out for an ungrateful bitch like you?[35]

What rules of fair fighting were violated? Notice that both members of the dyad had been storing up their grievances for some time. George R. Bach and Peter Wyden call this "gunny-sacking" and teach their clients to avoid the practice. In this case, when the sack broke open, Bill's attitude toward his mother-in-law as well as Mrs. Miller's negative view of Bill as a provider spilled out on what otherwise would have been a neat, clean argument about her being late.

Figure 4-3 Aside from being simply flashes of anger, arguments may serve positive, constructive purposes in communication. Nonetheless, rules for fair fighting help to ensure that the argument plays an effective part in the conflict and does not lead to further resentment and frustration. (Leonard Freed/Magnum Photos, Inc.)

The Institute of Group Psychotherapy recommends that, instead of employing the gunny-sack technique, the couple should fight when each issue arises — even if it happens in front of friends and children. They even recommend fighting before, during, or after intercourse. This way the marriage "books" can be kept up to date and can be balanced daily; the partners need not walk around with a gunny-sack full of unpaid bills.

Another rule for marital argument generated by Bach and Wyden is "Don't drop the atomic bomb on Luxembourg!"[36] The meaning of this rule can be explained by another incident described by Bach and Wyden. The James couple had been married for eight years, and tonight Mrs. James is in a quiet rage at Mr. James. He had refused to discuss an urgent financial matter at dinner. Later he had strewn his clothes messily all over the bedroom floor. After intercourse he also had the nerve to praise his own lovemaking ability. Without thinking, she reaches for an atomic bomb.

"You know, I never come. I fake it."[37]

Atomic bombs should not be used when a water pistol would suffice.

Bach and Wyden describe a systematic program for teaching the rules of fighting fairly. Space will not permit a fuller description of it here, but additional reading on the subject is recommended at the end of the chapter. Having taken a favorable attitude toward fighting, I want to balance this position with a few words about compromise. Fighting is better than silence, but there are alternatives to a constant win-lose orientation to interpersonal communication. The point of the most important dyad that the majority of us experience — that is, marriage — is the ideal of sharing. This suggests that there is wisdom in an occasional compromise as a form of sharing.

However, there is more to be learned about effective argumentation in an interpersonal situation than how to fight fairly. It is also valuable for individuals to understand how to influence one another in a dyadic situation. Let us consider, then, what is analytically necessary for one person to change the mind of another by argument.

The theory of argument, or argumentation, is an important segment of rhetorical theory. Although the theory of argument is usually discussed in terms of formal speaker/audience and debate situations, it is important to understand the role of argument in a dyadic situation. Two concepts from the theory of argument that need explanation are presumption and burden of proof.

Presumption.   _Presumption_ is a concept we know intuitively if not perfectly. In a criminal court case, the defendant is presumed to be innocent; hence, he or she enjoys the presumption. The defendant preoccupies the "ground" of innocence and will continue to do so until dislodged by sufficient reasons. Argument theory gives presumption to the status quo, or present conditions and institutions. If one wishes to institute new laws governing the use of, say, marijuana, one must accept that the current laws have the presumption, preoccupy the ground, and must be dislodged by arguments. In other words, existing laws and institutions will continue unless enough people are convinced by argument of the necessity of change; these laws and institutions have presumption.

Presumption in a natural dyadic argument differs somewhat. When alter and ego disagree, they do not formally decide which one has the presumption — even if they are lawyers or teachers of argumentation. In any case, it would not really matter who had the institutional presumption (that is, who believes in the status quo). In the natural state, if alter wants to change ego's mind, *ego enjoys the psycho-logical presumption*.[38] Ego's belief is the psychological status quo; it preoccupies the ground and can only be moved by sufficient reasons. Ego's belief — whatever it is — will continue to exist unless alter can provide sufficient arguments to cause ego to change his mind. In short, alter must grant presumption to ego in such a situation if he or she wishes to be effective.

Burden of Proof.   The *burden of proof* is the other side of the coin. When the state attempts to convict the defendant, it assumes the burden of proof. In a debate those who propose a change, such as new marijuana laws, assume the burden of proof. A person or group who seeks to change a law or institution in this country can do so only by assuming the burden of proof in order to convince enough people of the necessity of that change to bring it about. (Note that there is a conservatism, or resistance to change, within the legal system, argumentation theory, and social structures. This is a reflection of the way people behave naturally; that is, people — and their products such as laws and institutions — will continue to think and act as they have in the past, until convinced of the necessity or value of change. This fact proved frustrating to those involved in the antiwar movement of the 1960s and 1970s.)

To return to alter and ego, alter assumes the burden of proof by his or her attempt to change ego's belief. Generally speaking, in accepting the burden of proof, alter must (1) show that the existing idea or practice is faulty, and should not occupy the ground; and (2) recommend that a new idea or practice should be accepted in its place. Once accepted by ego, the new idea or practice would then occupy the ground and enjoy the presumption.

The burden of proof, thus, has two main points. They are sometimes called problem-solution, or need-plan. Most people would be unable to verbalize the arguments that should be proved in order to assume the burden of proof. When their beliefs are under attack, however, most people can quickly point out the weaknesses in that attack; people have an intuitive understanding of burden of proof. Therefore, ego will expect alter to show that something is faulty with the present idea, that the new solution (or plan) will remove the problem (or meet the need), and may well expect to be shown that advantages will accrue to him or her by adopting the new idea or practice. Ego and the rest of us seem to be saying: If you expect me to change my ways, show me not only what's wrong with my ways but also a better way. Otherwise, I'll continue with my ways.

Let me try to illustrate the ideas of presumption and burden of proof, not only for the sake of understanding the alter-ego dyad, but also because we shall return to the concepts in several subsequent chapters. Suppose that alter and ego are college roommates; suppose further alter is an English major, and ego is a business major. Alter sets out to persuade ego to change her major. Thus, ego has the psychological *presumption* (and would even if what alter were advocating had institutional presumption), and alter accepts the *burden of proof*.

> A1: Yes, you really ought to consider changing your major to one of the departments in the College of Arts and Sciences.

> E1: Oh you artsy-craftsy people. I want a job when I get out of this place, and a B.S. in business will do it for me.

> A2: I think you're wasting your educational opportunity. Did you realize that people who graduate with your major in management are not all getting jobs, and that some of the jobs they do get are below their level of preparation?

> E2: Well, at least some of them got jobs. That's better than you English lit. types do.

> A3: Perhaps. I know several people with majors in communication, economics, and mathematics who went on for a master's in business administration and got *really* good jobs.

> E3: I'll keep that in mind. Maybe I'll get an M.B.A.

> A4: But our School of Business gives preference to students with majors in the College of Arts and Sciences in accepting applicants for the M.B.A. program. Why don't you talk to your advisor in the Business School about it?

Although ego may not be completely persuaded by alter, ego does seem to be actively reconsidering her decision; alter assumes the burden of proof (1) by showing that the status quo, the existing state of affairs, is faulty (see A2); and (2) by recommending a new idea or practice (see A3). Alter also shows that the problems discussed (in A2) would be solved by the recommendation. Sensing that his ethos, or credibility, might not be sufficiently high, alter also recommends that ego talk to her advisor in the Business School as a check on the truthfulness of his remarks. This is an apparent indication that alter's end or intention has ego's interests in mind.

Although presumption usually lies with the status quo — or existing laws and institutions — and although those seeking change must assume the burden of proof, such is not necessarily the case in a dyadic situation. In a dyad the one seeking to convince the other has the burden of proof. The object of the persuasive attempt has the presumption, even if his or her views are radical and therefore contrary to institutional presumption. He or she will not change his or her mind until convinced of the necessity of that change. Thus, in the preceding example, ego (the persuadee) enjoyed psychological presumption, and alter (the persuader) had to assume the burden of proof. We will return to the concepts of presumption and burden of proof in later chapters. This concludes our discussion of the five approaches to dyadic or interpersonal communication. We shall now consider why dyads break up.

On Breaking Up

Although I am not advocating them, breakups of dating couples are to be preferred to divorces, and they do provide insight into some of the reasons for divorce. Those experiencing breakups often experience considerable pain, which they think no one else has experienced.

Charles T. Hill and associates conducted a two-year study of dating relationships among college students in the Boston area. At the end of the two-year study period, 103 couples (45 percent of the total sample) had broken up, ending relationships that ranged in duration from one month to five years. Several factors were related to the breakups.

First, the degree of attachment to the relationship made a difference. The greater the degree of "love," "liking," "closeness," and probability of marriage as reported by the couples, the better the chances for the relationship to survive. Interestingly, two measures of intimacy — having had sexual intercourse and having lived together — were totally unrelated to breaking up.

The second factor, an unequal degree of attachment to or identification with the relationship, tended to be followed by breakup. As the researchers put it, "Of the couples in which both members reported that they were equally involved in the relationship in 1972, only 23% broke up; in contrast, 54% of those couples in which at least one member reported that they were unequally involved subsequently broke up."[39] As one might expect, those who reported high attachment tended also to report equal involvement.

The third factor is similarity and matching. Similarity pertains to a variety of physical, intellectual, and social characteristics, as well as attitudes, and operates in both interpersonal attraction and mate selection. In this study, couples were more likely to stay together if the parties were similar with respect to age, intelligence, future educational plans, and physical attractiveness (as measured by judges' ratings of individual color photographs).

How do couples break up? What is the process by which the 103 couples ended their relationship? If due only to factors internal to the relationship (such as conflicting values), breakups should occur evenly throughout the calendar year. The 103 couples, however, broke up at key turning points of the school calendar year. They were more likely to break up in May–June, September, or December–January than at other times of the year. Because college students typically return home during the summer to live with parents and take a job, the change places a strain on the relationship. If one is already contemplating a breakup, it is possible to use a vacation as a convenient excuse for what would otherwise be a more trying confrontation. (The statement "I think we should date other people during the summer" is more easily accepted than "It's time to break it off.")

Timing is also related to another aspect of the breaking-up process. In most cases the breakup was desired more by the less involved party. In a minority of cases the partner who was more involved desired the termination (presumably because the "cost" of the relationship was more than could be borne). Hill and his associates found that the breakups desired by the less involved partner tended to take place before, during, and after the summer vacation (71.1 percent April–September versus 28.9 percent October–March). The breakups desired by the more involved partner were more likely to take place during the school year (59.1 percent October–March versus 40.9 percent April–September). Perhaps the best explanation is this thought from La Rochefoucauld, "Absence extinguishes small passions and increases great ones."[40]

Few breakups are mutually desired. In the study of 103 couples, 85 percent of the women and 87 percent of the men said that one partner had wanted to break up at least somewhat more than the other. Thus, there are two distinct roles in breaking up: "breaker-upper" and "broken-up-with."[41] The breaker-upper, whether male or female, felt freer, happier, and less lonely than the broken-up-with; however, he or she also felt guiltier. This is made somewhat cloudy by the fact that in some cases both partners claimed to be the one who desired the breakup. It seems to be easier to cope with a breakup if one views it as desired, rather than having been forced upon oneself (see Figure 4–4).

Indeed, we can speak of his or her breakups because the sexes handle the phenomenon differently. Romantic sexual stereotypes to the contrary, in respect to dating in middle-class America, "(a) men tend to fall in love more readily than women, and (b) women tend to fall out of love more readily than men."[42] In the 103 breakups, the woman was more desirous of breaking up in 51 percent of the couples, the man in 42 percent, and the desire was mutual in about 7 percent. This holds true whether the woman was more or less

Figure 4-4   Dyads end when the couple breaks up. A study of breakups among college students found that the separation was not usually sought equally by the partners. One member of the couple acted as "breaker-upper," the other as "broken-up-with." These opposing roles establish how each will respond to and recall the breakup. (© René Burri/Magnum Photos, Inc.)

committed than the partner. The partners were more likely to remain friends when the man precipitated the breakup (70 percent), or when it was mutual (71 percent), than when the woman precipitated it (46 percent). Men also seem to be hit harder emotionally than women by a breakup, finding it hard to reconcile themselves to the state of not being loved. In this study the men tended more to retain the hope that their rejectors really did love them after all.

 According to Hill and his associates, there are two explanations for the role played by the women in a breakup. The first may be changing because of the women's liberation movement, but the traditional economic explanation is that a man selects a helpmate for marriage while a woman selects a standard of living. She must be cold-blooded and mercenary in selecting a husband.

 The second explanation is that women have greater interpersonal sensitivity than men. Men are the traditional task-specialists while women are expert on the social and emotional matters (concepts explained in greater detail in chapter 6). Thus, women may be much more sensitive to interpersonal problems than men.

Hill and his associates concluded their study by noting the similarities and dissimilarities between breakups and divorces. As painful as they are, breakups before marriage are to be preferred to divorces after marriage. They also found, "it may be useful for couples to consider and create their own occasions for redefining and discussing their relationship. . . . Taking part in the study had the effects of clarifying participants' definition of their relationships and of facilitating disclosure of feelings, issues, and concerns. Other attempts to facilitate such self-examination and confrontation whether through college courses, counseling programs, or the mass media, are of potentially great value."[43]

Summary

This chapter has explored a cycle of dyadic communication. The cycle begins when the dyad gets together, progresses through different kinds of interpersonal communication, and ends when the dyad breaks up.

For the initial stage we have looked at the levels at which we know another person: description, prediction, and explanation. Consciously or unconsciously, we also use strategies to get acquainted. Among the most common are interrogation, self-disclosure, deception detection, environmental structuring, and deviation testing.

The five general approaches to, or aspects of, dyadic communication that we have considered are action-interaction, constructivism, self-disclosure, relational communication, and the argumentative approach.

I chose these five approaches for several reasons. They are consistent with the action (or interaction) stance of the book. The pattern variables were introduced as a heuristic device, or learning tool, which can be employed with or without the other approaches in analyzing dyadic communication. For example, we have shown how the pattern variables relate to self-disclosure. In addition, as contemporary society becomes more bureaucratized, interpersonal communication will be more characterized by particularism, performance, affective neutrality, and specificity. Constructivism is consistent with the action stance in stressing rhetorical skills in interpersonal communication and in emphasizing the self-concept in the perceptions relevant to interpersonal communication. Self-disclosure is a thoroughly researched topic of interest to most people, and the research suggests general guidelines for this kind of interaction. The relational approach emphasizes that dyadic communication involves more than people, namely relations, and poses the problem of control and compliance in dyads. The argumentative approach emphasizes the rhetorical (or psychological) skills required in interpersonal communication.

To see why dyads break up, we have discussed a study of couples who separated. This research provides some generalizations about why and how people break up, the timing of breakups, and the effects. By implication, the study also shows why and how people maintain relationships.

The following chapter adds another player, or agent, to interpersonal communication and examines triadic communication.

Questions for Essays, Speeches, and Group Discussions

1. Use the pattern variables to analyze the following dyads:

   teacher-student   chef-waiter
   brother-sister   priest-confessor
   doctor-patient   businessman-professor
   quarterback-fullback   attorney-psychiatrist

2. In each of the dyads above, specify the situations or scenes in which self-disclosure in depth would be appropriate and inappropriate.

3. If some persons have more categories than others by which to "construct" people, what differences (if any) would there be in ability to describe, predict, and explain?

4. Compare and contrast the notion of the "command" aspect of a message with the "speech act" theory of meaning discussed in chapter 3.

5. Is the concept of complementarity related in any way to the effect of pattern variables in a relationship?

6. Analyze one or more of the dyads in question 1 in terms of Burke's dramatistic theory using the pentad (see chapter 2).

Additional Readings

Cushman, Donald P., and Robert T. Craig. "Communication Systems: Interpersonal Implications." In *Explorations in Interpersonal Communication*, edited by Gerald R. Miller, pp. 37–58. Beverly Hills, Calif.: Sage Publications, 1976.

Gilbert, Shirley J. "Empirical and Theoretical Extensions of Self-Disclosure." In *Explorations in Interpersonal Communication*, edited by Gerald R. Miller, pp. 197– 215. Beverly Hills, Calif.: Sage Publications, Inc.

Millar, Frank E., and L. Edna Rogers. "A Relational Approach to Interpersonal Communication." In *Explorations in Interpersonal Communication*, edited by Gerald R. Miller, pp. 87– 103. Beverly Hills, Calif.: Sage Publications, 1976.

Rocher, Guy. *Talcott Parsons and American Sociology*. New York: Barnes & Noble, 1975.

Swanson, David L., and Jesse G. Delia. *The Nature of Human Communication*. Chicago: Science Research Associates, 1976.

Notes

1. Gerald R. Miller, ed., *Explorations in Interpersonal Communication* (Beverly Hills, Calif.: Sage Publications, 1976), pp. 9– 10.

2. Gerry Philipsen, "Enthymematic Discourse in Conversational Persuasion," Dimension Program Paper, Speech Communication Association Convention, Washington D.C., November 1977. See also Sally Jackson and Scott Jacobs, "Structure of Conversational Argument: Pragmatic Bases for the Enthymeme," *Quarterly Journal of Speech* 66(1980): 251– 65.

3. Charles R. Berger, Royce R. Gardner, Malcolm R. Parks, Linda Schulman, and Gerald R. Miller, "Interpersonal Epistemology and Interpersonal Communication," in *Explorations in Interpersonal Communication*, ed. Gerald R. Miller (Beverly Hills, Calif.: Sage Publications, 1976), pp. 149– 71.

4. Gerald R. Miller and M. Steinberg, *Between People: A New Analysis of Interpersonal Communication* (Palo Alto, Calif.: Science Research Associates, 1975), pp. 7– 25.

5. Charles R. Berger and R. J. Calabrese, "Some Explorations in Initial Interaction and Beyond: Toward a Developmental Theory of Interpersonal Communication," *Human Communication Research* 1(1975): 99– 112.

6. Berger et al., "Interpersonal Epistemology," pp. 163– 70.

7. Talcott Parsons, *The Structure of Social Action*. Copyright ©1968 by The Free Press, a Division of MacMillan Publishing Company, Inc. Reprinted by permission.

8. For example, Parsons's definition appeared in the first (1937) edition of *The Structure of Social Action*. Burke's pentad first appeared in 1945. Furthermore, Burke quotes Parsons's definition approvingly in his article "Dramatism," *International Encyclopedia of Social Sciences* 7(1968): 445– 52. Finally, Parsons acknowledged that Burke was "another scholar whose work has influenced me greatly," p. 521 (footnote 3), in "Theory in the Humanities and Sociology," *Daedalus* 99(1970): 495– 523.

9. Talcott Parsons, "The Theory of Symbolism in Relation to Action," in *Working Papers in the Theory of Action*, ed. Talcott Parsons, Robert F. Bales, and Edward A. Shils (New York: Free Press, 1953), pp. 31–62.

10. Edward C. Devereux, Jr., "Parsons' Sociological Theory," in *The Social Theories of Talcott Parsons*, ed. Max Black (Englewood Cliffs, N.J.: Prentice-Hall, 1961), pp. 25–26. Reprinted by permission.

11. Guy Rocher, *Talcott Parsons and American Sociology* (New York: Barnes & Noble, 1975), pp. 38–39.

12. Devereux, p. 41. Reprinted by permission.

13. David L. Swanson and Jesse G. Delia, MODCOM: *The Nature of Human Communication*. ©1976, Science Research Associates, Inc. Reprinted by permission.

14. Ibid., p. 14. Reprinted by permission.

15. Ibid. Reprinted by permission.

16. Ibid. Reprinted by permission.

17. Ibid., pp. 14–15. Reprinted by permission.

18. George Herbert Mead, *Mind, Self, and Society from the Standpoint of a Social Behaviorist* (Chicago: University of Chicago Press, 1934).

19. Swanson and Delia, p. 17. Reprinted by permission.

20. Ibid., p. 18. Reprinted by permission.

21. Paul C. Cozby, "Self-Disclosure: A Literature Review," *Psychological Bulletin* 79(1973): 74.

22. Ibid., p. 78.

23. Myong Jin Won-Doornink, "On Getting to Know You: The Association between the Stage of Relationship and Reciprocity of Self-Disclosure," *Journal of Experimental Social Psychology* 15(1979): 229.

24. Ibid.

25. Cozby, "Self-Disclosure: A Literature Review," p. 83.

26. Paul C. Cozby, "Self-Disclosure, Reciprocity, and Liking," *Sociometry* 35(1972): 151–60.

27. Cozby, "Self-Disclosure: A Literature Review," p. 88.

28. As reported in Cozby, "Self-Disclosure: A Literature Review," p. 88.

29. Paul Watzlawick, Janet H. Beavin, Don D. Jackson, *Pragmatics of Human Communication: A Study of Interactional Patterns, Pathologies, and Paradoxes* (New York: W. W. Norton & Company, 1967), p. 51. Italics in original.

30. Ibid., p. 54.

31. Ibid., p. 59.

32. Ibid., p. 56.

33. Ibid., p. 70.

34. Frank E. Millar and L. Edna Rogers, "A Relational Approach to Interpersonal Communication," in *Explorations in Interpersonal Communication*, ed. Gerald R. Miller (Beverly Hills, Calif.: Sage Publications, 1976), pp. 87–103.

35. George R. Bach and Peter Wyden, *The Intimate Enemy*. Copyright © 1968, 1969 by Dr. George R. Bach and Peter Wyden. Reprinted by permission of William Morrow & Company and The Sterling Lord Agency.

36. Ibid., p. 8. Reprinted by permission.

37. Ibid., p. 7. Reprinted by permission.

38. J. Michael Sproule, "The Psychological Burden of Proof: On the Evolutionary Development of Richard Whately's Theory of Presumption," *Communication Monographs* 43(1976): 115– 29.

39. Charles T. Hill, Zick Rubin, and Letitia Anne Peplau, "Breakups Before Marriage: The End of 103 Affairs," *Journal of Social Issues* 32(1976): 153.

40. As quoted in Hill et al., p. 158.

41. Hill et al., p. 158.

42. Ibid., p. 160.

43. Ibid., pp. 166– 67.

CHAPTER

5

Triadic Communication

Two is company and three is a crowd.
Proverb

*In married life three is company and
two none.*
The Importance of Being Oscar
Oscar Wilde

"Three's Company"
Television Situation Comedy

The Ubiquitous Three

It has probably occurred to you many times that things in our world appear in threes. Whatever the subject, public speakers often seem to find three points to make. This "threeness" may be a deeply embedded part of our thought process. It is certainly a standard framework of English prose; a classic "tripartite ending" is that most regal of sentences that resolves in three, well-balanced elements. In fact, this very chapter on triadic communication has three central parts. First, after setting the stage with a picture of the extensiveness of the triad, we shall provide a definition of the concept. Second, we shall explore the field of research, which shows how triads are formed and delineates the various types. Third, and finally, we shall look at important triads in society.

Nature itself may be a system of threes. Or something inherent in the human symbol-making capacity may force us to see and label things in sets of threes. Think back over the earlier chapters of this book. We have discussed Aristotle's three modes of proof and the three kinds of oratory. We have mentioned the three branches of the United States government. What are the three kinds of rules discussed earlier? The "triangle of meaning" in chapter 3 integrates three elements. We could have mentioned that speeches, essays, and other messages have three main parts: introduction, body, and conclusion. This book has three main parts; each part contains three chapters. The Holy Trinity; Freud's id, ego, and superego; and the Three Stooges provide three more examples.

The list could go on. Sonata form in music is an elegant use of threes.[1]

In a sonata (which itself usually has three movements), the first movement (A) follows the diagram in Figure 5–1. In the exposition section, three musical themes (a, b, c) are introduced. The first theme (a) is usually "dramatic" and in the tonic key. The second theme (b) is usually "lyrical" and in the dominant key. The third theme (c) is less important than the other two and is also in dominant keys.

In the development section (B) the composer is free to present the original themes in new and unsuspecting ways, and may choose to add new material; this section moves into new, "foreign" keys. In the recapitulation section the three original themes are quoted more or less literally from the exposition section, but the difference is that they are now in the tonic key.

We have developed this example of threes at more length than the others because music is a form of communication. Its theory and terminology are similar to rhetorical theory and terminology. As pointed out in chapter 2, the teaching of rhetoric in ancient Rome was so dominant that other arts imitated it. The rhetorical term *invention* is the ancestor of the musical term,

Figure 5-1   Sonata form. Note how the three movements of the sonata are each
in turn broken down into patterns of three musical themes. (From
Copland, *What to Listen for in Music*, p. 115.)

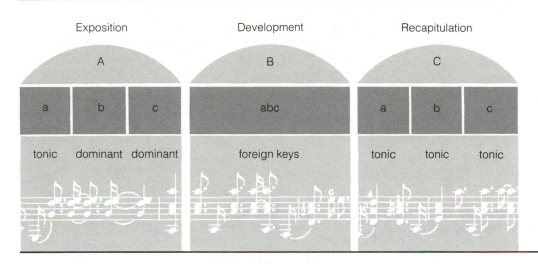

as in Bach's *Inventions*. In considering the first movement of a sonata as a
message, notice how much redundancy is built in; the themes a, b, and c will
be heard several times. That makes it possible for the listener to recognize
and remember a sonata.

Notice also that music, like rhetoric, can be persuasive. The totalitarian
government of Nazi Germany banned certain of its composers but honored
certain others such as Richard Strauss and Richard Wagner. The Soviet Union
forces its composers to write for the masses in relatively tuneful and melodic
ways. We speak of music having the power to create moods. Bach's music was
intended to keep the churchgoers faithful.

Notice also that the sonata form could be used as the method of
organizing a persuasive speech or essay. The themes or theses are introduced
to the receiver in the opening section (or introduction); they could be
developed by enthymeme and example in the second section (or body); and
the theses could literally be recapitulated, or summarized, in the final section
(or conclusion) and coupled with an appeal for action. In fact, there is an
exercise at the end of the chapter suggesting that you carry out such an
assignment in your class.

Our final example of the ubiquitousness, or "everywhereness," of
threes is the geodesic dome. Examined carefully, this structure is made of

contiguous, or touching, triangles. The man responsible for the geodesic dome is Buckminster Fuller. According to Fuller, "All nature's struggling, associating, and patterning must be based on triangles, because there is no structural validity otherwise."[2]

In the previous chapter about dyads we saw that, ironically, threeness has important implications for interpersonal communication. The two persons in communication are always being monitored, directly or indirectly, by society or by the "generalized other" of the parties. To put it another way, the two parties of a dyad are influenced by the values and rules of the social system. Another kind of threeness is important to interpersonal communication, and that is the subject of this chapter.

Triad Defined

"A triad is a social system containing three related members in a persistent situation."[3] "Social system" means that what happens to or is done by one usually affects the other two. "Related" means interdependent and assumes that they communicate among each other. "Persistent" means that they are not strangers meeting for the first and last time but will continue as an interacting system over a long period of time.

The reader should be reassured that we will not continue in this mode by having chapters on four-person, five-person, and six-person systems and so on. A chapter devoted to three-person systems is needed, however, because an important concept in rhetoric and communication can be most easily seen in triads.

I can remember vividly an evening spent with two friends fifteen years ago. Two of us (including me) were in our first year as Ph.D. holders and in our first year on a university faculty. The third person was older and wiser, a man of great wisdom and culture. We both valued his opinions. I am by nature argumentative; I enjoy disagreeing with others — when done in an agreeable way — because I learn that way. That evening I disagreed several times with our older colleague. In each instance, the other young colleague agreed not with me but with our older colleague. Despite my enjoyment of argument, and despite the fact that the issues were relatively trivial, a sense of uneasiness, tension, and even unpleasantness mounted with each instance. In frustration I began searching my mind for issues by which to divide them as a pair.

Research on Triads

Formation of Coalitions in Triads

Perhaps you have experienced the same feeling described in the preceding example. How can we explain this? "The most significant property of the triad is its tendency to divide into a coalition of two members against the third."[4] This observation was first made by Georg Simmel (1858–1918), a German generalist now considered to be a founding father of modern sociology. His observations have been carried forward through analysis and empirical research by contemporary social scientists. This work is totally consistent with earlier assumptions of this book concerning the dramatistic pentad and communication as action. The three actors or agents in the triad may be individuals, groups, organizations, or even nation states.

The tendency of a triad to organize into a pair against the other, or two against one, demonstrates again Burke's thesis that identification and division or cooperation and conflict are invariably found together in the human order. This tendency also creates another irony: the transformation of strength into weakness and weakness into strength. Let me illustrate this ironic transformation.

Suppose that Augustus (A), Brutus (B), and Caesar (C) are college roommates who organize to sell illegal substances. Suppose that Augustus is more powerful (physically and mentally) than either Brutus or Caesar; Brutus and Caesar are equal in power, and together are more powerful than Augustus. When it comes time to split up the loot, Augustus will want the lion's share. However, we can also expect the triadic tendency of a pair against the other to manifest itself.

We can predict that Brutus and Caesar will unite against Augustus, or a BC coalition. Several reasons for this prediction can be offered. Neither B nor C can dominate the other; each needs the protection of the other from A's power. An AB coalition could be dangerous for B if C should leave the triad for any reason (the same would be true of an AC coalition). More importantly, A could impose an unfair split on either B or C in an AB or AC coalition. Thus, A's strength is transformed into weakness, and the individual weaknesses of B and C are transformed into strength.

Types of Triads

Theodore Caplow, an American sociologist who has done extensive research on the theory of coalitions, argues that social interaction can best be under-

Figure 5-2 Power distribution in eight triads (From Caplow, "Further Development of a Theory of Coalitions in the Triad," p. 488.)

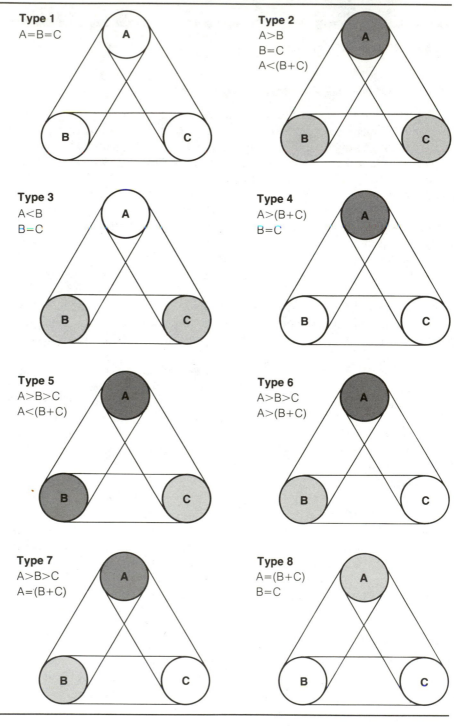

Type 1
A=B=C

Type 2
A>B
B=C
A<(B+C)

Type 3
A<B
B=C

Type 4
A>(B+C)
B=C

Type 5
A>B>C
A<(B+C)

Type 6
A>B>C
A>(B+C)

Type 7
A>B>C
A=(B+C)

Type 8
A=(B+C)
B=C

stood as triangular or triadic in nature. Although his work also deals with triads made up of three collectivities, such as three organizations, the research can be understood by examining three-person triads. Caplow has developed a typology, or classification, of eight different triads as depicted in Figure 5–2.[5] The differences are due to the power distribution (> means more powerful than; < means less powerful than).

W. Edgar Vinacke and Abe Arkoff conducted research on the first six types. Subjects were asked to play a game, pachisi, in which three persons competing for rewards move pieces around a board based on the throw of a single die. Two conditions, however, were added. First, all three players moved their pieces on each throw of the die. Second, each player was given a weight and moved his or her piece a number of spaces equal to the number thrown times the assigned weight. For example, in the type 2 triad: A received the weight of three, B received two, and C received two. The players quickly learned that without coalitions the outcome of the game was decided when the weights were assigned. Without coalitions neither luck nor skill could affect the final outcome. Figure 5–3 shows the assigned weights and predicted coalitions of each type of triad.[6] Each group of subjects played eighteen games, and ninety games were played according to the conditions of each triad type.

In general, the results conformed to the predictions. In type 1, all three coalitions were formed. In type 2, in 71 percent of the games the predicted

Figure 5-3   Assigned weights and predicted coalitions for six triads (From Vinacke and Arkoff, "An Experimental Study of Coalitions in the Triad," p. 408.)

Triad type	Assigned weights	Predicted coalitions
1	A=1, B=1, C=1	Any
2	A=3, B=2, C=2	BC
3	A=1, B=2, C=2	AB or AC
4	A=3, B=1, C=1	None
5	A=4, B=3, C=2	AC or BC
6	A=4, B=2, C=1	None

BC coalition materialized. In that triad, B can win by a coalition with either A or C, but he or she will be weaker than A and equal to C in the coalition. As predicted, players preferred BC. In type 3, the predicted coalitions were preferred (AB and AC), but for some unexplained reason the players chose AC more often than AB. No coalitions were predicted for type 4. B and C have no utilitarian, or strictly useful, motivation for a coalition because even combined they are weaker than A. Likewise, A has nothing to gain by a coalition. Thus, in over two-thirds of the games, no coalition was formed.

In type 5, both AC and BC were predicted, and this was the outcome. Interestingly, the BC coalition was the most popular one worked out by the subjects. C, the weakest member, was most likely to join a coalition (transforming weakness into strength) and chose most frequently the partner who would minimize the discrepancy in strength. B, weaker than A, minimized that discrepancy. In type 6, no coalition was predicted because A was stronger than B and C combined. In two-thirds of the games, no coalition was formed.[7]

Because of these coalitions and the resultant shifts in power and because in many situations different coalitions may be formed in the same triad, coalitions create strain in the relationships. As noted earlier, Burke argues that identification and division (or cooperation and conflict) invariably occur together in the human order. In the formation of triads, this simultaneous development of identification and division creates strain among the relationships within the triad. This concept will be considered again later in this chapter in relation to an important primary triad in society, the family.

Minimum Winning Combination. An important concept, called the "minimum winning combination," emerged in this and other studies. Notice that in type 5 the weakest member, C, chose B more often as a partner. Coalitions formed in real-life legislatures have been observed to follow this principle; that is, the coalitions will be made (with attendant compromises) *only* to the point where the winning number of votes have been gained. A similar phenomenon occurred in type 2. Consider C's perspective in that situation. C can win with either A or B, but will be inferior to A within an AC coalition and equal to B in a BC coalition. Thus, C (and B, who has the same perspective in that game) chose the minimum winning relationship.

Unexpected Results. In social science, averages or central tendencies are used either to confirm or to deny hypotheses. There can be many exceptions; however, if researchers can say "in general" the results confirm the hypothesis, the hypothesis is accepted. The exceptions in this case are worth examining.

For example, the theory (in the form of predictions) and the results of types 4 and 6 seem to weaken the original theory that triads tend to organize into the pair against the other. In those two types no coalition was predicted, and the results came out that way most, but not all, of the times. Thus, in such situations, the triads did not split into two against one.

Furthermore, in type 2, the predicted or rational (utilitarian) choice was BC. How can we explain the fact that in 28 percent of the type 2 games the players divided equally between AB and AC coalitions? The experimenters also thought that the players were "irrational" in dividing the loot according to the strength each brought to the coalition. According to the experimenters, "rational" behavior would be to divide the proceeds equally because in a winning coalition no partner is better or worse than another.

A Dramatistic Analysis.   The "irrationality" of the players can be explained in several ways. As we observed in chapter 2, Aristotle showed thousands of years ago that human decision-making is based on emotions (pathos) as well as upon rationality (logos). It should be clear that many of our coalitions, associations, and identifications are made partly on emotional grounds.

The thesis of this chapter, therefore, is that the uniqueness of the triad can be traced to the human need for identifying with another. In this way we transcend the loneliness and the separateness of the individual. The intensity of that coupling can be increased when united against another. The absence of a coalition in a triad could in reality be identification of three persons, united against another tight-knit triad.

Thus, we can overemphasize the tendency for triads to organize in the pair against the other. Three-way coalitions are possible as in the case of "My friend's friend is my friend." This state of balance or symmetry is itself the result of identification; we can in fact postulate a strain toward identification in triads that manifests itself in the pair or the trio.[8]

The so-called irrationality of the pachisi players can be viewed as rational behavior. Experimenters in social science often underestimate the role and effect of communication in their experiments. The coalitions formed in the experiments could be created only through a kind of communication called negotiation. When coalitions are likely in a triad, there is often one person—*tertius gaudens*, or "enjoying third"—who is invited by each of the other two to join them. This creates the conditions in which the enjoying third can negotiate for a best offer.

How can we handle the exceptional cases of coalitions that did not conform to the predictions? Associations, coalitions, and identifications are formed for other than strictly useful, or utilitarian, motives. In fact, they are sometimes formed in ways that run counter to such motives. Consider the person who takes the lesser paying of two job offers because of identifications. People vary in their interpersonal attractiveness, and, therefore, some are naturally more desirable as partners. People also identify with others when they are persuaded that their interests are joined—whether or not in fact they are. We can conclude that the tendency of the triad to form into the pair against the other, two against one, is probably less basic to human behavior than is the strain toward identification and division. Let us now consider some important triads in society.

Important Triads in Society

The Primary Triad

Most infants enter a world dominated by two extraordinary figures, mother and father. They are extraordinary in that they are bigger, stronger, and smarter than the baby. The child's perspective of the triad is clearly evident in the scene in Figure 5–4. As the infant grows and develops through communication with its parents, the power discrepancy slowly grows smaller and smaller. At some point the child learns that one parent has more power than the other. Historically speaking, in our culture the father often has held the greater amount of power, but this is changing. Regardless of that fact, each family is different in how the power is distributed.

At what age it is I do not know, but every child seems to learn that the parents do not always agree. The child also tries to get its way by making requests to individual parents rather than to the pair. The parent who accedes to the request may then become an ally in a coalition against the parent who would deny the request. The pair against the other will take very different forms from day to day. On Monday it may be the parents against the child. On Tuesday it may be mother and daughter against father. On Wednesday it may be father and son against mother. On Thursday it may be mother and son against father, and so on. These conditions even vary hour by hour.

At three years and two months, Emily learned to play with me what she called "the 'nother word game." I gave a word such as *head*, and she had to come up with a rhyme like *bed*. One evening, after persuading me to play, she turned to the third member of the primary triad and said, "Mommy, you can't play with us, right dad?" Naturally I disagreed with her. The reason I disagreed with Emily is probably a useful generalization about triadic communication. Aware of the divisive tendency of such groups, I resisted the unnecessary formation of the pair against the other. It is always easier to produce messages that divide a group, necessarily or unnecessarily, than it is to produce messages that unify.

As the child matures, he or she reaches a peak of power as the parents decline in power. A mother-son coalition may continue to win over the father, but the mother's power will sooner or later be matched by that of the child.

Figure 5-4   In most families the primary triad is the child and his or her mother and father. Families differ, however, in the way power is distributed. Coalitions frequently shift to match new circumstances, and coalitions may change as the child matures. (James Motlow/Jeroboam, Inc.)

The offspring will finally become more powerful than even a coalition of the two parents. This ultimate independence is the cause of much strain in the family; parents usually want it to come later, while the child wants it sooner. In general coalitions bring strains to triads, and this is part of the reason why the American family seems to be disintegrating. By contrast, pioneer families had powerful economic motives for sticking together. Each member helped to produce the crops by which needs were satisfied. In modern society most of our needs are satisfied outside the family. Given that fact and the strains provided by generation gaps and coalitions, the only force at work to hold the family together is love.

Additional Family Triads

I once heard a comedian define "mixed feelings" by the example of watching his mother-in-law drive off a cliff in his new car. Although it is a tasteless gag, it is representative of the mother-in-law jokes included in the repertoire of nearly every stand-up comic in our culture. That should be an indicator that the wife – husband – mother-in-law relationship is a problematic triad. If this triad is a problem in our culture, consider how much worse it is in other societies:

> In more than three-fifths of the world's societies, severe penalties follow upon the meeting of a man and his mother-in-law, and they shun each other accordingly. In northern Australia a man who speaks to his mother-in-law must be put to death. In parts of the South Pacific, both parties would commit suicide. In Yucatan, men believe that to meet one's mother-in-law face-to-face would render a man sterile for life, so he may travel miles out of his way over dangerous territory to avoid being near her. Navaho men believe that they will go blind if they see their mothers-in-law, so that she is not even allowed to attend the wedding.[9]

Such cultural norms are probably those societies' answer to the problems and conflicts that result from these family triads.

The tendency for coalition formation in triads can place the wife in an impossible situation. She will be torn between a coalition with her mother and with her husband. If a balanced, three-way coalition or identification cannot be achieved, avoidance may be the only solution; that is, the husband and wife will maintain the minimal level of face-to-face communication with the mother. Although the husband-wife-wife's mother triad has been the subject of most of the research and theory, these same principles hold for the wife-husband-husband's mother triad.

There are many other possible triads within the family. In patrilineal societies (that is, where males are dominant), the son, father, and mother's brother are said to form the "natural" triad. Following the terms of the pentad, we can visualize triads of father, mother, and the children as coagents. Siblings often act in unity against the parents.

Other Triads

Groups can profitably be seen as triads of coagents. A nine-person group could become a triad in which three coagents constitute each of the parties to a triad. American industrial society can be viewed as a triad. The aggressive, often unfair practices of big business helped to create a strong opposing force, big unions. The only third party that could possibly dominate those two parties, as well as mediate between them, is big government. When the Republican party controls the federal government, it usually identifies more with big business; the Democrats identify more with big labor.

Business organizations are often thought of as three parties: top management, middle management, and the workers; or as management, foreman,

Figure 5-5 At the end of World War II the Allied leaders—Winston Churchill, Franklin Roosevelt, and Joseph Stalin (*l* to *r*)—met to discuss a peace plan for Europe. Since this postwar period, international relations have generally been triadic; opposed to one another ideologically, the Soviet Union and the United States have vied for the alignment of other nations. (British Prime Minister Sir Winston Churchill, President Franklin Roosevelt, and U.S.S.R.'s Joseph Stalin at Yalta. The Bettman Archive)

and worker. The foreman in that triad is in a difficult position, not unlike the wife in the husband-wife-wife's mother triad. To be effective, the foreman has to be able to identify with both management and the worker.

International relations since World War II can also be considered triadic in nature. As one actor or agent the Soviet Union and its satellites has been opposed to the United States and its allies. Each agent has tried to get other countries to join it in opposition to the other (see Figure 5–5). A large number of nations, however, have resisted the advances of each superpower and have constituted what is now called the "Third World." United States-Soviet detente, the opening of the United States-Chinese relationships, and Euro-communism indicate that basic changes are taking place in these power relationships.

Summary

Triads appear frequently in our world. This phenomenon may be due to our human capacity for symbol making in threes. In this chapter we have used

Theodore Caplow's definition of a triad: a social system containing three related members in a persistent situation.

Triadic communication is marked by a tendency to organize into a pair against the other. Minimum winning combinations are formed such that coalitions are made only to the point that the winning number of votes or degree of power is gained. This book submits that this pairing is due not to an innate characteristic of triads; rather it is due to the human need to identify with others. When it is not possible to form a three-way identification, the pair against the other allows identification to occur with a simultaneous division. Groups, organizations, and even nations also develop triads as the result of identification and coalition-formation.

Textbook writers, including this one, assume that knowledge is carried from one chapter to the next. The unique nature of the triad does not cancel out the principles presented in the chapter on dyadic communication. In some scenes or circumstances, the triad is potentially a set of three dyads. Certainly the pattern variables applies to triads as well as dyads; the same is true of the principles of constructivism and the relational approach. Self-disclosure presents a different twist. Your steady lover or fiance probably does not talk about your relationship in the presence of a parent in the same way that he or she does in the parent's absence. That may be still another strategy for getting to know the other.

How does communication change when more members enter the triad? In chapter 6 we shall expand the number of players even further and examine group communication.

Questions for Essays, Speeches, and Group Discussions

1. Analyze the relationships among Othello, Desdemona, and Iago (in Shakespeare's play *Othello*) by means of triadic theory.

2. Defend or attack the thesis that the strain for identification is stronger than the strain to form the pair against the other.

3. What threesomes in history have succumbed to the tendency to form the pair against the other or have resisted this tendency by means of a balanced relationship?

4. How could members of a triad act so as to resist the unnecessary formation of the pair against the other?

5. Organize a persuasive speech following the pattern of sonata form. Prepare an outline of the speech in which you indicate in the left-hand

margin of the paper which points illustrate the musical terms of sonata form. Evaluate the speech in terms of the effectiveness of the organization for oral communication.

Additional Readings

Caplow, Theodore. *Two Against One: Coalitions in Triads*. Englewood Cliffs, N.J.: Prentice-Hall, 1968.

Zajonc, Robert B. "The Concepts of Balance, Congruity, and Dissonance." In *Foundations of Communication Theory*, edited by Kenneth K. Sereno and C. David Mortensen, pp. 181–96. New York: Harper & Row, 1970.

Notes

1. Aaron Copland, *What to Listen for in Music*, rev. ed. (New York: McGraw-Hill Book Co., 1957), p. 115. Reprinted by permission.

2. As quoted in Theodore Caplow, *Two Against One: Coalitions in Triads* (Englewood Cliffs, N.J.: Prentice-Hall, 1968), p. v.

3. Ibid., p. 1.

4. Ibid., p. 2.

5. Theodore Caplow, "Further Development of a Theory of Coalitions in the Triad," *American Journal of Sociology* 64(1959): 488. Reprinted by permission of The University of Chicago Press.

6. W. Edgar Vinacke and Abe Arkoff, "An Experimental Study of Coalitions in the Triad," *American Sociological Review* 22(1957): 408. Reprinted by permission of The American Sociological Association.

7. Ibid., pp. 406–14.

8. The reader may want to compare this postulate with the "strain toward symmetry" postulated by balance theory. See Robert B. Zajonc, "The Concepts of Balance, Congruity, and Dissonance," in *Foundations of Communication Theory*, ed. Kenneth K. Sereno and C. David Mortensen (New York: Harper & Row, 1970), pp. 181–96.

9. John M. Shlien, "Mother-in-Law: A Problem in Kinship Terminology," in *Marriage, Family and Society*, ed. Hyman Rodman (New York: Random House, 1965), pp. 198–99.

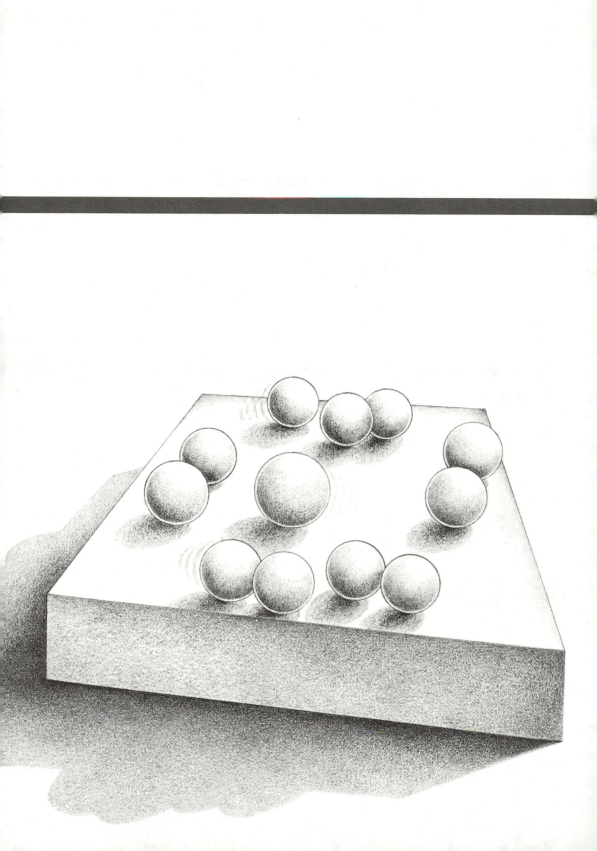

CHAPTER

6

Group Communication

The most intensely social animals can only adapt to group behavior. Bees and ants have no option when isolated, except to die. There is really no such creature as a single individual; he has no more life of his own than a cast-off cell marooned from the surface of your skin.

The Lives of a Cell: Notes of a Biology Watcher
Lewis Thomas

I know professor-colleagues who regularly teach courses in group dynamics, group communication, group problem-solving, and group leadership. In these courses my colleagues tell their students with sincere solemnity how important groups are and how important it is that students learn to make them effective. Later, relaxing with colleagues over a cup of coffee, the same professors can be counted on to say, "Oh my god, we have another committee meeting tomorrow!"

As a professor who has chaired numerous committees, a faculty senate, and a university department, I have been truly perplexed by this paradox. Having to call unwanted meetings is almost as painful as having to chair them. To make the problem even more perplexing, consider how professors tend to react to autocratic administrators.

"I see they have done it again," the professors say. "They've made

Figure 6-1   Do the men in this painting, who have apparently gathered in a park to discuss the affairs of the day, constitute a group? We cannot tell if this cluster satisfies the five necessary characteristics of a group, but the arrangement of the men and their facial expressions indicate that they share an interest and that they are communicating. (David Fredenthal: *The People* [no date] The University of Arizona Museum of Art, Gift of Mr. and Mrs. C. Leonard Pfeiffer.)

another important decision without consulting the faculty." In other words, on such occasions professors sound as if they most value and look forward to faculty meetings in which they participate in decision making. How can we make sense of these perplexing paradoxes?

Professors are a highly individualistic category (note that I did not say "group") of persons. Think of all the time they spend alone, grading papers, preparing lectures, and writing articles and books. These are the communicative activities by which they achieve security (tenure) and status. Most group activities intrude on these individual activities and are quite naturally resented. On the other hand, most professors value "collegiality," a belief that they should be involved in or at least be consulted on decisions having an impact on the educational process. Thus, professors have an ambivalent attitude toward discussion groups. My observation is that professors readily accept their group responsibilities when meetings are conducted in such a way as to raise important issues and to permit the participants to solve significant problems.

In order to cover the subject of group communication adequately, it will be necessary first to define the concept of group. Second, we shall consider the methods and findings of a system used to categorize communicative acts in groups called interaction process analysis. Third, we shall consider a system called reflective thinking by which groups rationally solve problems. Fourth, we shall trace the historical development of the theory of group leadership. Fifth, and finally, we shall attempt a summary and synthesis of these topics.

Definition of a Group

Group Characteristics

What is "groupness"? Neither a *category* (all professors, teenagers, or felons) nor an *aggregation* (audiences at concerts and athletic events) is the same thing as a group. The reason is that each lacks one or more of the following characteristics that define *groups*.

1. *Shared Interest*. Each member of a group has at least one interest shared by all other members. The common interest in a chess club, stamp club, or sailing club is quite obvious. In other groups the interest is not so obvious, and one must look for the common values or goals of the group, as in the Kiwanis Club. Figure 6–1 shows a circle of men who appear to share an interest.

2. *Communication*. Unlike either the category or the aggregation, the members of a group must communicate with each other about the group and its activities. Indeed, it is through communication that people discover those common interests that can serve as the basis for a group's formation.

3. *Hierarchy*. As indicated in chapter 1, humans are by nature hierarchical. Thus, groups must by definition have this quality. Even if not done consciously and explicitly, members do rank each other from top to bottom on the criterion of usefulness to the group. This individual status may be formal (titles in an academic department) or informal. A person's rank in a group may be inferred from the communication patterns in the group. For example, high status members tend to address the group-as-a-whole more often than do low status members. Low status individuals tend to address individuals, often those with high status.

4. *Identification*. The members of the group must have a sense of group-ness. The degree of identification may be operationally defined as the extent to which members, in contemplating several alternatives to individual action, weigh the consequences of the potential act upon the group.

5. *Long Life*. A group is capable of living longer than even the longest living individual in the group. We shall elaborate on this characteristic later in our attempt to fix the number of members in a group.

In a book on communication as action, the second defining characteristic in this list has to be considered the most important. Without communication there could be no known shared interest, no hierarchy, and no identification; indeed, without communication there would be no group. Many theorists have indicated that the two basic and interrelated functions of a group are (1) task functions, or actions for accomplishing the goal of the group, and (2) social-emotional functions, or actions for maintaining effective relationships among members of the group. Both functions require communication. A group can form and maintain itself only by means of communication.

Group Size

You might think that, if it is possible to define a group, it should be possible to specify the number of members. It is possible to do so, but there is no agreement about it by the experts. The upper limit is sometimes set at fifteen, sometimes at twenty. There is no good reason for selecting one number over the others in fixing the upper limit. In a group, however, each member must be able to communicate directly with every other member of the group. This becomes increasingly difficult, if not impossible, when groups are larger than twenty, so I shall arbitrarily adopt this as the upper limit. (The limits of the size of a group will be discussed more fully in chapter 7 when we consider the limitations of intercommunication in organizations.)

There are reasons for fixing the lower limit of a group's size. It makes no sense to speak of a group of one. It is possible to have a group of two; a dyad may have a common interest, communication, hierarchy, and identification. A dyad is terminated, however, if either of its members drops out. A marriage does not "continue" if a widow remarries; a new marriage is created. A triad, however, has the potential to survive as a group even if one member drops out. If a new third is added, we can say that the group continues. We shall, therefore, specify that a group contains between three and twenty members. Logically speaking, then, the preceding chapter on triads was an introductory chapter on group communication; the principles of coalition formation discussed in that chapter are applicable to larger groups. Consider a fifteen-member group, for example, as a potential set of three parties, agents, or collective actors of five persons each.

Thus, the range of three to twenty members allows us to explain how certain groups achieve a condition approaching immortality not enjoyed by individual members. The Supreme Court of the United States, for example, has been functioning continuously for about two hundred years even though all the original members are long dead. All but the current justices have been replaced one at a time during that judicial group's existence (see Figure 6–2).

Having defined groups and considered their potential for immortality, we shall turn our attention to interaction process analysis.

Interaction Process Analysis

This system of analyzing groups, which was worked out by Robert F. Bales, has been in existence for thirty years and is one of the most frequently discussed research programs in group communication. You may have already encountered this scheme or system. Let me ask you to look at it one more time and to make connections with concepts presented earlier in this book that you have probably not considered before.

Bales's Categories

Bales set out to understand how groups work by analyzing interaction within them. Groups of two to seven members were asked to take part in four, forty-minute problem-solving discussions. As they worked through their problems and solutions, the group members were observed through a one-way mirror. Happily enough, the system for observing member behavior was consistent with the action orientation of this book. Each remark made by group members was classified within a few seconds by trained observers looking through the one-way glass. Each unit of interaction, whether nonverbal or verbal, was classified as an act. These acts, similar to the concept of speech acts in chapter 3, were coded as questions, answers, and positive and negative reactions to the questions and answers. Figure 6–3 shows the system of categories.[1]

The twelve categories require little additional discussion. An interesting question to contemplate is how Bales could wind up with twelve categories after beginning with eighty-seven categories.[2] Furthermore, notice the symmetrical nature of the four blocks of categories. These four blocks of categories were selected *before* the observations from the action theory of Talcott Parsons (see chapter 4). In an essay coauthored with Parsons, Bales explained how the categories were discovered:

> The essential approach was to think of the small group as a functioning social system. It was held that such a system would have four main "functional problems" which were described, respectively, as those of *adaptation* to conditions of the external situation, of *instrumental* control over parts of the situation in the performance of goal oriented tasks, of the management and *expression* of sentiments and tensions of the members, and of preserving the social *integration* of members with each other as a solidary collectivity. In relation to this complex of system-problems, a classification of types of action was worked out,

Figure 6-2 The Supreme Court illustrates the immortality of a group. The Court has existed for over two hundred years, despite the fact that year by year individual members may retire and others join the Court. (United Press International.)

Figure 6-3   The system of categories used in observation and their relation to major frames of reference. (From Bales, "A Set of Categories for the Analysis of Small Group Interaction," p. 258.)

Social-Emotional Area: **Positive Reactions**	**A**	1. Shows solidarity, raises other's status, gives help, reward **f**
		2. Shows tension release, jokes, laughs, shows satisfaction **e**
		3. Agrees, shows passive acceptance, understands, concurs, complies **d**
Task Area: **Attempted Answers**	**B**	4. Gives suggestion, direction, implying autonomy for other **c**
		5. Gives opinion, evaluation, analysis, expresses feeling, wish **b**
		6. Gives orientation, information, repetition, confirmation **a**
Task Area: **Questions**	**C**	7. Asks for orientation, information, repetition, confirmation **a**
		8. Asks for opinion, evaluation, analysis, expression of feeling **b**
		9. Asks for suggestion, direction, possible ways of action **c**
Social-Emotional Area: **Negative Reactions**	**D**	10. Disagrees, shows passive rejection, formality, withholds help **d**
		11. Shows tension, asks for help, withdraws out of field **e**
		12. Shows antagonism, deflates other's status, defends or asserts self **f**

Key

a. Problems of orientation   d. Problems of decision
b. Problems of evaluation   e. Problems of tension management
c. Problems of control   f. Problems of integration

falling into twelve categories as given in [Figure 6-3]. It will be seen that they fall into four groups of three each, and further that the total set is symmetrically arranged according to whether its significance is "positive" or "negative" from the point of view of what the occurrence of the act indicates about the state of solution of the particular system problem it deals with. This is the distinction between those above (1-6) and those below (7-12) the central line. In the second place each half is divided into those which are most directly relevant to the problems of adaptation and instrumental control (4-9) and those primarily relevant to the problems of expression of emotional reactions and tensions and maintenance of group integration (1-3, 10-12).[3]

If you have encountered Bales's system of interaction analysis earlier, you may have considered it an atheoretical counting system. As we have seen, however, the four blocks and the twelve categories were discovered because they reflect "functional" problems successful groups must solve.

•

Prudential Rules for Committees

If this were a more advanced text on group communication, we would also show how Parsons linked, in a highly complex way, the four pattern variables discussed in chapter 4 to the four functional problems facing groups and other social units. (Additional readings are listed at the end of this chapter for those who want to pursue the matter.) Closer to our purposes in this chapter and book is the practical guidance provided by Bales's findings. After studying many problem-solving groups (the problems were problem cases in administration and human relations), the groups gave an indication of the degree to which they were either satisfied or dissatisfied with their solutions. This gave Bales a chance to compare and contrast interaction patterns between "good" and "bad" groups. This comparison allowed Bales to list ten "rules of thumb," for people who either appoint or participate in groups and committees. Some of the "rules of thumb," or what I called prudential rules in chapter 3, are self-explanatory. Others will require additional discussion.

1. Avoid appointing committees larger than seven members unless necessary to obtain representation of all relevant points of view. Try to set up conditions of size, seating, and time allowed so that each member has an adequate opportunity to communicate directly with each other member.

2. Avoid appointing committees as small as two or three members if the power problem between members is likely to be critical.

3. Choose members who will tend to fall naturally into a moderate gradient of participation. Groups made up of all high participators will tend to suffer from competition. Groups made up of all lows may find themselves short on ideas.

4. Avoid the assumption that a good committee is made up of one good "leader" and several "followers." Try to provide the group with both a task leader and a social leader, who will support each other. It is probably not a bad idea to include a "humorist" if the social leader does not have a light touch. A few strong but more silent men add judicious balance to the group.

A group of otherwise balanced composition can probably absorb one "difficult" member — one of the type, for example, who talks too much, is short on problem-solving ability, tends to arouse dislike, and cannot be changed by ordinary social pressures. If such a member must be included, probably the best strategy is to "surround" him.

5. In actual procedure, start with facts if possible. Even where the facts are thought to be well known to all members, a short review is seldom a waste of time. A good general procedure is probably to plan to deal with three questions on each major agenda item:

"What are the facts pertaining to the problem?"

"How do we feel about them?"

"What shall we do about the problem?"

This is probably the preferred order. Take time to lay the groundwork before getting to specific suggestions, the third stage. It may be noted, by the way, that the order recommended is the exact opposite of that which is characteristic of formal parliamentary procedure.

6. Solicit the opinions and experiences of others, especially when disagreements begin to crop up. People often think they disagree when actually they simply are not talking about the same experiences. In such cases they do not draw each other out far enough to realize that, although they are using the same *words*, they are thinking about different *experiences*. Try to get past the words and general statements the other man uses to the experiences he is trying to represent. Members of the group may agree with his experiences.

7. When somebody else is talking, listen, and keep indicating your reactions actively. Most people are not much good at reading your mind. Besides that, they need the recognition you can give them by your honest reactions, whether positive or negative.

8. Keep your eyes on the group. When you are talking, talk to the group as a whole rather than to one of your cronies or to one of your special opponents. Search around constantly for reactions to what you are saying. A good deal of communication goes on at a subverbal level. Nothing tones up the general harmony of a group like a good strong undercurrent of direct eye contact.

9. When you scent trouble coming up, break off the argument and backtrack to further work on the facts and direct experience. In some

instances the best way to get started on a cooperative track again after a period of difficulty is to agree to go out and gather some facts together by direct experience.

10. Keep your ear to the ground. No recipe or set of rules can substitute for constant, sensitive, and sympathetic attention to what is going on in the relations between members. Do not get so engrossed in getting the job done that you lose track of what is the first pre-requisite of success — keeping the committee in good operating condition.[4]

Rules 1 and 2 flow from the fact that groups of five and seven members tend to be the most effective. Notice also that the numbers five and seven are within the limit of "chunks" we can handle in the short-term memory. Notice that each is an odd number; even numbers can produce a stalemate. Rule 3 takes cognizance that some people talk more than others; effective groups tend to be made up of talkative people ("high participators") and people who are less talkative ("lows").

Rule 4 grew out of Bales's findings that some people specialize in the task (categories 4–9), while others specialize in social-emotional matters (categories 1–3, 10–12). Few people can contribute in both areas. Hence, Bales advises that both a task leader and a social leader be included in the group so that it can solve its "functional" problems. We shall return to the question of group leadership in the final section of this chapter.

Rule 5 has to do with the chronological order in which an effective group goes about its business. We shall expand on this rule also in a following section. Rule 6 recognizes the importance of meaning in interaction and urges participants to be sensitive to differences in meanings. Rule 7 recommends that members communicate their honest reactions, whether positive or negative, to the remarks made by other members. Rule 8 advises the speaker to address the entire group and to scan all group members for verbal and nonverbal reactions, for feedback from others. Rules 9 and 10 advise committee members to be sensitive to the effect of social-emotional factors on the group's ability to perform the task.

Let us turn now from these observations about the actions of groups to the psychological requirements of effective group functioning.

Reflective Thinking

In the discussion on interpersonal communication in chapter 4, we introduced the concepts of presumption and burden of proof. If there are psychological requirements for convincing an individual, are there comparable requirements for a group? The answer is a qualified yes. Social scientists become angry and upset if they think a writer has even hinted at believing in the concept of "group mind." I am not suggesting that there is such a thing as a group mind, but a group is made up of individual minds, and these collective individuals do, generally speaking, grant presumption to the status quo. They also require that, if a change is to be made, a problem must be established and an appropriate solution advanced. Even if the group formed because the members recognized the existence of a problem, the group must first analyze that problem to establish a shared perspective; only then can they find an appropriate solution.

For example, consider Bales's findings with problem-solving groups. After comparing "good" and "bad" groups, Bales recommended three main questions for each agenda item:

"What are the facts pertaining to the problem?"

"How do we feel about them?"

"What shall we do about the problem?"

You may recognize that in these three questions we have the essential elements of the burden of proof.

Textbooks in group communication have been recommending this agenda for problem solving for many years. In fact, they were recommending such a method at the same time Bales discovered it in his laboratory.[5]

The Steps of Reflective Thinking

Barnlund and Haiman claim that

> reflective thinking was first described in a slim volume written by John Dewey which appeared in 1910 and was destined to become something of a classic. It was called, simply, *How We Think*. It was an attempt on the part of this well-known philosopher to distinguish among the various kinds of mental activity in which human beings engage in solving a wide variety of problems. Not only did the author describe how we *do* think — using intuition, reverie, creative imagination — but he also formulated how we *ought* to think.[6]

Reflective thinking, then, has been presented as both a *descriptive* (how we do think) and *prescriptive* (how we should think) *system*; it is similar to the burden of proof and to the stages Bales observed in his problem-solving groups. The following are the five steps in the process of reflective thinking.

1. *Occurrence of Some Difficulty*. Without a difficulty felt by the group, there will be little or no motivation to find better ways of acting. This step is characterized by a malaise, a feeling that something is not the

way it should be. It may be ineffable, difficult to put into words. Nonetheless, if the group does agree that further consideration of the problem would be desirable, it moves to the next step.

2. *Location and Definition of the Problem*. In this step, members of the group locate and analyze the problem. From an action perspective a problem is something that is preventing the group from realizing its end or its desired state of affairs. In order to find the best solution the group members must carefully analyze the obstacle or problem. They will need to assess the facts, or the symptoms of the problem, as well as its underlying causes. A group could "solve" the symptoms of the energy problem by manufacturing gasoline instead of home heating oil. Summer motorists would then escape long lines at the service station, but a long cold winter would follow. In other words, the group would not have solved the underlying causes of the problem.

3. *Formulation of Possible Solutions or Actions*. At this point the group asks, What should we do? They might also ask, What action or actions on our part would allow us to reach our end or the desired state of affairs? In the interest of assembling all possible solutions, members should avoid evaluation of solutions or actions at this point; evaluation may stifle the development of new, creative, nontraditional solutions. Avoiding evaluation at this point also allows for a more systematic appraisal of all possible actions at a later point.

4. *Generation of Criteria*. It is impossible to discriminate between and among solutions without applying criteria. In the United States we tend to rank people according to social classes; the criteria or values employed are economic wealth and education. Some criteria used in evaluating a solution are topic specific; that is, they relate to the specific problem being analyzed. Other criteria are atopical; these "stock" criteria can be employed in the analysis of almost any set of solutions or actions. Stock criteria include: Is the solution practical? Can it be adopted within our time frame? Is the action financially feasible? Will the action solve the problem? It is probably best to make such criteria explicit, even formal, before evaluating the solutions. In this way all the possible solutions can be fairly evaluated in relation to the criteria. As a consultant to the National Aeronautics and Space Administration (NASA) during the research and development stages of Saturn V, the moon rocket, I watched scientists and engineers apply reflective thinking to technical problems. They tended to apply reflective thinking as a check on their more intuitive problem-solving processes. They went as far as assigning numerical weights to the various criteria used in the evaluation of solutions.

5. *Application of Criteria to the Solutions and Selection of the Best One(s)*. This is a straightforward process of analyzing each solution to determine how well each one measures up to the criteria, thus allowing the group to determine which is the best solution. In a real-life group this

step would also include the consideration of how to implement the selected action(s). One of the many advantages to group problem solving is that the participants will work harder for the success of a group-chosen solution as compared to a solution imposed on them from above. The system allows for the fact that sometimes no solution is adopted; in some cases the best action is no action.

Limits of Reflective Thinking

If this process seems somewhat artificial, particularly in classroom discussions of academic problems, there is nonetheless a pedagogical, or educational, justification for its use. It is best to learn the rules before taking the liberty of breaking them. In that way you have a chance to gain insight into the spirit of reflective thinking and to learn to avoid what Barnlund and Haiman call the "slavish devotion to the *pattern* of reflective thinking."[7]

Furthermore, it is a useful exercise to apply the steps of reflective thinking and discover the limits of rationality. A slavish devotion to both the spirit and pattern of reflective thinking will still fail to achieve total rationality. Human action must fall short of objective rationality for three reasons:

1. Rationality requires a complete knowledge and anticipation of the consequences that will follow on each choice. In fact, knowledge of consequences is always fragmentary.

2. Since these consequences lie in the future, imagination must supply the lack of experienced feeling in attaching value to them. But values can be only imperfectly anticipated.

3. Rationality requires a choice among all possible alternative behaviors. In actual behavior, only a very few of all these possible alternatives ever come to mind.[8]

This triangle of limits on rationality led Nobel laureate Herbert A. Simon to argue that even our careful decisions "satisfice," or yield courses of action that are merely "satisfactory" or "good enough." Despite Kenneth Burke's observation that we are rotten with perfection, our actions are products "of human beings who *satisfice* because they have not the wits to *maximize*."[9]

The context of Simon's remarks indicates he was talking about decisions made by individual administrators, but they apply to group decision-making as well. Perhaps the closer groups get to practicing the spirit of reflective thinking, the more they move from satisficing toward maximizing in their decisions.

Reflective thinking, even when not perfect, can be realized by a group only if it has effective leadership, which is the next topic of this chapter on group communication.

Leadership

At the risk of dating this book, I must indicate that as it is being written there is a general clamor in the United States for leadership. Much of this craving for old-fashioned leaders, I suspect, is a kind of nostalgia for youth. Parents look smaller to the child of twenty-one than to the child of eleven; similarly, the leaders of one's youth seem in retrospect to be larger, wiser, and stronger than the leaders of one's own generation.

We also tend to forget that wishing for stronger leadership is meaningless unless one also wishes for strong followership. Those unwilling to follow are unrealistic in desiring people to lead. Leadership is impossible unless followers grant to their leaders a degree of ethos, credibility, or trust. Without that trust we are bound to flounder. Just as our money has undergone a steady inflation since the early 1960s, our trust in leaders has undergone a sharp deflation in that same period. According to the newsmagazine *Time*, "A report issued in September [1976] by the Public Agenda Foundation noted that trust in Government declined from 76% in 1964 to 33% today; that 83% of American voters say they 'do not trust those in positions of leadership as much as they used to': that confidence in Congress, the Supreme Court, business, college presidents, the military, doctors and lawyers dropped sharply from the mid-60's to the mid-70's."[10] This trend has certainly continued in the 1980s.

In addition to nostalgia and a deflation of trust (accompanied by a rise in the "me-first" ethic of interest groups and social movements), the public seems to be catching up with the changing conceptions of leadership advanced by those who scientifically study leadership in small groups. This change indicates that leadership is still alive and well; the difference is that it manifests itself in less dramatic ways. Let's examine the historical changes in theories of small group leadership by means of Burke's dramatistic pentad (see chapter 2).

A Pentadic Analysis

Theories of small group leadership are accounts of human action. A pentadic analysis (act, scene, agent, agency, purpose) of such accounts can reveal emphases, even misplaced emphases, allowing us to decide whether or not they can be regarded as well-rounded accounts of theories of action. Many scholars of group communication have divided the theories and research of leadership into four categories or perspectives on leadership: traits, styles, situations, and functions.[11] Roughly speaking, this is also the chronological order of the development of leadership theory.

Traits.   The assumption of this perspective is "the belief that a leader is a unique individual possessing some innate ability which allows him to assume a leadership position in any social system. Further assumed is the belief that leaders are born and not made."[12] This can be regarded as a counterpart to the so-called great man theory of history; that is, great men are born, not made, and they possess certain traits and qualities that make them natural leaders and that, in turn, affect historical outcomes to a significant degree. Abraham Lincoln, shown in Figure 6–4, might be an example of this theory.

Scholars associated with the trait approach sought to determine the traits leaders possessed that made them leaders and, therefore, different from their followers. Intelligence tests and personality tests were given to subjects to determine whether there were significant differences between leaders and followers. Traits researched included such factors as intelligence, physical appearance and health, dominance or submission, and self-confidence. Most of these studies of leadership traits were done in the first half of this century. After that time, however, the trait approach was considered to be inadequate as an explanation of leadership.

However, in his review of trait research, R. D. Mann indicates that many studies show positive and significant correlations between leadership and intelligence. Only the magnitude of the correlation has been called into question; that is, "the magnitude of the relationship is less impressive, no correlation reported exceeds .50 and the median r is roughly .25."[13] (By squaring a correlation you get the percentage of common variance needed to make a perfect prediction of one variable to another; thus a correlation of .50 gives you 25 percent of the information to predict leadership perfectly from intelligence.) Similar correlations have been found for various personality traits such as integration or adjustment. In his review of 100 studies of traits related to leadership, R. M. Stogdill reported that only 5% of the traits reported as characteristics of leaders were common to four or more studies.[14] Although this suggests that the research on traits of leaders has failed to establish consistent evidence of the importance of certain traits to leadership, it is worth considering another finding of Stogdill. He found that three general categories of traits were repeatedly found to be significantly corre-lated with leadership: (1) *abilities* including such factors as intelligence, knowledge of how to get things done, and verbal ability; (2) *sociability* including such factors as social perception, dependability, and cooperation; and (3) *motivation* including such factors as initiative and persistence.[15]

Although the trait approach has fallen into disrepute and is considered to be an inadequate explanation of leadership, it should be remembered that many studies found significant but low magnitude correlations between cer-tain traits and leadership. In addition, certain categories of traits (that is, abili-ties, sociability, and motivation) were found to correlate repeatedly with leadership. Thus, it would be unwise to reject completely the concept that traits of an individual are related to leadership.

There are probably many reasons why the trait approach failed to produce more consistent and higher magnitude findings. In his review of leadership Cecil Gibb suggests that

> The failure to establish a definitive relation between personality and leadership may be due to one or more of four factors:

Figure 6-4   The traits theory of group leadership maintains that leaders possess a number of inherent qualities that make them leaders. Thus, great men (or women) are born, not made. Abraham Lincoln, depicted here delivering the Gettysburg Address, had the kind of personal traits that helped him overcome personal misfortune and social calamity to become a great leader. (William H. Johnson: _Lincoln at Gettysburg III,_ ca. 1939–42. Courtesy of National Museum of American Art, formerly National Collection of Fine Arts, Smithsonian Institution, Gift of the Harmon Foundation.)

1. Personality description and measurement themselves are still inadequate. It may be that in leadership research the really significant aspects of personality have not yet been investigated.

2. The groups studied have usually been markedly different from one another, and this may have had the effect of concealing a relationship between personality and the exercise of leadership within a more homogeneous set of groups or family of situations.

3. Situational factors may, and sometimes do override personality factors. . . .

4. Leadership itself is known to be a complex and probably not consistent, pattern of functional roles.[16]

Other factors probably also limited the effectiveness of the research on traits. For example, Stogdill points out that evidence suggests leaders and followers cannot be too different from one another. Thus, we may want a leader who is a little more intelligent, perceptive, or persistent than we are—but not too much so. In our society, if a person is perceived to be too intelligent, he or she may be thought of as an egghead or dreamer rather than as a good leader. This suggests that the relationship of leadership to certain traits may be a curvilinear one (see chapter 4). Yet most of the studies of traits assumed the relation to be a linear one.

In addition, comparing leadership and the rhetorical concept of ethos can illuminate another weakness of the trait research. The constituents of ethos—good sense, good character, and goodwill—are traits. However, no rhetorician has even tried to measure a rhetor's ethos by asking him or her to complete a written test, the very method used in leadership trait studies. The explicit assumption since Aristotle is that the traits must be perceived and/or construed by auditors in the rhetor's verbal and nonverbal acts. There are many explanations as to why a measured trait might not be perceived by others, and almost as many explanations as to why a trait might be perceived even though it had not been measured. We would be greatly surprised if an approach to leadership that measured relevant traits as perceived by others (followers) failed to produce high, positive, and significant correlations.[17] We would also be surprised if the Aristotelian constituents of ethos failed to emerge as salient perceived traits.

Even if we did rehabilitate the traits perspective, it would still be an inadequate theory because it is *agent-centered* and, thereby, excludes scene, act, agency, and purpose.

Styles. Explaining the failure of the trait approach to discover a "definitive relationship between personality and leadership," Gibb pointed out that leadership is a "complex and probably not consistent pattern of functional roles." Thus, in order to understand leadership, the behavior of the leader, not merely the traits, must be studied. In the styles approach to leadership, researchers examined the behavior of leaders and its effects on the group. The scope of the behavior examined, however, was restricted to the leader's use of authority. The research began with comparison of democratic, autocratic, and laissez-faire styles of leadership.[18] A democratic or participatory style of leadership implied a sharing of leadership among the leader and members of the group. Autocratic or authoritarian leadership meant a strong, directive role maintained by the leader; members here mainly follow orders. Laissez-faire style of leadership was soon dropped because of definitional problems. It was judged not to be a leadership role at all because such a leader merely supplies materials and information when asked but otherwise does not participate in the group.

The democratic style of leadership was usually found to produce higher satisfaction among group members. Despite the democratic bias of some researchers, however, the autocratic style was often found to be more efficient and productive.[19]

The findings of the styles approach to leadership, like those of the trait approach, were limited in value. Perhaps in order to gain clear-cut findings, researchers tended to examine only the extreme styles of leaders. The structure of their research characterized the behaviors of the leaders as either extremely autocratic and authoritarian or as extremely democratic and participative. Little consideration was given to the situations in which the leaders, whatever the style of leadership, functioned.[20]

The styles approach, like the trait approach, seems to place primary emphasis on the leader (or agent) and could therefore be considered another agent-centered theory. However, the behavior of the leader is emphasized in the styles approach. It is *agency-centered*. Burke uses *manner* as a synonym for *agency*, and my thesaurus lists *manner* as a synonym for *style*. Furthermore, if there were no agency-centered perspective, the logic of the pentad would require us to create one. Nonetheless, a style perspective on leadership is inadequate on its own to explain behavior across situations.

Situations.   This approach to leadership considered not only the leaders but the situations in which the leaders must function. Fred E. Fiedler and his contingency model of leadership can serve as a good example of the situational approach to leadership. The contingency model considers not only the leader and his or her style of leadership, whether autocratic or democratic, but also considers the situation in which the leader functions. A study in *Communication Monographs* claims to provide support for the contingency model and quotes Fiedler in this way: Effective group performance "depends just as much on the group *situation* as it does on the leader. . . . If we want to improve organizational performance we must deal not only with the leader's style but also with the factors in the situation."[21]

To quote a popular article by Fiedler, "From our research, my associates and I have identified three major factors that can be used to classify group situations: (1) position power of the leaders, (2) task structure, and (3) leader-member personal relationships."[22] In short, Fiedler has given us a situational perspective, a *scene-centered* theory of group leadership. It should be acknowledged that he has incorporated style into his theory; thus, a more precise characterization might be that the theory is *scene-agency-centered*. That fact no doubt explains the broad appeal of the theory. It does not emphasize one term to the exclusion of all others, and the merit of this approach will be discussed later.

Fiedler's work, nonetheless, is not general enough to satisfy. His research has been limited to task-oriented groups. In addition, no theory provides a complete taxonomy of situations.

Functions.   In this approach, emphasis shifts from the person in the leadership role to the communicative behaviors that must be performed by the leader (or other group members) for the group to move toward its goal. Primary exponents of this approach include D. Cartwright and A. Zander, C. D. Mortensen, Dean G. Barnlund and Franklyn S. Haiman, and Robert F. Bales.[23] To provide some historical context, I should add that Chester Barnard was the first to provide a systematic analysis of leadership functions, albeit executive leadership, as the title of his book, *The Functions of the Executive*, and date of publication (1938) suggest.[24] Dean Barnlund also wrote a pioneering functional study of small group leadership.[25]

Although this approach is very popular today, it is important to note that no consistent set of leadership functions has been found. Moreover, the functions listed by most theorists are quite general. Specific behaviors or acts that would fulfill those functions in specific situations are seldom made clear or explicit. The functions perspective shifts emphasis from the agent to the behavior of the agent, his or her acts. Thus it is an *act-centered* theory. As such, it cannot explain the consistent finding, mentioned earlier in discussing Bales's work, that task functions and social-emotional functions cannot often be performed by the same person; it is also clear that some people are unable to provide leadership for even the most mundane group discussion. These findings suggest that different people (agents) are needed in different situations. Because the theory lacks any consideration of agent or scene, it is unable to explain adequately these and other findings of leadership in small groups.

Purpose.   We are in the awkward situation of having a pentadic term with no corresponding theory or perspective. The pentad would suggest that either we search for one hidden in the implicit assumptions of other perspectives or create one if none exists. The functional approach to leadership does seem to have a built-in concept of purpose or goal. A leadership function cannot be identified without making a means-ends judgment; the function must be perceived as assisting the group achieve its end, purpose, or goal. Otherwise it would not be leadership. Prudential rules in other textbooks advise would-be leaders that the purpose of a group meeting — whether problem-solving, informational, or communion — dictates the kind of leadership acts required. Common sense suggests that this is the case. Thus, the functional approach can be more clearly identified as an *act-purpose-centered* theory. Like Fiedler's situational theory, the functional approach actually incorporates two terms of the pentad. Again, perhaps this explains the popularity of the two approaches; they simplify less than the other theories.

This pentadic analysis has shown that no well-rounded theory of small group leadership now exists. If it was not clear in the preceding discussion, it must be emphasized here that each of the perspectives (with the possible exception of purpose) has generated scientific evidence in its support. The support is certainly partial, as in the case of the median r of .25 between intelligence and leadership, but it is statistically significant. Therefore, unless we deny both the logic of the pentad and the scientific evidence, it would seem to be unwise to adopt a strategy of totally rejecting any of the perspectives.

A New Theory of Leadership

The preceding argument, however, runs counter to my own intuition because I have a bias for the functional perspective. The functional perspective, for example, can be easily integrated with the ethos-inspired approach discussed earlier. From the leadership functions or acts, others can infer or construct desired traits in the agent. That could be the key to the perplexing question as to why some people attempt to perform functions and fail to achieve followership from the group, while others with high credibility or ethos attempt the identical functions and are successful.

Our analysis suggests the basis of the popularity of Fiedler's contingency model and the functional approach. Rather than a one-dimensional approach to action, Fiedler's theory stresses both scene and agency, and the functional approach stresses act and implies purpose. For these reasons, then, the most satisfactory theory of leadership would speak to each and all of the terms. Leadership will truly be understood only when all of the essential elements of human action are taken into account. That is not to say that existing theory on each dimension is without need of improvement. A suggestion was made earlier about the approach to traits. Stogdill has recently called for "a taxonomy of situation dimensions and for research on the reaction of leaders and groups to variations in the situation."[26]

I am not prepared to present a perfectly well-rounded theory of leadership at this moment, but I shall offer a definition of the phenomenon in the hope of inspiring your thinking along these lines. From a pentadic perspective, leadership is defined as *the successful execution of a function* (act) *that helps a group achieve its goal* (purpose), *performed by a person* (agent) *who is perceived by others to have the traits and style* (agency) *appropriate to the situation* (scene).

Let's now try to explain that definition in search of practical advice for group leadership. The functions needed to be performed by a problem-solving group may be found in Figure 6–3. Categories 6 and 7 solve the function or problem of *orientation*; this might involve asking for or supplying the group's goal, objective, or end. Categories 5 and 8 solve the function or problem of *evaluation*; this includes asking for or giving opinions about the problem, criteria, or proposed solutions. Categories 4 and 9 solve the function or problem of *control*; examples might include asking for or supplying directions so that the group might move forward in seeking its objective. Categories 3 and 10 solve the function or problem of *decision*; typical acts here would be expressing either agreement or disagreement with another member. Categories 2 and 11 solve the function or problem of *tension-management*; this might include both the expression of tension and the release of tension. Categories 1 and 12 solve the function or problem of *integration*; one can either show antagonism or solidarity (identification). Notice that no single leader could possibly perform all of these functions. Even if a group has a designated leader, he or she will need assistance from the other members. It is the wise leader indeed who encourages others to assist in the performance of these functions. As a result, such a leader would lack the visibility and centrality of the tyrant or even of the old-fashioned leaders for whom so many people today express nostalgia.

The purpose of a discussion group may vary from problem solution to problem analysis to the sharing of information. Member acts (means), of course, will vary as objectives (ends) vary. The agent who performs these acts may be either the designated leader or a member so long as he or she is perceived to have the traits (for example, good sense, good character, goodwill) and style (either directive or nondirective) appropriate to the situation. As the situation changes it will call for different kinds of leadership styles. For example, following Fiedler, we can expect directive leadership to be more effective when (1) the position power of the designated leader is very strong or very weak in comparison to the group members, (2) the structure of the task is either very simple or very complex, and (3) the leader-member personal relationships are either very good or very bad. We can expect nondirective leadership to be more effective when the three conditions mentioned above are between the extreme positions, conditions that seem to be most prevalent in group deliberations.[27]

Summary

This chapter has defined a group as three to twenty people who have shared interests, engage in communication with each other, are organized into either a formal or informal hierarchy, and identify with each other; these conditions must prevail over a continued period of time. A system of interaction analysis has shown the categories of action within a group. This analysis has led to prudential rules for group participation. Reflective thinking is a descriptive and prescriptive system that outlines the steps by which groups solve problems. Finally, this chapter has subjected leadership theories to pentadic analysis, illustrating the weaknesses of each of the present theories of leadership in isolation and the need for a well-rounded theory that accounts for all of the terms of the pentad. This analysis, in turn, has yielded a definition of leadership for small group communication that incorporates the five elements of the pentad.

The following chapter uses the analysis of the group to examine an orderly, systematic group—the organization.

Questions for Essays, Speeches, and Group Discussion

1. With six other classmates in your group, discuss the question, "How can the future energy problems of the United States best be solved?" After the discussion answer the following questions:

   a. Did certain members contribute more to the task than others? Did certain members contribute more to the social-emotional climate than others? Did anyone contribute significantly in both areas?

   b. Assuming the group was satisfied with the outcome, can you identify the steps of reflective thinking employed by the group?

2. Without using criteria, attempt to rank in order of quality the top five rock groups now recording music. After the discussion try to recall the use of disguised criteria—for example, the use of enthymemes (see chapter 2) such as, "I like the Rolling Stones because of their unique rhythm."

3. Go to the library and read the story on leadership in the United States, published in *Time* magazine, November 8, 1976. You will find that famous leaders are quoted about leadership; classify each quotation

according to the terms (act, agent, agency, scene, and purpose) of Burke's pentad (see chapter 2 and the leadership section of the present chapter).

4. Support or attack this thesis: Historical changes have forced leadership to be exercised differently today than in the past. (If possible, ask your parents and grandparents for ideas and examples about this thesis.)

Additional Readings

Bales, Robert F. "A Set of Categories for the Analysis of Small Group Interaction." *American Sociological Review* 15(April 1950): 257–63.

Bales, Robert F. "In Conference." *Harvard Business Review* 32(1954): 48–52.

Barnlund, Dean C., and Franklyn S. Haiman. *The Dynamics of Discussion*. Boston: Houghton Mifflin Company, 1960.

Fisher, B. Aubrey. *Small Group Decision-Making: Communication and the Group Process*. New York: McGraw-Hill Book Co., 1974.

Gibb, Cecil A. "Leadership." In *Handbook of Social Psychology*, 2nd ed., edited by Gardner Lindzey and Elliott Aronson. Reading, Mass.: Addison-Wesley Publishing Co., 1968.

Parsons, Talcott, and Robert F. Bales, "The Dimensions of Action-Space." In *Working Papers in the Theory of Action*, edited by Talcott Parsons, Robert F. Bales, and Edward A. Shils (New York: Free Press, 1953), pp. 63–110.

Notes

1. Robert F. Bales, "A Set of Categories for the Analysis of Small Group Interaction," *American Sociological Review* 15(1950): 258. Reprinted by permission.

2. Robert F. Bales, *Interaction Process Analysis: A Method for the Study of Small Groups* (Cambridge, Mass.: Addison-Wesley Press, Inc., 1951), p. viii.

3. Talcott Parsons and Robert F. Bales, "The Dimensions of Action-Space," in *Working Papers in the Theory of Action*, ed. Talcott Parsons, Robert F. Bales, and Edward A. Shils. Copyright 1953 by The Free Press. Reprinted by permission.

4. Robert F. Bales, "In Conference," *Harvard Business Review* 32(1954): 49–50. Copyright © 1954 by the President and Fellows of Harvard College; all rights reserved. Reprinted by permission of the *Harvard Business Review*.

5. For example, see James H. McBurney and Kenneth G. Hance, *Discussion in Human Affairs* (New York: Harper and Brothers, 1950), pp. 11–13, 65–93.

6. Dean G. Barnlund and Franklyn S. Haiman, *The Dynamics of Discussion* (Boston: Houghton Mifflin Company, 1960), p. 84.

7. Ibid., p. 85.

8. Herbert A. Simon, *Administrative Behavior*, 3rd ed. (New York: Free Press, 1976), p. 81.

9. Ibid., p. xxviii. Italics in original.

10. *Time*, 8 November 1976, p. 30. Copyright Time Inc. 1976. Reprinted by permission from *Time*, The Weekly Newsmagazine.

11. For example, see B. Aubrey Fisher, *Small Group Decision Making: Communication and the Group Process* (New York: McGraw-Hill Book Co., 1974), pp. 74–82. Similar, but not identical, categories of perspectives are discussed by James B. Spotts, "The Problem of Leadership: A Look at Some Recent Findings of Behavioral Science Research," in *Leadership and Social Change*, 2nd ed., ed. William R. Lassey and Richard R. Fernandez (La Jolla, Calif.: University Associates Inc., 1976), pp. 44–63; and in Marvin E. Shaw, *Group Dynamics: The Psychology of Small Group Behavior* (New York: McGraw-Hill Book Co., 1971), pp. 267–78.

12. Fisher, p. 74.

13. R. D. Mann, "A Review of the Relationships Between Personality and Performance in Small Groups," *Psychological Bulletin* 56(1959): 248.

14. R. M. Stogdill, "Personal Factors Associated with Leadership: A Survey of the Literature," *Journal of Psychology* 25(1948): 67.

15. Ibid., p. 69.

16. Cecil A. Gibb, "Leadership," in *Handbook of Social Psychology*, 2nd ed., ed. Gardner Lindzey and Elliot Aronson (Reading, Mass.: Addison-Wesley Publishing Co., 1968), p. 227.

17. For example, see John G. Geier, "A Trait Approach to the Study of Leadership in Small Groups," *Journal of Communication* 17(1967): 316–23.

18. For example, see K. Lewin, R. Lippitt, and R. K. White, "Patterns of Aggressive Behavior in Experimentally Created 'Social Climates,'" *Journal of Social Psychology* 10(1939): 271–99.

19. For example, see M. E. Shaw, "A Comparison of Two Types of Leadership in Various Communication Nets," *Journal of Abnormal and Social Psychology* 50(1955): 127–34; and N. C. Morse and E. Reimer, "The Experimental Change of a Major Organizational Variable," *Journal of Abnormal and Social Psychology* 52(1956): 120–29.

20. A unique approach to the study of styles of leadership can be found in Michael Maccoby, *The Gamesman: The New Corporate Leaders* (New York: Simon and Schuster, 1976), pp. 46–120. Unlike other researchers who have

viewed leadership styles as a dichotomy or continuum between autocracy and democracy, Maccoby has determined that there are four types or styles of leaders in modern corporations: the Craftsman, the Jungle Fighter, the Company Man, and the Gamesman.

21. C. W. Downs and T. Pickett, "An Analysis of the Effects of Nine Leadership-Group Compatible Contingencies upon Productivity and Member Satisfaction," *Communication Monographs* 44(1977): 221. Italics added.

22. Fred E. Fiedler, "Style or Circumstances: The Leadership Enigma," *Psychology Today* 2(1969): 41.

23. D. Cartwright and A. Zander, eds., *Group Dynamics: Research and Theory*, 3rd ed. (New York: Harper & Row, 1968), pp. 538–50; C. D. Mortensen, "Should the Discussion Group Have an Assigned Leader?" *Speech Teacher* 15(1966): 34–41; Barnlund and Haiman, pp. 275–92; R. F. Bales, *IPA; A Method for the Study of Small Groups* (Cambridge, Mass.: Addison-Wesley Press, 1950).

24. Chester I. Barnard, *The Functions of the Executive* (Cambridge, Mass.: Harvard University Press, 1938).

25. D. Barnlund, "Experiments in Leadership Training for Decision-Making Discussion Groups," *Speech Monographs* 22(1955): 1–14. Barnlund reports evidence that training in leadership can lead to improvement in leadership behavior.

26. A 1975 statement quoted in Downs and Pickett, p. 220.

27. Fiedler, pp. 41–43.

Three

Macro-Communication Settings

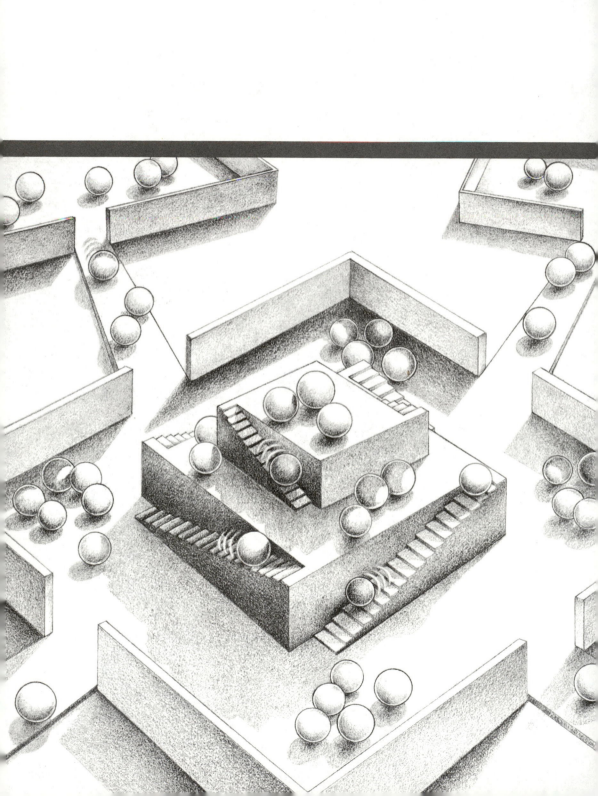

CHAPTER

7

Organizational Communication

Communication technique shapes the form and the internal economy of organization. This will be evident at once if one visualizes the attempt to do many things now accomplished by small organizations if each "member" spoke a different language. . . . In an exhaustive theory of organization, communication would occupy a central place, because the structure, extensiveness, and scope of organization are almost entirely determined by communication techniques.

The Functions of the Executive
Chester I. Barnard

Most Americans begin life as the customers of organizations — hospitals. After a short stay there, they go home to join the family. "Well baby" visits to a pediatric clinic are often followed by trips to day-care centers and nursery schools. Compelled by law to attend school at the age of five, children voluntarily join such organizations as 4-H, scouts, and the YWCA. While still in childhood they are the targets of concerted communication campaigns launched by advertising organizations on behalf of toy, candy, and cereal manufacturers. Almost half of all Americans go from high school to a college or university, whether private or state-supported; the others go to work for an organization or collect unemployment compensation from a government agency. Undergraduates go on to professional schools, join firms, form families, and even create new business organizations. After the inevitable, churches, synagogues, and mortuaries provide the final services.

We spend our lives as members of organizations. Notice the diversity of organizations referred to in the preceding paragraph: service groups (hospitals, day-care centers), voluntary organizations, manufacturers, schools, families, and government agencies. Our lives are touched, even formed, by organizations to an extent few of us realize. That touching, contact, or forming, of course, is accomplished by messages from organizations to us as individuals.

The theme of this chapter is that organizations are constituted by communication; that is, communication creates the internal and external bonds of organization. In developing this theme we shall consider the following points. First, we shall look at two ways of classifying organizations in our society: one way is by the kind of functions performed by organizations for society; the other is by how an organization communicates with its employees. Second, we shall look at how groups are integrated into an organization by means of communication. Third, we shall consider how organizations interact with their environments. Here we shall combine points two and three to develop a model of internal and external organizational communication. Fourth, we shall look at traditional and modern theories of management — with special attention to Douglas McGregor's Theory X and Theory Y, W. Charles Redding's Ideal Managerial Climate, and Chester I. Barnard's Functions of the Executive. Finally, I shall close with a discussion of organizations I have studied.

Definition and Classification of Organizations

In keeping with our action orientation, and to link organizations with our analysis of groups, we shall define an organization as "a social system which is organized for the attainment of a particular type of goal; the attainment of that goal is at the same time the performance of a type of function on behalf of a more inclusive system, the society."[1] Just as the actions of individual members of a group were classified by Robert F. Bales as solving problems or functions for the group, so the actions (or "outputs") of organizations are seen here as solving the problems or functions of the larger society.

Classifying Organizations by Functions

Talcott Parsons saw four functions performed or problems solved by organizations for the larger society.[2] He cautioned, however, that in applying these to concrete organizations we should think of the *primacy* of function and not think that an organization performs any one function exclusively.

1. *Organizations Oriented to Economic Production*. The most frequent example here is the business firm. Such an organization is governed by the values of economic rationality (see Figure 7–1). Profits are both a symbol of success and a condition of continuing operation. Organizations of this type produce services as well as products. Business firms are expected to pay their own way by paying for their costs out of their own proceeds or loans taken in the private sector. Employees are paid what the market deems they are worth.

2. *Organizations Oriented to Political Goals*. This type of organization is oriented to the attainment of valued goals and to the generation and allocation of power in society. This includes most organs of government; because the banking system creates and allocates power in a business economy, it is included by Parsons in this category. Military organizations, as an example, are supported by taxes. At times employees are conscripted, or drafted, and paid at less than market levels. Duty and service are stressed. Unlike business employees, the members cannot leave whenever they want for higher offers. Discipline and control are high, even coercive if need be.

3. *Integration Organizations*. These organizations adjust conflicts in society that would otherwise paralyze society. They include the court system and the legal profession. The political parties, in mobilizing support for political figures, also belong to this category. Interest groups, which attempt to influence the outcome of congressional adjustments of disputes and conflicts, are another example.

4. *Pattern-Maintenance Organizations*. The cases in this category are devoted to "cultural," "educational," and "expressive" functions. Obvious examples are churches and schools. The university, for example, "socializes" its students by teaching them their past as well as what will be expected of them in the future. The university collects part of its

Figure 7-1 One of the four social functions performed by organizations is economic production. The men and women here are working in a Massachusetts textile mill in 1935. (American Woolen Co., Lawrence, Massachusetts, 1935, Margaret Bourke-White/*Life* Magazine, 1935. ©Time Inc.)

costs by charging tuition, but the bulk is provided by taxes and contributions. It is less authoritarian than the other types of organizations.

If these categories appear to be too conservative or too devoted to the status quo, let's correct that impression with the following reasons. First, economic organizations are constantly seeking out new goods and services to produce, as well as new methods of production. Second, the general trend of adjusting conflicts by the courts and Congress over the past forty years or so has been to side more with labor, workers, and minorities rather than with business, management, and the majority; this has produced considerable societal changes. (These would include the rise of organized labor and increased civil rights.) Third, pattern-maintenance organizations also have responsibility for the modification of the cultural tradition by supporting "research" and the "arts."

To summarize, just as the acts of individuals fulfill needs or perform functions for groups, so groups perform the needs of organizations and organizations perform the functions or needs for society. Thus, the individual actions of an individual are tied through groups and organizations to the needs of society.

Classifying Organizations by Their Communication Strategies

Amitai Etzioni has developed another system, called *compliance theory*, for classifying organizations.[3] The theory distinguishes between organizations on the basis of how the organization gains compliance from the lower participants or employees. Compliance is defined by Etzioni as referring "both to a relation in which an actor behaves in accordance with a directive supported by another actor's power, and to the orientation of the subordinated actor to the power applied."[4] Power is divided into three categories: coercive, remunerative, and normative.

Coercive power rests on the use or threat of force to gain compliance or obedience. *Remunerative* (or *utilitarian*) *power* rests on the distribution of material rewards such as wages and salaries to gain compliance. *Normative power* rests on the ability to use persuasion (or rhetoric) to gain compliance. Nearly every organization uses all three kinds of power, but most of them emphasize one kind of power over the others.

For example, an army or prison would stress its coercive power in communication with soldiers or inmates (see Figure 7–2). A factory or building contractor would stress its remunerative power in communicating with workers. A political party or charitable organization would stress its normative power in communicating with its members.

Perhaps you noticed that Etzioni's definition of compliance specifies both the superior's use of power and the subordinate's response to it. Different kinds of power by superiors beget different kinds of involvement by subordinates. Coercive superiors produce *alienated* subordinates, such as prisoners and many soldiers. Remunerative or utilitarian power produces *calculating* subordinates, such as a factory worker who may be constantly looking for a higher paying job. Normative superiors produce *moral* subordinates, such as church members or volunteers.

The three kinds of power can be combined with the three kinds of involvement to produce nine sets of relations. The three combinations just mentioned — coercive-alienating, remunerative-calculating, and normative-moral — are called *congruent types* and are found more frequently than the other six types. The other six are called *incongruent types*; and an example would be normative-alienative, in which normative power expressed through persuasion by superiors would be met by alienation on the part of subordinates.

Why are the congruent types found more often than incongruent organizations? Etzioni's compliance theory explains this by its "dynamic

Figure 7-2 Organizations gain compliance from participants through various kinds of power. These WACs undergoing an officer's inspection are experiencing the military's coercive power to enforce obedience and instill discipline. (Mary Ellen Mark/Archive Pictures, Inc.)

hypothesis": "Organizations tend to shift their compliance structure from incongruent to congruent types and organizations which have congruent compliance structures tend to resist factors pushing them toward incongruent compliance structures."[5] As you might guess, some types have greater legitimacy or societal approval. Normative power is most likely to be seen as legitimate, coercive power least, and remunerative or utilitarian is in between.

This system of classifying organizations is particularly useful to students of communication. There is, however, a certain circularity to the method. For example, if you look at how an organization communicates with its lowest members and find coercive power producing alienation, you would classify it as coercive-alienative. Follow-up research on the organization would, predictably, find coercive messages producing alienation. Nonetheless, this system has produced some less obvious findings. For example, communication blockages between lowest superior and subordinates can be useful and functional to a coercive-alienative organization because the human needs of the subordinates are not relayed to the superiors. If a superior understood subordinates' needs and problems, it would be more difficult to use coercive power and coercive messages.

Next we shall examine the relationship between groups and organizations.

Groups and Organizations

Rensis Likert has found that successful organizations tend to function according to the diagram in Figure 7–3.[6] Note that there is a hierarchical pattern (the shape of a pyramid or triangle) to the overall organization. Note the vertical and horizontal lines; these represent the *formal channels of communication* without which organizations would be aggregations. We speak of downward, upward, and horizontal communication.

An organization generates subdivisions by the way in which it divides its overall task. A manufacturer of outhouses might have a seat department, a roof department, and so on; perhaps there would even be a department responsible for carving half-moons in the doors. These departments or units can come into existence by subdividing existing units or by adding new ones. There is no other way.

The case in Figure 7–3 is one of four-person groups; nonetheless, they could, and do, vary in size as circumstances require. The executives, managers, and supervisors (those who have subordinates) have an important

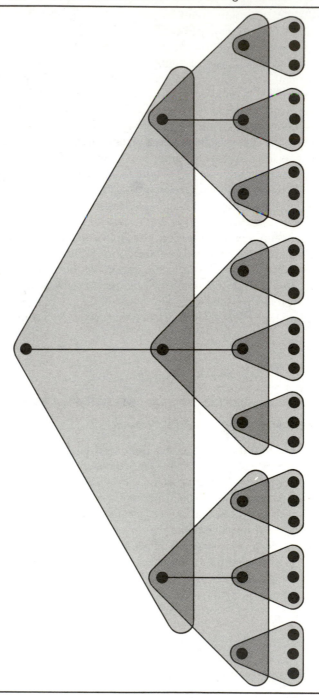

decision to make about their communication action: whether to deal with subordinates mainly in a one-on-one (person-to-person) relationship or as members of a group. Likert recommends the latter, the group approach, with these remarks:

> As our theoretical derivation has indicated, an organization will function best when its personnel function not as individuals but as members of highly effective work groups with high-performance goals. Consequently, management should deliberately endeavor to build these effective groups, linking them into an overall organization by means of people who hold overlapping group membership [Figure 7–3]. The superior in one group is a subordinate in the next group, and so on through the organization. If the work groups at each hierarchical level are well knit and effective, the linking process will be accomplished well. Staff as well as line should be characterized by this pattern of operation.[7]

(The reference to "staff" and "line" in the quotation by Likert may be explained in this way: In our outhouse factory the people assembling the product are line employees; those who perform such tasks as making out paychecks and carrying out sawdust and trash are staff employees.) Likert is recommending that organizations be set up as a group of groups tied together by the overlapping membership of supervisors. A supervisor is in a leadership role in one group and in a subordinate or membership role in another. This crucial integration function Likert calls the "linking-pin function." In summarizing research on the rhetorical or persuasive ability of supervisors, Likert says the "results demonstrate that *the capacity to exert influence upward is essential if a supervisor (or manager) is to perform his supervisory functions successfully.*"[8]

Likert probably overemphasizes the value of group loyalty. If members of an organization identify almost totally with their work group, serious problems can develop. If they cannot see the "big picture," if they see only how their efforts satisfy a part of the organization's needs, they will have a distorted view of the common enterprise. Organizational "statesmanship" requires in part that an actor have a balanced view of the organization's efforts. Nonetheless, Likert shows us in a slightly different way how groups fit into that "big picture," as well as the communicative requirements of supervisors (that is, the need for supervisors — foremen, managers, and executives — to listen and speak or to persuade and be persuaded). Likert is also an effective advocate for full and open communication within work groups, up and down the hierarchical scale.

Having seen how groups interact with other groups to produce a larger organization, it is now time to consider how organizations interact with their environments. Before doing that it is necessary to discuss the distinction between an organization and its environment.

Organizations and Environments

It is not easy to draw the line, or to describe the boundary, between an organization and its environment. According to William H. Starbuck, an authority on organizations, "Assuming organizations can be sharply distinguished from their environments distorts reality by compressing into one dichotomy a melange of continuously varying phenomena."[9]

The problem can be tracked back to our earlier distinction between state and process definitions (see chapter 3). Organizations have historically been defined as states with such elements as members, purpose, hierarchy, communication, and so on. This definition has even had a geometric aspect in that organizations have been defined as triangles or pyramids. A triangle or pyramid enclosing certain elements can be easily distinguished from their environments.

A process definition of an organization, on the other hand, would stress the fact that organizations import materials and energy while exporting goods and services. They buy and sell from people in the environment, influence people and groups in the environment, and are, in turn, influenced by such "external entities." The most important part of an organization's environment is other organizations. We need a model to explain how an organization interacts with other organizations or interacts with other persons, who are representatives of other organizations.

Boundary Role Persons

J. Stacy Adams has identified the *boundary role person* (or BRP) as the agent or actor formally responsible for representing an organization in its communication with the environment. The BRP's are found in offices and departments bearing such labels as marketing, sales, purchasing, recruitment, admissions, advertising, and public relations. BRP's also include collective bargaining negotiators and anyone whose responsibilities require them to interact with the environment on behalf of the organization. They would include the park ranger shown in Figure 7–4.

According to Adams, the BRP has three characteristics that are derived from the role and its relationship to other roles. The first is *distance*. The BRP frequently travels or is even stationed away from the home office. Looking outward and dealing with outsiders, the BRP may have psychological distance between him or her and the organization. The BRP is often aware of this distance and begins to wonder how he or she is being perceived by the organization. The organization may well react to this distance by developing suspicion of the BRP and may even want to develop ways of checking up on the BRP. The more hostile the environment, the more suspicious the BRP's constituents will be.

The second characteristic, according to Adams, is that the BRP is the *representative* of the organization to members of the environment. The BRP must know the external organizations he or she deals with and reflect that knowledge inwardly to his or her own constituents. Conversely, the BRP must know and reflect outwardly his or her own organization. The BRP must manage the impressions formed by both the external organizations and the internal constituents. At times the BRP distorts or conceals information. For example, the BRP in the sales department may exaggerate apathy of external clients to justify low sales when interacting with constituents.

The third characteristic of the BRP is as an agent of *influence*. The BRP must persuade external organizations to accept his or her organization's position. Conversely, as a successful negotiator, the BRP must also persuade his or her constituents to accept the position of the external organization(s). For example, a labor relations negotiator may see that it is wise to accept from a labor union a compromise offer that his or her constituents see as unfavor-

Figure 7-4   A boundary role person (BRP) represents the organization to the public and to other organizations. A park ranger, for instance, is the National Park Service's representative. For these park visitors this ranger is the living embodiment of the larger organization. (© Frank Balthis/Jeroboam, Inc.)

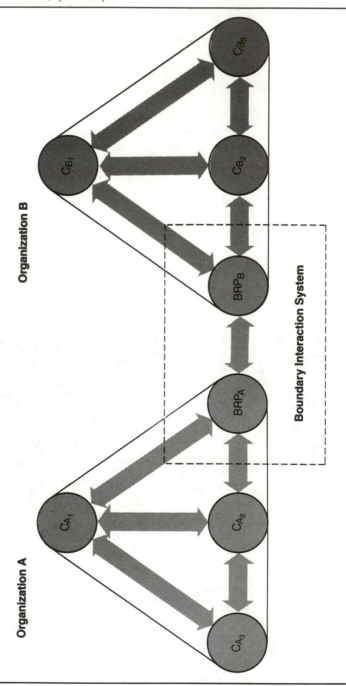

able. The BRP is thus caught in the middle between constituents and BRP counterparts in other external organizations. Although Adams did not seem to realize it, he has described — in a horizontal way — the functions performed vertically by Likert's linking pin.

Figure 7–5 represents my adaptation of Adams's model.[10] Notice that BRP_A represents organization A in interaction with BRP_B, the representative of organization B. The arrows pointing to and from each BRP represent their reciprocal influence on each other. C_{A1} and C_{B1} are the top managers of their respective organizations and are, respectively, the most important constituents for each BRP. Other constituents are represented by C_{A2}, C_{A3}, C_{B2}, and C_{B3}. There are, of course, more constituents than represented in the model.

Notice also that the arrows between constituents and BRP's indicate again a reciprocal influence. Just as BRP's must influence and be influenced by each other in external interaction, constituents and BRP's must influence and be influenced by each other in their internal interaction. (There should be a line with two arrows linking each BRP with C_3 in each organization. This line is not depicted for esthetic reasons.)

This model provides us with a dynamic process definition or model of how an organization interacts with its environment.

Internal and External Organizational Communication

Figure 7–6 is a dynamic model of internal and external organizational communication.

The key difference between this figure and Figure 7–5 is that C_{A3} is linked with reciprocal arrows to C_{A4}, C_{A5}, and C_{A6} to indicate further how vertical interaction flows up and down the entire organization; this vertical interaction is ultimately influenced by and influences the external interaction. The same is indicated for organization B.

Notice also that the dotted lines indicate the entire organization is linked by the same processes. Thus, this model combines the vertical process of internal influence with the horizontal process of external influence. Just as supervisors perform as linking pins to integrate the internal groups into an organization, the BRP links one organization to another. In reality, BRP's link a single, focal organization with many external organizations. Indeed, there can be complications deriving from "third party" organizations. An example would be two suppliers and a customer or a government agency intervening in a labor dispute. In such cases the triad theory discussed earlier (see chapter 5) can help us understand these interactions. The model does, however, depict the basic processes of organizations. It indicates how organizations import personnel, materials, services, and energy; it also indicates how subgroups are organized to perform transformations that, in turn, be-

Figure 7-6 Model of internal and external organizational communication. This figure represents the interaction flowing up and down each organization; that interaction influences and is influenced by the external interaction between organizations.

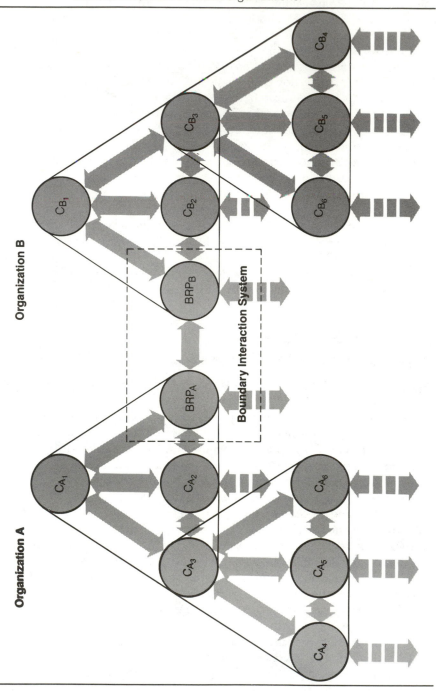

come the products, by-products, and services exported to the environment. It should be clear that the central process in all of this is communication and influence — that is, persuasion. We shall turn now from the theory of organizational communication to management communication theory and the question of how to make organizations work well.

Traditional and Modern Theories of Management Communication

We are at the end of the second century of industrialism. During that period a number of theorists have attempted to capture the essence of human organization and how to manage these organizations. These theorists probably did not realize that they were continuing in the tradition of rhetorical theory. The management theory of the Roman empire, for example, was the rhetorical theory we discussed in chapter 2. Rhetorical theory provided the Romans with their theory of decision making, justice, politics, and persuasion.

Since then theorists have developed theories of management. Rather than write another history of management thought in this chapter, I have decided to quote a summary of them through the writings of Douglas McGregor. Following that I shall examine the theories of W. Charles Redding and Chester I. Barnard.

McGregor: Theory X and Theory Y

Douglas McGregor divides the body of management theory into two groups. The first he calls "the traditional view of direction and control," or Theory X. These assumptions about human nature and human action are drawn by McGregor from the theories and writing of such people as Max Weber, Henri Fayol, and Frederick Taylor.

1. The average human being has an inherent dislike of work and will avoid it if he can.

2. Because of this human characteristic of dislike of work, most people must be coerced, controlled, directed, threatened with punishment to get them to put forth adequate effort toward the achievement of organizational objectives.

3. The average human being prefers to be directed, wishes to avoid responsibility, wants security above all.[11]

These assumptions add up to a managerial strategy of communication, as McGregor puts it, "admirably suited to the capacities and characteristics of the child rather than the adult."[12] But look around you, continues McGregor, and you will see that many of our organizations (or bureaucracies) are built to pursue such strategies. They are "rational" to the point of being like machines; workers are treated like parts of the machine. Soon they may begin to act (react or move) as expected. This, in turn, provides managers with fresh evidence by which to prove Theory X.

To understand interpersonal communication in such an organization, we can recall the four pattern variables described in chapter 4. The first characteristic would be *affective neutrality*. Communication, even relationships, should be regarded as means to an end in a Theory X organization. Feelings should not be a part of such communication; they are irrelevant (if negative feelings do develop, they should be concealed). Second, interpersonal communication in such organizations would have the attribute of *specificity*, not diffuseness. Employees deal with only one aspect of others — the other as worker, expert, boss, subordinate — rather than with the total personality. Third, such organizations require that we take notice of another's *performance* rather than his or her human qualities. I care not about who you are, only what you do. It matters not that you have unused abilities, it matters only that you perform as directed. Fourth, and finally, bureaucracy or Theory X organizations require that we apply *universal* rather than particular standards to others. Job applicants must either pass the civil service examination or show they have earned the appropriate diplomas and degrees. To apply particular criteria to an individual would be "irrational," and such an act would even be regarded by fellow employees as unfair, an act of favoritism. Universalism is, after all, more "professional" than particularism.

Theory Y is offered by McGregor as an alternative to Theory X. It is based on the social scientific work of such writers as Chris Argyris, Abraham Maslow, and Rensis Likert. The assumptions of Theory Y are

1. The expenditure of physical and mental effort in work is as natural as play or rest.

2. External control and the threat of punishment are not the only means for bringing about effort toward organizational objectives. Man will exercise self-direction and self-control in the service of objectives to which he is committed.

3. Commitment to objectives is a function of the rewards associated with their achievement.

4. The average human being learns, under proper conditions, not only to accept but to seek responsibility.

5. The capacity to exercise a relatively high degree of imagination, ingenuity, and creativity in the solution of organizational problems is widely, not narrowly, distributed in the population.

6. Under the conditions of modern industrial life, the intellectual potentialities of the average human being are only partially utilized.[13]

It should be clear that Theories X and Y differ on a number of assumptions. Perhaps the most central difference is that X assumes people must be directed and controlled by a central authority; Y, by contrast, assumes that management should create conditions in which employees can pursue their own goals by participating in how the organization can pursue its own ends. The implications for management communication are, of course, profound. Theory X would have managers "order" all work. Theory Y would favor persuasion, suggestion, and even asking questions such as, How can we best do this job?

There are other implications for interpersonal communication. Employing the pattern variables again, we may assume that a Theory Y organization would encourage members more often than Theory X to opt for positively *affective* relationships; *diffuseness* rather than specificity; *qualities* rather than performance; and *particular* rather than universal standards.

As regards group communication within X and Y organizations, Theory Y stresses group decision making; Theory X favors one-on-one, superior-subordinate communication. We would expect Theory X organizations, because they do not promote group identification, to force workers to find such satisfactions in informal groups and labor unions.

In regard to informal groups, it came as a shock to Theory X managers when a team of researchers from Harvard University found informal groups developing their own group work rules.[14] These rules were contrary to the rules and expectations put forward by management. The same kind of group satisfactions were also achieved in Theory X organizations when workers organized labor unions. By joining such a union the worker did gain some control over the work environment through collective bargaining (a "we" against "they") and the grievance procedure. My thesis is that *when management fails to encourage group identification, the workers will find their own way of doing so —whether by informal groups or labor unions.*

Theories X and Y are not scientific theories; they are theories only in the sense of being organized sets of belief statements. McGregor does seem to have placed the angels on one side and the devils on the other. In addition, each set of belief statements oversimplifies the two groups of management and organization theories. It is no doubt true that Theory X is true of some workers in the United States, Theory Y of others. In a study of communication practices in a NASA field center during the Apollo Project I found evidence of both kinds of management among highly educated employees.[15]

Redding: Ideal Managerial Climate

W. Charles Redding of Purdue University, one of the authorities on organizational communication, has derived a hypothesized consensus of leading authorities. He calls this the "Ideal Managerial Climate" (IMC). The IMC's five main components are briefly summarized here.[16]

1. *Supportiveness*. This term is used in the sense of its dictionary definition, which is the furnishing of support or aid. Redding relies on Likert somewhat in discussing this concept. Likert himself used a cluster of terms in describing how a supportive manager communicates with subordinates: "supportive, friendly and helpful rather than hostile . . . sensitive, considerate . . . just . . . he shows confidence in the integrity, ability and motivation of subordinates . . . he expects much, not little . . . he coaches and assists employees. . . ."[17]

Citing J. R. Gibb, Redding lists six terms that are paired with their opposites, thereby denoting the contrasting manifestations of defensive and supportive climates (see Figure 7–7).[18] We shall not explain these terms in depth here because they are readily understandable. In Redding's IMC coworkers should be descriptive rather than evaluative in dealing with each other; be oriented toward the solving of problems rather than toward dominating others; deal with others as the needs of the situation suggest rather than by a campaign of manipulation; realize that impersonality is defensive while concern for the other is supportive (the neutrality versus empathy pair is quite similar to the pattern variable of affectivity-affective neutrality in chapter 4); relate as peers rather than "talking down" to each other; and acknowledge that what one of us knows may not be the final answer. In a sentence, a supportive climate is such that each member of the organization feels that he or she can maintain a sense of personal worth and importance.

2. *Participative Decision Making*. This component of IMC is closely re-

Figure 7-7 Behavioral characteristics of supportive and defensive climates.

Defensive climates	Supportive climates
1. Evaluation	1. Description
2. Control	2. Problem orientation
3. Strategy	3. Spontaneity
4. Neutrality	4. Empathy
5. Superiority	5. Equality
6. Certainty	6. Provisionalism

lated to our discussion of group communication and problem solving (see chapter 6), and does not require repetition here. The essence of participative decision making is that individual employees should engage in making decisions that affect them. This, of course, implies that a certain amount of conflict is necessary, even desirable, if Redding's IMC is to be realized and an organization is to be effective. The qualifications we identified while discussing Fiedler's contingency approach (see chapter 6) apply here also.

3. *Trust, Confidence, and Credibility*. Redding regards the three concepts in this component as "close cousins." He does this for good reasons. Although some writers consider credibility to be a dimension of interpersonal trust in the communication process, others view trust as a dimension of credibility. We can claim still another relative — this one a parent rather than a cousin — in the Aristotelian concept of ethos (see chapter 2). The traditional view of ethos and credibility has been that of the audience's (or receiver's) construction of the speaker (or source). It also works the other way. If a source has a high degree of trust or confidence in the receiver, it will encourage him or her to be more candid in disclosing information that could be "used against" the source. For example, a researcher studied fifty-two pairs of superiors and subordinates and found that the more ambitious the subordinate, the more about his problems he concealed from his boss. Also, the less he trusted the boss, the more he concealed.[19]

It is clear that Redding means that the IMC requires a high level of trust, confidence, and credibility. Indeed, it is difficult to conceive of an organization surviving for long with a low level of this component.

4. *Openness and Candor*. When introduced to this component, many students conclude that it is identical to self-disclosure, which was discussed in chapter 4. If that were the case, we could refer the reader to that passage and be done with this component of the IMC. Upon reflection, however, it's clear that there are differences and similarities between self-disclosure, on one hand, and openness and candor, on the other. For the concepts to be identical, one would have to expand the concept of self to include every possible topic of discussion in an organization. Although you and I may know a few individuals with such an expanded ego, most of us include less than, say, the General Motors Corporation under our heading of self. Redding gives this factor another twist in this remark:

> Further, it is emphasized that (a) openness is a concept which should be applied to *both* message-sending (telling) and message-receiving (listening); and (b) openness should be examined in all three of the familiar dimensions of communication in a hierarchical organization: (1) from superior to subordinate, (2) from subordinate to superior, and (3) from peer to peer. A final word: . . . one could say that any company setting out to improve the climate of openness must examine its system of rewards and penalties. Management must somehow find ways of

generating *clearly visible rewards* for behaviors which manifest true openness of communication. Mere lip service will not only be inadequate, it can easily undermine credibility (see the preceding section) and thus produce a boomerang effect.[20]

Perhaps it is worth reemphasizing that Redding is saying that it takes *at least two* — and at best the entire organization — to practice openness and candor. Every student of organizations has a briefcase full of anecdotes about organizations that discouraged the upward flow of bad news, about employees who were fired for telling the truth, and about organizational failures that resulted from a "coverup."

Indeed, there is a relevant phenomenon in modern organizational life called "whistle-blowing." An individual who communicates bad news up the line to the boss, and to the boss's boss, is often frustrated by the absence of a meaningful response. If the problem has serious consequences to the larger public — such as unsafe products being produced, the environment ravaged, or the taxpayers' money wasted — the individual often feels the ethical need to blow the whistle and to bring the problem to the attention of the public by talking to the press. "Whistle-blowing" often leads to the firing of the person who "went public" with his or her complaints.

If the discussion of these four main components of the IMC has led you to believe that the organization contemplated by Redding was a Brownie troop, a sensitivity group session, or a wedding reception, let's hasten to the fifth and final main component.

5. *Emphasis upon High Performance Goals*. Certainly this factor should be included in a discussion of the organizational ideal. Redding's interest in this component, however, was whether organizational communication can produce high organizational performance. He surveyed considerable evidence and expert opinion that support a positive answer to that question when various combinations of the first four components were practiced.

There is a second question: "*Should management mount persuasive (or "inspirational") campaigns in order to achieve acceptance of high performance standards*? On this matter the evidence is mixed."[21] Rather than consider all of the mixed evidence, we shall conclude our discussion with a quotation Redding thinks should hang on the office walls of all students and practitioners of organizational communication:

> *Give the employee credit for being conscientious in his job. Don't insult his intelligence and self-esteem with childish promotional gimmicks; do recognize him for his own worth, as a responsible worker.*[22]

In conclusion, it is important to note, first, that the components of the IMC are statements about communication. Second, we should note that such an ideal climate could exist only in Heaven, where presumably the members need neither organization nor management. Third, although such an ideal cannot be achieved on earth, it is presented by Redding as a set of standards by which to measure how far and in what ways actual practice deviates from the ideal.

We turn now from the ideal managerial climate to the functional perspective on management communication put forth by Chester I. Barnard.

Barnard: Functional Perspective on Management Communication

Barnard has provided a highly regarded theory of organization as well as a theory of management. His work will receive special attention for two important reasons. The first is that Barnard, more than any general theorist of organization or management, was explicitly a communication theorist. The quotation from his work at the beginning of this chapter helps to prove this point. The second reason is that his theory is a reasonable compromise or bridge between the extreme positions represented by Theory X and Theory Y.

Barnard was not the typical academic theorist. Rather, he was a successful executive, in both business and voluntary organizations, who reflected carefully on his observations and experiences. He said that only after he relegated economic theory and economic interests to a secondary, though indispensable, place did he understand organizations and organizational behavior.[23]

In considering Barnard's pioneering work we shall consider his definition of organization, his theory of the "birth" and growth of organization, and the informal organization. In addition we shall see how his theory of authority is related to classical terms in rhetorical and communication theory. Barnard's seven principles of organizational communication will be enumerated and explained before looking at his theory of decision making. We shall conclude with a discussion of his famous functions of the executive.

Definition of Organization. Earlier in this chapter we quoted Parsons's definition of organization because we wanted to emphasize the functions organizations perform for society. At the risk of breaking a textbook writer's rule ("Never give different definitions of the same concept!"), Barnard's definition of organization will be quoted in order to emphasize processes internal to the organization: "A system of consciously coordinated activities or forces of two or more persons."[24] A system in this sense is something that should be thought of as a whole because each part is significantly related to every other part.

Birth and Growth of Organizations. Barnard identified the ways in which organizations come into existence, and communication is involved in each way. First, the birth of an organization can be spontaneous, as when a group of people get an idea for producing goods or services and create an organization in order to implement their idea. Second, an organization can come into existence as the result of any person's concerted effort to organize. In college I knew a young man who made pizzas in his family's grocery store; he got a good response from customers and set out to create the organization now known as Pizza Hut. Third, a parent organization sometimes sets free an infant body to let it make it on its own. Fourth, existing organizations are sometimes segmented by fights, rebellions, or the legal authority of the United States Justice Department. Standard Oil was once one organization; several new organizations were created by the "break up" ordered by the Justice Department. The common elements in all four "methods of birth" are *communication* and *collective purpose*.

Once born or created, organizations can grow in only two ways. An organization can grow by combining units already in existence, as when a local bakery buys a competitor. The second method of growth is by creating new units of organization that are added to the existing complex, as when our local bakery creates a new department devoted to making ice cream. Barnard's analysis in support of the claim that these are the only two methods of growth is based on his idea of the *unit organization*. The unit organization is the building block of complex organizations. The unit organization has a size limitation.

To quote Barnard, "the limitations are inherent in the necessities of intercommunication."[25] If the number of people in the unit gets above fifteen, according to Barnard, there are so many potential channels of communication that the supervisor cannot keep track of them; he or she cannot communicate with the individuals, dyads, triads, and groups that will inevitably develop. Exceptions to the rule of fifteen, according to Barnard, are symphony orchestras and large audiences gathered to hear public speakers. (In these two exceptions note that the subordinates, musicians and listeners, are usually subject to a rule prohibiting verbal communication while the unit organization is functioning. This allows the conductor or speaker to coordinate their efforts consciously without concern for intercommunication.)

Informal Organization. Barnard also gave close attention to informal organization and communication. The formal organization is the hierarchy depicted by the organization chart and official channels linking its various levels or groups. The informal organization is "the aggregate of the personal contacts and interactions and the associated groups of people."[26] The number of persons with whom any individual is linked informally is rather small, but because these links produce endless chains external as well as internal to the organization, the whole society is formed by these chains of interaction and their norms, rules, and customs.

Although we generally think that only the opposite is true, informal organization (and communication) gives rise to formal organization. To understand this important point, try to imagine creating a formal organization next week. To whom would you turn? Clearly it would be to people you already know. Imagine the difficulty of creating a formal organization without prior contact and communication among those who are creating the organization. It is impossible to conceive.

Once formal organizations are established (and this is our usual way of thinking), they, in turn, create new informal organizations. As an additional means of effective communication and cohesion, informal organization is necessary to the very operation of formal organizations.

Authority. One of Chester Barnard's more famous definitions is part of his theory of authority: "Authority is the character of a communication (order) in a formal organization by virtue of which it is accepted by a contributor to or 'member' of the organization as governing what he does or is not to do so far as the organization is concerned."[27]

With this communicative definition of authority, the decision as to whether or not an order has authority is made by the receiver, not the source. As with ethos or credibility, authority resides in the consent of message receivers. According to Barnard, there are four conditions that must be satisfied before a receiver will accept the message as authoritative: (1) the receiver must understand the message; (2) the receiver must not believe the order to be inconsistent with organizational purposes; (3) the receiver must believe the order is compatible with his or her personal interests; and (4) the receiver must be mentally and physically able to comply with the order.

Principles for Evaluating an Organization. Logically, the lines of communication in any organization are also the lines of authority. The lines of communication and authority give any organization its shape or structure. We discussed Barnard's distinction between effectiveness and efficiency in chapter 3. In the interests of organizational effectiveness and efficiency, Barnard offers seven principles by which to evaluate an organization.

The first is that the channels of communication should be known by the organization's members. The second is that every member of the organization should be reached by a formal channel; otherwise, there would be a breakdown of authority. The third principle is that the line of communication should be as short as possible; otherwise, messages will be delayed and distorted.

The fourth is that the complete line of communication should usually be used; bypassing levels of authority leads to confusion and weakens authority. The fifth principle is that the communication centers — executives, heads, or supervisors — must be competent; that is, persons with supervisory responsibility must have both technical and communicative competence.

The sixth principle is that the line of communication should not be interrupted when the organization is functioning. Some organizations function seasonally, some for eight hours a day, and still other organizations (such as hospitals, armies, and police stations) never stop functioning. However the period of functioning is punctuated, vacant offices in a line of communication can cause the informal organization to break up and the formal organization to break down.

The seventh principle is that every message should be authenticated. The receiver should know that it is within the organizational authority of a source to issue an order. This principle explains the need for dramatizing a person's entry into an important office. Induction and inauguration ceremonies tell other persons that the new officeholder has the authority to issue orders on behalf of the organization.

Decision Making.   Decision making is also approached by Barnard from the perspective of communication theory. There are three occasions that call for a decision to be made: A superior may ask or order a subordinate to make a decision; a subordinate may refer a case to a superior with a request for decision; and the individual may make decisions on his or her own initiative.

Barnard also distinguishes between positive decisions — to do something — and negative decisions — decisions *not* to decide. The negative decisions are as important as the positive. *"The fine art of executive decision,"* wrote Barnard, *"consists in not deciding questions that are not now pertinent, in not deciding prematurely, in not making decisions that cannot be made effective, and in not making decisions that others should make."*[28]

Leadership.   Barnard's theory of leadership is the final of his contributions that we shall consider. Barnard was one of the first theorists to adopt a functional approach to leadership. The functions of the executive are "first, to provide the system of communication; second, to promote the securing of essential efforts; and, third, to formulate and define purpose."[29]

Let me try to explain each function in great detail. Barnard is saying that executives or organizational leaders must act in such a way as to produce the essential elements of an organization: *communication, efforts,* and *purpose.*

The first function is to make organizational communication possible. To provide a system of communication does not mean merely buying bulletin boards and telephones — although these are important. It means selecting the right people and the right positions and putting them together in a system of communication. It is through this system of communication that executives consciously coordinate the work of organizational members.

The second executive function is to secure essential efforts from other people. This takes place in two stages: recruitment and motivation. People must be recruited into a cooperative relationship with the organization; once recruited, they must be motivated to do the tasks required by the organization.

The third executive function involves the formulating and expressing of organizational purposes. Once formulated, such purposes can be expressed in words and actions. In fact, the actions of executives may at times speak louder about objectives than their words. In short, objectives can be communicated verbally and nonverbally. Notice that, although the necessity of communication is made explicit in the first function, the necessity of communication is implicit in the other functions as well; effective communication is essential for fulfilling all three executive functions.

Rather than summarize Barnard, we shall conclude this chapter with an application of Barnard to two historically important organizations that I have studied: Kent State University and the George C. Marshall Space Flight Center, the largest of the field centers within the National Aeronautics and Space Administration (NASA).

Two Case Studies

Although I made my study of organizational communication at NASA's Marshall Space Flight Center (MSFC) before making a study of Kent State University, I shall reverse the order in discussing them in this chapter. There is only one reason for this reversed order. The one story is a tale of tragedy; the other is a chronicle of success. I would rather not close with an organizational example of failure and tragedy.

Kent State University

Summary of Events.   Colleges and universities in the United States were very different places in the late 1960s than they have been since. The most striking difference is in the methods and modes of communication. Student dress and appearance then were intended to be a counterstatement against the establishment. Long hair, headbands, beards, and shabby clothes adorned with slogan-bearing buttons all proclaimed a "we-ness" in opposition to much of the rest of the world.

Other modes and methods of communication different in the 1960s from those seen in the years since would include posters figuratively shouting out from any surface the protests of the moment; audiences reversing tradition by speaking to, even literally shouting down, the speaker; all-night vigils for war victims, mass rallies and marches. Even the classroom became a medium for expressing discontent; sometimes buildings in which classes were housed became flaming messages of outrage. Obscenities became public clichés.

Kent State University (KSU) was similar to the scene I just described; it was much quieter than many campuses, quieter no doubt than most of its size. KSU enrollment had grown from 12,000 students in 1963 to 21,000 in 1970; the ratio of townspeople to students had changed from nine to one in 1930 to almost one to one in 1970. Although it was relatively quiet, KSU had experienced two notable disturbances during the late 1960s.

In November 1968, members of the Black United Students (BUS) and the Students for a Democratic Society (SDS) staged a sit-in to protest the presence of recruiters from the Oakland, California, Police Department (long a bitter foe of the Black Panthers). The administration threatened disciplinary action; 250 black students walked off campus demanding amnesty; no charges were brought, and the students returned.

Among a number of relatively minor incidents in 1969, one stands out. After a scuffle between members of the campus police force and members of the SDS in April 1969, the administration suspended before hearings the individual students and revoked without hearings the campus charter of the SDS. By these acts the administration succeeded in alienating a large proportion of the faculty and students, who were overwhelmingly unsympathetic to the SDS, for acting in violation of the Student Conduct Code and for failing to listen to responsible members of the university community.

In contrast to other campuses, the academic year 1969–1970 was so quiet that administrators thought they would reach the summer vacation without a major confrontation between protestors and officials. Then the crisis quickly developed. The main cause for protest, of course, was the Vietnam War, which was highly unpopular with students and many other Americans. In late April government officials revealed that the United States had expanded the war by an incursion into Cambodia.

President Nixon addressed the American public on television on the evening of Thursday, April 30, 1970, in an attempt to justify the apparent reversal of his policy to wind down the war. The speech failed to justify the invasion and failed to persuade those critical of the war.

Events happened rapidly in response to the ineffective presidential rhetoric. On Friday, May 1, an estimated five hundred persons attended a rally at the center of the KSU campus. True to predictive rumors circulated at this noon rally, there was some "street action" in downtown Kent, Ohio, that night. Store windows were smashed, a bonfire was set, and police cars were pelted. The mayor of Kent declared a state of emergency and ordered that bars primarily patronized by students be closed shortly after midnight. Students and other customers were turned out onto the streets and were herded to the edge of campus, where they dispersed during the early morning hours.

At 5:28 P.M. on Saturday, May 2, the mayor of Kent secured the commitment of the Ohio National Guard to come to the aid of the city and campus. The National Guard troops arrived in Kent at 9:30 P.M. and were in time to see a sky made bright by the blaze of a burning ROTC building on campus. University officials had not been consulted in the decision to call in the guard and were surprised by their deployment on campus.

On Sunday, May 3, many KSU students returning from a weekend away were shocked to find the campus circled by armed guardsmen and their military vehicles. The University president, who had been away for the weekend, also returned on Sunday. A crowd gathered on the edge of campus that night and was told the president and the mayor would meet with them. When the crowd was later informed that these two men would not meet with them, they felt double-crossed. They cursed and threw rocks at guardsmen and police; tear gas was fired at the crowd. Injuries were sustained on both sides.

On Monday, May 4, I crossed the line of guardsmen at the edge of the campus on the way to my office. A glass door to the building was shattered. Posted on another door was an injunction prohibiting destruction to the campus. There was a hand-scrawled poster on a first floor bulletin board calling for a rally on the campus at noon.

I asked a secretary to call the provost's office to determine whether or not classes had been cancelled. The answer was no. Classes were meeting as usual. It did not occur to me to ask whether my right of assembly had been waived. Finding my office too cool to work in, and deciding against attending the rally because of the need to grade student papers for a late class, I returned home.

Nearly everyone knows what happened at Kent State University that noon. The rally took place. The guardsmen tried to break it up. Confusion followed: four students killed, nine wounded. As the news flashed around the world, campuses closed in protest. Some thought President Nixon would face a second front, or a second war at home in addition to the war in Vietnam.

A Communication Analysis. I still feel a sense of outrage about the National Guard for their actions on May 4, 1970. As all the evidence has since indicated, the shooting was unjustified. It was my purpose, then and now, however, to examine the role of the university during this crisis. How well did KSU operate as a communication system during the crisis?

It hardly functioned at all. Soon after the tragedy the president of KSU appointed me to serve as chairman of a task force on communication and as a member of a university commission. With help from colleagues I began a research project in which we interviewed the president, four vice presidents, nine deans, and twenty-nine chairpersons. In addition, we interviewed 120 faculty members and 225 students. The results were published.[30]

We asked our interviewees what they knew during the crisis. Although 58 percent of the faculty (75 percent of the students) knew a rally was scheduled for noon on Monday, May 4, a smaller percentage, 44 percent (56 percent of the students), knew the rally had been prohibited. Only 37 percent of the faculty (34 percent of the students) were aware that the guardsmen had live ammunition in their weapons. Finally, 53 percent of the faculty and chairpersons said they would have behaved differently had they known the facts. They would have used their influence to "cool" the situation and to dissuade students from confronting the guardsmen. As interviewees told us, ignorance deprived many of the right of choice.

Why did these organizational members know so little during the crisis? The president, operating on faulty upward communication, had left town on Friday without delegating authority to an acting president. Indeed, the academic vice president and provost, who should have been in charge during the president's absence, did not know the president had left town. As far as we could determine, only two attempts were made to communicate to the organization. The first was a statement on the campus radio station; the second was the release of twelve thousand leaflets, mainly placed in student mailboxes, saying that the governor had taken control of the campus and had prohibited demonstrations and rallies. These two forms of communication were almost totally ineffective. The informal organization responsible for the Monday rally was more effective in communication than the formal organization, that is, the university.

The lines of authority or communication running from president to vice president to deans to chairpersons to faculty were not used during the crisis period.

In summary, Kent State University suffered a total breakdown in communication during those days in May. The president was invisible, authority was not delegated, and the lines of communication were not used. Why?

During our interviews we asked interviewees to tell us about the routine functioning of KSU. Somewhat to our surprise, we learned that the routine functioning was also characterized by ineffectiveness. As we concluded in the book:

> The disintegration of Kent State University during the crises of May, 1970, can be traced to certain organization-communication *imperatives* which were present in the routine functioning of the university: a highly centralized and indecisive administration which operated "blind" because of inadequate upward-directed communication; a President with little appreciation for his communication responsibilities; the absence of a two-way system of communication designed to integrate all seg-

ments of the rapidly expanded university; academic officers who were shut out of administrative decision making.[31]

Our final conclusion was that the president "had failed in his first function as an executive: *to develop and maintain a system of communication*. His inability to delegate authority to his Vice Presidents let the latter refer to themselves as 'assistants to the President.' The academic officers, the deans, were almost unanimous in the judgment that they had been blocked from providing 'academic input' into the central administrative decision making process."[32]

In brief, Barnard's first function of the executive had not been performed. The lines of authority or communication did not function well on a day-to-day basis. The disintegration of the organization during the crisis period did not represent a qualitative change in effectiveness; it was a change in the importance of the ineffectiveness. I have not repeated all of the details included in our book, but it is conceivable that this tale might have had a happier ending with more effective organizational communication and with a competent performance of Barnard's executive functions.

Marshall Space Flight Center

Let's establish at the beginning of this case study that it is about a successful organization, one that helped bring about several of the great technological achievements of this century. One of those achievements was development of the Saturn V, the "moon rocket" by which American astronauts reached the moon.

The research and development of the Saturn V was managed by the George C. Marshall Space Flight Center (MSFC) at Huntsville, Alabama, the largest of the National Aeronautics and Space Administration (NASA) field centers. I served as consultant in communication to MSFC and its director, Dr. Wernher von Braun, in 1967 and 1968.[33]

The fact that I was asked to serve as a consultant and allowed full freedom to gather data for a diagnostic study of the organization—find problems and suggest solutions to them—is an indication that the managers of the organization were concerned about communication and open to criticism.

My method of gathering information was by observation and in-depth interviews with the top fifty managers in MSFC. Only the remarks of the top manager, von Braun, were on the record. All other interviews were confidential. This allowed me to get frank answers without jeopardizing the standing of the interviewees.

Although I did find communication problems and proposed solutions to them, the bigger challenge was to explain the successes this organization had enjoyed. My thesis here is that the director and his fellow managers were extremely conscious of Barnard's first function: to provide the system of communication. In fact, von Braun regarded management to be synonymous with organizational communication.

In particular, von Braun emphasized upward communication. He explained this in an interview with me by means of analogy:

> This is like being in the earthquake prediction business. You put out your sensors. You want them to be sensitive enough, but you don't want to get drowned in noise. We have enough sensors, even in industry. There are a lot of inputs about trouble. Some are too sensitive; they overreact. Someone else might underestimate. You want to know the name of the guy. Is he one of the perennial panic makers? Some guys always cry for help. You need balance in the system — to react to the critical things. Exposure teaches you how to react. Some create problems and then proudly announce they have solved them. Others make a lot of noise just to get the mule's attention.[34]

That quotation emphasizes upward communication. In addition, this successful manager was also emphasizing the critical importance of the source's ethos or credibility.

This twin emphasis on upward communication and sensitivity to the credibility of the source (or sensor) is illustrated by another story told me by a deputy director of one of MSFC's research and development labs. Even if the story isn't factual, it captures von Braun's philosophy of management communication. The reader must realize that, like von Braun himself, many of his subordinates were Germans brought to this country after World War II. According to the interviewee who told me the story, von Braun was asked during a meeting in Washington, "What is your reliability figure for this particular stage of the rocket?"

> "I don't know," von Braun is said to have replied, "but I'll find out when I return to Huntsville and let you know by telephone."

> After his return to Huntsville, von Braun made the call. The NASA official at the other end of the line heard von Braun's reply as "five nines" (or a reliability figure of 0.99999).

> "Fine," said the official. "How did you arrive at that figure?" "Well," answered von Braun, "I called Walter Haeussermann in the Astrionics Lab and asked him, 'Are we going to have any problems with this stage?' He answered, 'Nein.' Then I called Karl Heimburg in the Test Lab and he said, 'Nein.' I kept at it until I got five neins."[35]

Monday Notes. One of von Braun's most innovative communication techniques was called the "Monday Notes." Because of the increased size of MSFC during the research and development of the Saturn V, he created two major divisions within the organization. Research and Development Operations (RDO) was composed of the engineering offices and laboratories. Industrial Operations (IO) was a collection of offices that managed specific programs and projects such as rockets, rocket stages, and rocket engines. IO also served as liaisons between MSFC and aerospace contractors. Dr. von Braun thought this added size and complexity called for an innovation — the "Monday Notes." The idea came to him when one of his subordinates was assigned to Cape Canaveral. He asked this man to send a weekly one-page note to Huntsville describing the previous week's progress and problems. Here I quote at length from my own earlier description of this system.

> Finding that he looked forward to reading the weekly note, von Braun decided that a similar note from other key managers would help keep him informed. Therefore, he asked almost two-dozen of his managers (lab directors and program managers, all of whom were subsequently interviewed) to send him a weekly, one-page note summarizing the week's progress and problems. Simplicity was the key. There was no form to be filled out. The requirement was: no more than one page headed by the date and name of the contributor. A layer of management was *bypassed* (in the sense that the Directors of RDO and IO did not edit them). They were due in the Director's office each Monday, hence "Monday Notes."
>
> As the Director read each note he initialed his "B" and gave the date of his reading in the top right hand corner. (The first time I saw a set of the notes, the teacher in me automatically flipped through them looking for an "A" paper.) He also added a considerable amount of marginalia in his own handwriting; asking questions, making suggestions and awarding praise. The notes for 10 July 1967, for example, include a question directed to a manager about vehicle cost figures in a note. "Have we passed this on to (a NASA Headquarters official)? B" To another manager there is the marginal suggestion that a new computer mentioned in his note "could be immensely useful for earth resources surveys from orbit. . . ." To a lab director whose earlier recommendations about the superiority of one kind of weld over another had been rejected, and who had reported additional evidence which supported his original position, von Braun wrote, "Looks like you won after all! Congrats. B"
>
> These collected and annotated notes, arranged in alphabetical order by the authors' surnames, were reproduced and returned as a package to all of the contributors. What was the organizational effect of this simple and innovative communication technique? That was a question I put to each of the contributors. The answer was: an almost totally unqualified praise for the Monday Notes. The reasons offered to me in support of this judgment are worth examining. The first advantage was obvious — the boss was kept informed.
>
> There were many other reasons why the Monday Notes were judged to be a successful technique. For example, the managers pointed out during the interviews that the notes performed a crucial horizontal or

lateral function. That was because each lab director knew each week what all other laboratories had been up to (and up against); in addition, units in IO knew about the activities of RDO and vice versa. This also stimulated further horizontal interaction between the two major divisions. This can be illustrated by a remarkable coincidence which occurred during the interviewing period. A lab director mentioned to me that the recently arrived notes of that week had revealed to him a need to telephone a program manager in IO about a mutual problem. By chance, my next interview happened to be with that manager. While talking about the Monday Notes he volunteered that he had discovered in the notes of that week a suggestion and the need to telephone the lab director I had just left.

The marginalia supplied by the Director made the notes "the most diligently read document" at MSFC. This crucial *feedback* function was mentioned by nearly every contributor. One saw not only how the boss reacted to the week's work of his own group, but how the boss responded to the notes of the other contributors.

Another desirable effect mentioned by most of the contributors was closely related to this feedback function. Because von Braun found it increasingly necessary to travel to Washington, California, the Cape and other locations, the Monday Notes "kept the channels open" during a period of decreased face-to-face communication.

The notes also served as an antidote to the sterile, formalized procedures which dominated most of their activities. The contributors derived considerable satisfaction from the personalized nature of the notes that rather than using a code-numbered, official MSFC-NASA form designating lab or office, each note was headed simply by the individual's name. They also derived satisfaction from the informality, quickness and frankness of the notes. In regard to the latter, some rather fierce arguments among the contributors were carried out in the notes. One unit's note of the previous week might be challenged by this week's note from another unit. This controversy, said one lab director, gave the notes their particular "charm." Indeed, one lab director told me with a smile, "We sometimes misuse them — to get attention." In short, the notes provided a kind of court of last resort in which one could file a public brief asking the highest judge to reverse a previous decision.

During my interviews I discovered that the notes had had a more profound communication impact on the organization than had been imagined by the participants. Curious as to how the contributors generated the content of the weekly note, I systematically probed for these procedures. In almost every case the lab director would ask his subordinates, called division chiefs, to provide him with a Friday Note of their week's activities. (During the summer of 1968 I had the opportunity to interview fourteen division chiefs; most of them reported that they requested a similar note from their subordinates, called branch chiefs, and so on). In some cases the directors organized meetings to determine the contents of the next week's notes and to discuss von Braun's responses to the previous packet of notes. Relevant portions of the annotated notes were reproduced for distribution down the line. In short, von Braun's request for a weekly note produced an almost *iron-like discipline of communication* within the organization. Once a week, almost all of the supervisors of the entire organization paused to reflect upon what needed to be communicated up the line, to read what others had communicated to the Director and how he had responded. "Excellent"; "Best thing we do"; "Remarkable innovation," were some of the evaluations made to me by the interviewees. One former military officer said that such a practice — with its conscious bypassing — could not have been tolerated in the military. It is difficult for one to imagine such a practice in, say, the Post Office or other civil service organizations. One comment prompted by a discussion of the Monday Notes demonstrates von Braun's atypical emphasis on upward-directed communication as opposed to downward-directed communication. Said one manager in IO, "If we only had something coming down the line as powerful as the Monday Notes."

There is still another communication principle which von Braun exploited in general which is specifically embodied in the Monday Notes: the principle of redundancy. The principle of redundancy was built into the system not in the normal sense of syntactic or semantic redundancy — as a property of messages — but rather in the sense of redundant *channels* of communication. That is, to insure that nothing "fell through the cracks," more channels than were ideally necessary had been designed into the system.[36]

Automatic Responsibility.   There is another concept in von Braun's philosophy of organizational communication that was highly innovative. It was called "automatic responsibility." In practice it meant that an engineer working in one of the labs assumed automatic responsibility for any problem the engineer perceived. This applied whenever the engineer had the technical competence to solve the problem — whether or not the engineer's unit organization had been given a task assignment related to the problem. An engineer who assumed responsibility for such a problem was expected to stay with the problem until the solution was reached.

If the engineer who perceived a problem lacked the technical ability to see it through to its solution, he or she assumed responsibility for communicating word about the problem up the line. Top management, so alerted, could then direct other specialists to give attention to the problem.

I hope that my reader has already seen that automatic responsibility is directly related to McGregor's Theory Y. That theory rested on several assumptions, one of which was that "the average human being learns, under proper conditions, not only to accept but to seek responsibility."[37] My point is not that automatic responsibility proves this assumption of Theory Y. The employees at MSFC were probably not "average" in intelligence and education. Perhaps average and below average workers could not accept automatic responsibility, but keep in mind that McGregor qualified the assumption with the words "under proper conditions," and such conditions were realized with the case of MSFC employees.

To summarize this case study, MSFC was a successful organization. Part of this success can be explained by its attention to Barnard's functions of the executive. This is illustrated by the emphasis on upward communication, credibility, the Monday Notes, and automatic responsibility. Dr. von Braun considered communication and management and organization to be synonymous terms.

Summary

The theme of this chapter is that organizations are constituted by communication. The chapter has examined two ways of classifying organizations: Talcott Parsons's classification by the organization's function and Amitai Etzioni's classification by the way in which the organization communicates with its employees. Parsons sees four functions: economic production, political goals, integration, and pattern-maintenance. Etzioni's compliance theory distinguishes an organization's communicative strategy according to its power: coercive, remunerative, or normative.

We have also discussed Rensis Likert's theory and diagram of how groups interact with organizations. Looking at organizations and their environments, we have discussed the concept of boundary role person, or BRP, the agent or actor formally responsible for representing an organization in its communication with the environment and vice versa. This led to a model of internal and external communication.

To get a broad perspective on theories of management communication, we have explored three theories. Douglas McGregor's Theories X and Y divide management theory into two very different strategies of communication. W. Charles Redding formulates an Ideal Managerial Climate that operates with five components: supportiveness; participative decision making; trust, confidence, and credibility; openness and candor; and an emphasis on high performance goals. Chester I. Barnard focuses on the functions of the executive that facilitate communication.

The chapter ended with two case studies of organizational communication: Kent State University and the Marshall Space Flight Center.

Next, in chapter 8, we shall look at social movements, groups that differ markedly from organizations.

Questions for Essays, Speeches, and Group Discussions

1. Classify the following organizations by means of both the Parsons and Etzioni systems: (a) your college or university; (b) National Republican party; (c) General Motors; (d) Chase Manhattan Bank.

2. Pick a local business organization and try to identify the linking pins and the BRP's. Draw up some predictions about their communication actions, and test them by observation and/or interviews.

3. Defend or attack these statements: (a) College students would have low morale if they worked in Theory X organizations; (b) Automatic responsibility will work only in a few exceptional organizations; (c) MSFC achieved the Ideal Managerial Climate.

Additional Readings

Farace, R. V., P. R. Monge, and H. M. Russell, *Communicating and Organizing*. Reading, Mass.: Addison-Wesley Publishing Co., 1977.

Jablin, F. M. "Superior-Subordinate Communication: The State of the Art." *Psychological Bulletin* 86(1979): 1201–22.

Johnson, B. *Communication: The Process of Organizing*. Boston: Allyn and Bacon, 1977.

Redding, W. C. *Communication within the Organization*. New York: Industrial Communication Council, 1972.

Tompkins, P. K. "Organizational Communication." In *Handbook of Rhetorical and Communication Theory*, edited by C. Arnold and J. W. Bowers. Boston: Allyn and Bacon, in press.

Notes

1. Talcott Parsons, *Structure and Process in Modern Societies* (Glencoe, Ill.: Free Press, 1963), p. 56.

2. Ibid., pp. 45–58.

3. Amitai Etzioni, *A Comparative Analysis of Complex Organizations*, rev. ed. (New York: Free Press, 1975).

4. Ibid., p. 3.

5. Ibid., p. 14.

6. Rensis Likert, *New Patterns of Management* (New York: McGraw-Hill Book Co., 1961), p. 105. Reprinted by permission.

7. Ibid., pp. 104–105.

8. Ibid., p. 115. Italics in original.

9. William H. Starbuck, "Organizations and Their Environments," in *Handbook of Industrial and Organizational Psychology*, ed. Marvin D. Dunnette (Chicago: Rand McNally College Publishing Company, 1976), p. 1069.

10. J. Stacy Adams, "The Structure and Dynamics of Behavior in Organizational Boundary Roles," in *Handbook of Industrial and Organizational Psychology*, ed. Marvin D. Dunnette (Chicago: Rand McNally College Publishing Company, 1976), p. 1180. Reprinted by permission of Marvin D. Dunnette.

11. Douglas McGregor, *The Human Side of Enterprise*. Copyright © 1960 by McGraw-Hill Book Company. Used with the permission of McGraw-Hill Book Company. Italics in original.

12. Ibid., p. 43. Reprinted by permission.

13. Ibid., pp. 45–57, quotation from pp. 47–48. Reprinted by permission. Italics in original.

14. F. J. Roethlisberger and W. J. Dickson, *Management and the Worker* (Cambridge, Mass.: Harvard University Press, 1949), pp. 379–84, 511–24.

15. Phillip K. Tompkins, "Management Qua Communication in Rocket Research and Development," *Communication Monographs* 44(1977): 1–26.

16. W. Charles Redding, *Communicaton within the Organization* (New York: Industrial Communication Council, 1972), pp. 139–422.

17. Likert, p. 100.

18. Jack R. Gibb, "Defensive Communication," *Journal of Communication* 11(1961): 143. Reprinted in Redding, p. 140. Reprinted by permission.

19. William H. Read, "Upward Communication in Industrial Hierarchies," *Human Relations* 15(1962): 3–15.

20. Redding, pp. 405–406.

21. Ibid., p. 411. Italics in original.

22. Gerald V. Barrett and Patrick A. Cabe, "Zero Defects Programs: Their Effects at Different Job Levels," *Personnel* 44(1967): 46. Also quoted in Redding, p. 421. Italics in original.

23. Chester I. Barnard, *The Functions of the Executive* (Cambridge, Mass.: Harvard University Press, 1938), p. xxxi.

24. Ibid., p. 81.

25. Ibid., pp. 105–106.

26. Ibid., p. 115.

27. Ibid., p. 163.

28. Ibid., p. 194. Italics in original.

29. Ibid., p. 217.

30. Phillip K. Tompkins and Elaine VandenBout Anderson, *Communication Crisis at Kent State* (New York: Gordon and Breach, Science Publishers, 1971).

31. Ibid., p. 119.

32. Ibid., p. 120.

33. A full report of these activities can be found in two articles: Phillip K. Tompkins, "Management Qua Communication in Rocket Research and Development," *Communication Monographs* 44(1977): 1–26; Phillip K. Tompkins, "Organizational Metamorphosis in Space Research and Development," *Communication Monographs* 45(1978): 110–18.

34. As quoted in Tompkins, "Management Qua Communication," p. 7. Reprinted by permission.

35. Ibid., p. 8. Reprinted by permission.

36. Ibid., pp. 8–10. Reprinted by permission.

37. McGregor, p. 48.

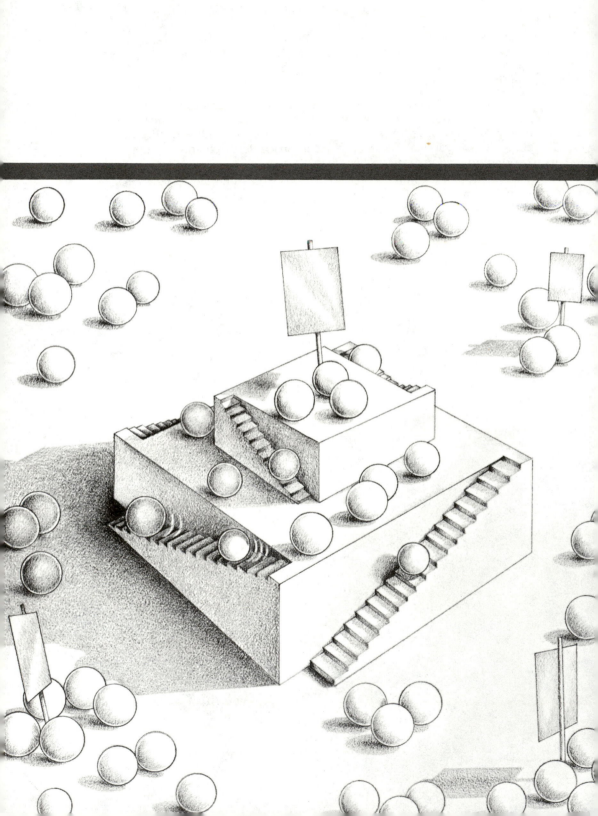

8

Communication and Social Movements

O conspiracy
Shamest thou to show thy dangerous
     brow by night,
When evils are most free? O, then by day
Where wilt thou find a cavern dark
     enough
To mask thy monstrous visage? Seek
     none, conspiracy;
Hide it in smiles and affability.

Julius Caesar
act 2, scene 1, lines 77 – 82
Shakespeare

For many years students of rhetoric created theories that would explain how one speaker persuaded audiences to adopt new ideas and practices. They also produced a good many scholarly studies of single speeches. These students began to grow uneasy, however, when they realized that single persuasive speeches rarely have lasting influences on society. More often whole campaigns are needed in order to move society. Elections, for example, are not decided by single speeches. Campaigns are needed to gain nominations and, eventually, to gain office. Even new toothpastes are introduced by massive advertising campaigns. Thus, in the 1950s and 1960s many students of rhetoric and communication turned their attention to campaigns and movements.

If a new toothpaste cannot be sold in a single speech, think how ridiculous it would be to assume that reformist and revolutionary ideas can be "sold" that way. This chapter will consider the movements that attempt to "sell" reforms and revolutions to a modern society. Here the analysis is more on how to understand than how to act. Our analysis will again reflect the thinking of Kenneth Burke, Talcott Parsons, and other thinkers in an attempt to explain how social movements change society. It will also be necessary to explain why so many movements fail and why so few succeed.

We shall first compare movements with organizations to see what they do and do not have in common, and we shall distinguish between reform movements and revolutionary movements. One theory of movements considers them in terms of the periods they pass through; we shall look at these periods to see the various adaptations of a movement. How does a movement interact with the status quo? We shall examine a number of strategies for resistance to movements. Finally, we shall discuss how the stage is set for revolution and what conditions are necessary.

Differences and Similarities Between Organizations and Movements

Characteristics of Movements

In the previous chapter the concepts of communication and organization were brought together. In this chapter communication and movement are brought together. To understand how an organization is similar to and different from a movement, we must first ask, What must the leader of a social movement do to become successful? There are three crucial functions or responsibilities such a leader must fulfill.

1. The first is to *formulate the purpose and objectives* of the movement. Followers and potential followers need to know what reforms would be made and what vision of the future the leader holds.

2. The second is to *secure essential services* from the members or followers of a movement. Such services might include passing out leaflets or participating in rallies and demonstrations. In order to secure such services the leader must persuade people to join the movement; once they do join, the leader must persuade them to perform the necessary tasks.

3. The third function of the leader is to *establish a system of communication*. The leader must develop a system through which to give orders to the followers, and through which to hear about their successes and failures. Having the right people in the right places, able to talk to and listen to each other is vital to any social movement.

The reader, who has read the previous chapter on organizational communication, will not be surprised to learn that these activities are well known as the *functions of the executive*, the activities required of the managers of business, industry, and government.[1]

There is a second similarity between organizations and movements. They are both subject to what Kenneth Boulding calls the principle of *"increasingly unfavorable environment"* and the principle of *"increasingly unfavorable internal structure."*[2] The single movement or organization is subject to these principles in the following ways. If you and I were to begin a new movement tomorrow to promote a new religion, we would probably expand our movement easily up to a point. We would quickly bring into the movement those people who had been waiting for such a sect or who were most likely to be attracted to us. After a point, however, we would have reached all of these people. We would experience resistance from those who are organized around other beliefs and religions. The principle of increasingly unfavorable environment would begin to operate, making it difficult to expand our movement.

New business organizations are subject to the same principle. Suppose we organize to sell mass-produced peanut butter and bacon sandwiches. Once we had promoted our new product, we would no doubt experience a growth of sales as we attracted all those waiting for something different to eat. At some point, however, the principle of increasingly unfavorable environment would halt our sales growth. Having reached what the economists call an imperfect market, we would have to reduce our costs or prices — or both — in order to stimulate growth.

The principle of increasingly unfavorable internal structure would also apply at some point to our hypothetical movement and business. As these units grew in size, we would reach a point where internal communication would begin to cause problems. Our leaders and executives would become more and more distant from the followers and workers. As we saw in the case of Kent State University, this distance can cause failures. The "Monday Notes" at MSFC/NASA were instituted in response to increased size, indicating that to succeed an organization must invest more time, energy, and other resources to internal communication as it increases in size.

Thus, organizations and movements are similar in at least two aspects: (1) the leaders must perform the same or similar functions; and (2) the environment and the structure of both movements and organizations are subject to a powerful check on growth. There are, however, important differences between organizations and movements.

The business executive, for example, can offer high salaries and expense accounts to recruit new members and can pay bonuses to those members who perform well. The executive can also take these away by firing people. The movement leader rarely if ever has such material rewards and threats to use. In addition, the movement leader is often faced with hostility from the press, police, and politicians. In short, a movement leader must often do more than a business leader with less in the way of material resources.

Herbert W. Simons, a communication theorist, put it this way:

> Shorn of the controls that characterize formal organizations, yet required to perform the same internal functions, harassed from without, yet obligated to adapt to the external system, the leader of a social movement must constantly balance inherently conflicting demands on his position and on the movement be represents.[3]

Movements have largely voluntary followings and enjoy fewer resources than do organizations. They seek reforms and revolutions and should be distinguished from "panics, crazes, booms, fads, and hostile outbursts, as well as from the actions of recognized labor unions, government agencies, business organizations, and other institutionalized decision-making bodies."[4]

Reform and Revolutionary Movements

Reforms are, of course, different from revolutions. Reform movements seek partial solutions; revolutionary movements seek total solutions. A reform movement can achieve its objective without either toppling or replacing the power structure. Violence is more likely to be employed or provoked by a revolutionary movement. This often calls for greater secrecy on the part of revolutionary movements than of reform movements.

Martin Luther King, Jr., for example, led the civil rights movement in the direction of reforms, while more militant Black Power leaders seemed to desire a revolution. The civil rights movement began when King organized a

Figure 8-1   Martin Luther King, Jr. will be remembered in this country as one of the great leaders of nonviolent protest in support of social reforms. The words reproduced here in Shahn's portrait are part of a prophetic speech King delivered to his followers the night before his assassination in 1968, and they demonstrate King's own special power as a rhetor. (Ben Shahn: *Martin Luther King, Jr. ". . . I Don't Know What. . ."*, 1968. ©Estate of Ben Shahn Collection New Jersey State Museum.)

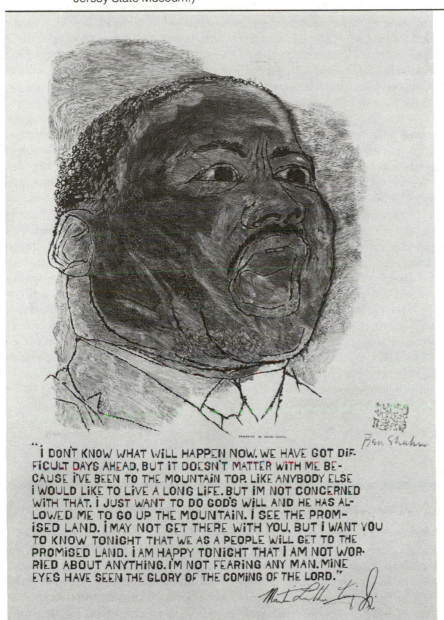

"I DON'T KNOW WHAT WILL HAPPEN NOW. WE HAVE GOT DIF-FICULT DAYS AHEAD, BUT IT DOESN'T MATTER WITH ME BE-CAUSE I'VE BEEN TO THE MOUNTAIN TOP. LIKE ANYBODY ELSE I WOULD LIKE TO LIVE A LONG LIFE. BUT IM NOT CONCERNED WITH THAT. I JUST WANT TO DO GOD'S WILL AND HE HAS AL-LOWED ME TO GO UP THE MOUNTAIN. I SEE THE PROM-ISED LAND. I MAY NOT GET THERE WITH YOU, BUT I WANT YOU TO KNOW TONIGHT THAT WE AS A PEOPLE WILL GET TO THE PROMISED LAND. I AM HAPPY TONIGHT THAT I AM NOT WOR-RIED ABOUT ANYTHING. I'M NOT FEARING ANY MAN. MINE EYES HAVE SEEN THE GLORY OF THE COMING OF THE LORD."

successful boycott of segregated buses in Montgomery, Alabama, in 1956. This experience pushed him into prominence as a leader of the movement (see Figure 8–1).

In 1963, 200,000 black and white citizens assembled in Washington, D.C., for a rally at the Lincoln Memorial. The purpose of the rally was to symbolize the civil rights struggle in general and to demand specific reforms such as the Civil Rights Act and the Voting Rights Act. King's brief speech, "I Have a Dream," was the climax of the rally. In this eloquent address King aligned his movement with the highest values of the American society such as justice, equality, and freedom, as well as their sources in the Constitution, the Declaration of Independence, and organized religion.

The Civil Rights Act was passed in the following year, 1964, and the Voting Rights Act was passed in 1965. These specific reforms were achieved in large part by the civil rights movement. Although he rejected the violent tactics and revolutionary aims of Black Power, King began to seek broader reforms. In 1967 he spoke out against the Vietnam War; he was organizing a "poor people's march" on Washington when he was assassinated in 1968.

The successes achieved by the civil rights movement inspired other movements: the student movement, the women's liberation movement, the gay liberation movement, and others. These movements have produced changes, some temporary and some more permanent. For example, although the nation's consciousness may have been raised about discrimination against women, the Equal Rights Amendment has not been ratified as of this writing.

Let's look at the life (and death) of political movements to understand why some fail, why some succeed, and of equal importance, why movements are inevitable. Our examination will be theoretical; the theory has been derived by Leland M. Griffin from the writings of Kenneth Burke.[5] The reader will be better prepared for this section by reviewing Burke's definition of [hu]man in chapter 1. The words that follow assume an understanding of the definition and its key terms.

A Dramatistic Theory of Movements

This (Griffin-Burke) theory of movements looks at the phenomena diachronically, or over periods of time, in three main periods. The first period is the inception (beginning) period, which is broken down into three main phases. Each of the first two phases calls for two rhetorical strategies. The final phase is a response to three grave dangers with which a movement will have to deal. The second period is the crisis period, a moment of transformation. The third period is called consummation, and it calls for two rhetorical strategies on behalf of the movement.

Inception Period

A movement has to have an inception, or beginning, and the *inception period* is one of widespread alienation or unhappiness with the existing order of society. Movements begin when an individual says no. As others join to express the negative, the movement becomes an organization of opposition. Thus, in the 1960s and 1970s antiwar protestors expressed their opposition to the draft by chanting, "Hell no, we won't go."

The initial act of the movement is its expression of a stand, an ideology. According to Griffin, "It may be called a constitution, manifesto, covenant, program, proclamation, declaration, tract for the times, statement, or counterstatement."[6] The American Declaration of Independence and the Communist Manifesto come to mind as initial acts of revolutionary movements. These documents even today reveal the equations of pro and con, "we" versus "they," are the "angels" against the "devils." The American colonists stood against the tyrannical George III and his ministers; the alienated workers in chains were claimed to stand against the evil capitalists.

The rhetoric of the movement during the *first phase* of the inception period pursues two strategies. The first strategy is to reach as large an audience as possible with the message that problems exist and that the existing order is unjust. More and more hearers must be shown that the leaders of the establishment are corrupt and should be rejected. The second rhetorical strategy is to provoke conflict between the movement and the "power structure." The power structure must be goaded into striking back or into engaging in the rhetoric of a countermovement. The countermovement provides not only a struggle but also a bad side, a foil, "a rhetorical Vile Beast to be slain" by the movement.[7]

In the *second phase* of the inception two more rhetorical strategies are employed. The first strategy is to convert the masses to the movement. This strategy is self-explanatory. The second strategy is to move the converted to action, to move them to cry no to the countermovement. This action is thought to endow the members with a new identity.

During its inception period the movement faces three grave dangers, any one of which may destroy it. The first danger is the possibility that the countermovement will triumph by being more effective with the masses. The second danger is that the leaders of the movement will fail to adapt or change their appeals to changing conditions. Unforeseen events will inevitably take place, and leaders will have to adjust their tactics accordingly. The third danger is that as the movement grows new members will bring slightly different motives to it. These different motives will create a tendency for the movement to "splinter" into quarreling subgroups. This failure to achieve solidarity will result in many incompatible visions instead of the one.

The *third, and final, phase* of the inception period is the movement's attempt to circumvent these three grave dangers. Using their rhetoric, the leaders of the movement must win the competition with the countermovement for the minds of the masses. At the same time the leaders must be sensitive to the changes in circumstances and adapt their appeals to these changes. The rhetoric directed to new members must be intensified in the effort to transcend the tendency to splinter.

Crisis Period

If successful in averting these dangers, the movement arrives at a moment or period of crisis. The *crisis period* is a time of transformation from the old order to the new order. The new order is a new social ladder, and as Griffin put it, "the birth of the new order is but the birth of a new hierarchy, a new system of authority."[8] People under its authority will now have a new identity.

Consummation Period

The crisis period is followed by a *consummation period*. Outlooks are now reversed. The movement began when conditions were bad enough to alienate many people. In the consummation period conditions are good. Leaders of the movement, now leaders of the new hierarchy, must say yes rather than no. The movement was anti, but the new order is pro. The rhetorical efforts of the new powers now seek assent and allegiance by following these two strategies: "Its first strategy is to arouse, and to gratify, the natural appetite for obedience. Its second is to strive, to the utmost, to actualize the 'perfecting myth' of the movement: to achieve the incarnation, or embodiment, in the actualities of the material world. . . ."[9]

In the consummation period the movement comes to an end. However, because it is impossible to achieve the perfect vision that motivated the movement, and because communication up and down the social ladder is imperfect, there will always be new sources of alienation. A new movement may spring up to say no. The process repeats itself.

The reader must have sensed in reading this dramatistic theory of social movements that it too suffers from our human striving for perfection. As a general theory it is too "perfect" to fit all political and social movements. For example, although one movement may fail in the inception phase and another in the crisis period, they may both endure and have some success. In some cases the leaders may use violence early in the movement's life, in some cases violence may come later, and in some cases — as was true of Gandhi and Martin Luther King, Jr. — violence is never part of the movement. Nonetheless, the theory does emphasize the rhetorical problems that movements and countermovements must solve in the complete life cycle. It is, therefore, a kind of common denominator for examining movements and countermovements for their differences as well as their similarities.

Movements Versus the Status Quo

Presumption and Burden of Proof

Let's consider what the necessary and sufficient conditions are for a revolution in any society. In chapter 4 we introduced the rhetorical concepts of presumption and burden of proof and showed how they can be applied to interpersonal communication. In this context we shall consider how the concepts apply to a group (or movement) and its mass audience(s). The presumption is with the status quo, and the status quo occupies the ground. A reformist or revolutionary movement must assume the burden of proof. As you recall, we defined it earlier in this way: The movement "must (a) show that the existing idea or practice is faulty, and should not occupy the ground; and (b) recommend that a new idea or practice should be accepted in its place" (see chapter 4).

When we defined the burden of proof in this way, our concern was with interpersonal communication between two parties, alter and ego. There is an important difference, however, between alter persuading ego to change majors, and, for example, the American Socialist party persuading the American voters to accept a socialist government. The difference is that the establishment and the forces of control, who are in general the defenders of the status quo, take a deep interest in criticism of themselves as well as in proposed changes that would alter their privileged position.

In short, as a revolutionary movement attempts to make its case to the mass audience, the hierarchy will put up resistance at every opportunity. It can minimize the degree to which problems are claimed to be "faulty," it can discredit the movement's proposed solutions, it can discredit the movement's leaders, and it can even use force to suppress the movement. Thus, a revolutionary movement faces resistance not only from its audience (as in the interpersonal communication example) but also from the hierarchy it would replace or modify.

Strategies for Resistance

There are several types of resistance used by the hierarchy against a revolutionary movement. In the proper circumstances we can expect the establishment to use force, coercion, imprisonment, and even executions in destroying revolutionary movements. In the realm of rhetorical resistance Andrew A. King has identified four strategies (or the "Ideo-Topoi of Power Maintenance," as he calls them) that can be expected from past experience.

Ridicule: Humor as Counterrevolution.

The opponents can be treated as clowns and ludicrous figures unworthy of serious consideration.[10] Ridicule can strike against the movement's sense of identity and can appeal to the hierarchy's sense of superiority. Andrew King quotes ridicule directed at the women's movement during the nineteenth century in this way: "How . . . funny it would be if Lucy Stone [a leader of the movement], pleading a cause, took suddenly ill in the pains of parturition, and gave birth to a fine, bouncing boy in court."[11] Opponents of the women's movement in the 1970s made many a joke about bra burning. This strategy can backfire if the movement has already been taken seriously by a broad segment of the public.

Crying Anarchy.

Andrew King uses the word *anarchy* in this strategy as a synonym for whatever the public fears most at any given moment.[12] If that is anarchy, the establishment accuses the movement of seeking anarchy. If the greatest fear is atheism, the establishment accuses the movement's leaders of being atheists. If the greatest fear is Communism, the establishment accuses them of being Communists. If the rulers can make such charges believable, a movement can be destroyed; at least the leaders of the movement will be diverted from their main tasks by the need to prove that they are not anarchists.

Setting Impossible Standards.

"It is an old truism," Andrew King continues, "that whoever is able to define the terms of a conflict situation wins. A common application of this is controlling the rules of a game in a way that shuts out or intimidates interlopers [outsiders]."[13] Socrates dominated his dialectical challengers precisely at the moment they accepted his definition of terms. In our electoral system the Republicans and Democrats have defined the election rules in such a way as to discourage third parties. In 1980, John Anderson ran hard to get on the presidential ballot (see Figure 8–2). Even when he succeeded, however, many political leaders predictably tried to discourage voters from turning to him simply because he was representing neither the Republican nor Democratic party. If Mr. Anderson had been a radical candidate, he would probably have experienced even greater difficulty.

Co-optation. When pressure from a movement becomes overwhelming — even if it is humorous, anarchistic, cannot measure up to standards, and has been so denounced — the movement can always be assimilated.[14] The movement can be assimilated in many ways. Its leaders can be welcomed with open arms and then forced into figurehead status. Radical student leaders are often invited to join college and university committees where they can be outvoted. The movement's ideas, in a weakened and compromised version, can be assimilated by legislative approval.

These are only some of the rhetorical strategies the establishment can use to defeat a movement. It's well to keep in mind, however, that the establishment can win without saying a word in response to the movement or without even taking notice of the movement. That is so because reformist and

Figure 8-2 Hierarchies set impossible standards in order to discourage opponents. For example, America's two-party political system discourages third-party presidential candidates, such as John Anderson who ran in 1980, by maintaining rigid election rules and by operating precinct vote-getting organizations around the country. (United Press International.)

revolutionary movements have the burden of proof. The present conditions, or status quo, will continue functioning unless the movement fulfills the demands of the burden of proof, thereby bringing change.

Conditions for Revolution

Parsons's Four Conditions

With this understanding of presumption and burden of proof in mind, consider what the late Talcott Parsons called the "four major broad sets of conditions which must be present if such a [revolutionary] movement is to spread widely and gain ascendancy in a social system."[15]

1. "The first condition is the presence in the population of sufficiently intense, widely spread and properly distributed alienative motivational elements."[16] This is the "need" or "problem" step of the burden of proof: a problem of such magnitude that it alienates large numbers of people. The problem cannot be distributed randomly; it must be clustered about particular issues such as inflation, recession, and unemployment. Widespread problems, however, can lead to crime and psychosomatic illness rather than revolution. A second condition is required.

2. "[The second condition is] namely, the organization of a deviant subcultural group or movement."[17] This second condition, the organization of a movement, has been discussed earlier, and it is included in the burden of proof by the assumption that someone will express this need or problem. The movement's leaders perform this function; the members provide security for each other through solidarity. Organizing a movement is not, however, enough to generate a revolution.

3. The third condition is "the development of an ideology — or set of religious beliefs — which can successfully put forward a claim to legitimacy in terms of at least some of the symbols of the main institutionalized ideology."[18] Parsons is saying that a "new idea or practice," a solution or plan, should be accepted in place of the old. In addition, Parsons is saying that the movement must propose an ideology that is consistent with the highest values of the society. The reader will recall from our analysis of the Declaration of Independence in chapter 2 that the values of this document's enthymeme were not even contested

by the British king; what was contested was the king's abuse of these values. For an opposite example, during the 1960s and early 1970s certain revolutionary movements in the United States produced no clear-cut plan or ideology, and seemed even to be proud of producing a "counter-culture."[19] Parsons was prophetic in seeing that such movements were doomed to failure. As early as 1951, Parsons predicted, "If, however, the culture of the deviant group, like that of the delinquent gang, remains merely a 'counter-culture' it is difficult to find the bridges by which it can acquire influence over wider circles."[20]

In short, Parsons was predicting in 1951 that revolutionary groups who are "counter" to the culture — counter in dress, action, and appeals — can never have wide enough appeal to gain ascendancy in the social system. Only by proposing an ideology *consistent with* (instead of *counter to*) the highest values of the society can they gain enough support to rise to the top.

4. "The fourth set of conditions concerns the stability of the aspects of the social system on which the movement impinges, and their relation to the equilibrium balance of the society."[21] This statement by Parsons also requires some "translation." Although there have been Socialist and Communist revolutions during the twentieth century in Russia, China, and Cuba, there have been no such "revolutions of the left" in any highly industrialized countries such as the United States, Japan, and Great Britain. The stability of industrial societies seems to be maintained by a power structure — a network of business, industrial, military, and banking leaders — which is not easily toppled or pushed over. By contrast, in prerevolutionary Russia and China the power structures were "peculiarly unstable" and easily pushed over.

Lenin's Plan

Edmund Wilson, a critic and historian, has paraphrased, with occasional quotations, the kind of revolutionary organizing and communicating called for by one of history's most famous revolutionaries — Lenin. I quote it at length so as to end as well as begin this chapter with a comparison and contrast between movements and organizations.

> The general organization of those working for revolution is to be dominated by a small band of persons, by the smallest number of persons possible, who have devoted their lives to this aim. It is easy for the political police to demoralize however large a movement which is loose and uncentralized; but it will be difficult for them to fight a movement directed by a permanent and secret staff who have themselves been trained, as the police have been, objectively to judge situations and to keep out of the hands of the authorities. This will set the

mass membership free to circulate illegal literature and engage in other forms of agitation—since the police, unable to catch the leaders, will have to give up trying to curb the activity—as well as guarantee them against the dangers of being diverted by demagogues, while [Lenin says] the "dozen experienced revolutionists will concentrate all the secret side of the work in their hands—prepare leaflets, work out approximate plans, and appoint bodies of leaders for each town district, for each factory district, and for each educational institution." "I know," he adds in a parenthesis, "that exception will be taken to my 'undemocratic' views, but I shall reply later on at length to this altogether senseless objection." The central committee will thus hold in its hands all the threads of the subsidiary bodies, but it will remain always apart from them and above them, set off from them by a sharp demarcation. This, so far from restricting the scope of the movement, will make it possible to include the greatest variety of revolutionary organizations—and not only working class organizations: trade unions, workers' circles for self-education and the reading of illegal literature; but also socialist and even simply democratic circles in all the other layers of society. And beyond these will be the fringe of sympathizers who are to be found in all walks of life: "office employees and officials, not only in factories, but in the postal service, on the railroads, in the Customs, among the nobility, among the clergy, even in the police service and at the Court," who will help them when they can. The party would not be in a hurry to admit such sympathizers as these to the heart of the organization; "on the contrary, we should husband them very carefully and should train people especially for such functions, bearing in mind that many students could be of much greater service to the party as 'abettors'—as officials—than as 'short-term' revolutionists."

Such a system, Lenin says, does not imply that the "dozen" will "'do the thinking' and that the rank and file will not take an active part in the movement. On the contrary, the crowd will advance from its ranks increasing numbers of professional revolutionists." As for the talk about the "broad principles of democracy," you cannot under a despotism like Russia's, have democracy in a revolutionary party any more than anywhere else. For democracy, you need first full publicity, and, second, election to all functions. The German Socialists can afford to have democracy, because even their party congresses are public; but how can there be anything democratic about a group which has to work in secret and which requires from its revolutionary following even a good deal more secrecy than it gets? How on earth can you have democratic elections where it is not possible for the rank and file really to know much about the outstanding workers, where even their identity is not known to most?[22]

Lenin's analysis of the requirements for organizing a revolutionary movement in Tsarist Russia is, ironically, no doubt applicable to the Soviet

Union today. The despotism brought about by Lenin's successful revolution in the Soviet Union requires the same kind of secret, disciplined, and undemocratic movement to be successful in bringing about another revolution.

At the time of writing, the situation in Poland suggests that the movement called Solidarity (a synonym for identification) may well have failed. The passage of time and study and analysis will help to explain why. Perhaps the movement and its leaders saw themselves as seeking reform while the Soviets and their satellite governments saw them as seeking revolution (see Figure 8–3). Perhaps totalitarian governments tend to view systematic attempts at change from outside government channels as revolution — something to be feared and crushed completely. And finally, if that is true, perhaps as Lenin suggested in the preceding quotation, a reform or revolutionary movement in a totalitarian state must act in a secret, disciplined, and undemocratic manner if it is to be successful.

Figure 8-3   Poland's union movement, Solidarity, drew worldwide attention in 1980-1981 when it defied the socialist government in a series of protest strikes. The group illustrates a deviant movement, Parsons's second condition for revolution. Here Solidarity's leader, Lech Walesa, is shown being carried through the streets of Warsaw during a rally in 1981. (United Press International.)

Summary

This chapter has noted similarities and differences between organizations and movements. The similarities include (1) the functions of leadership — formulation of purpose, securing essential services, establishing a system of communication — which must be performed in each unit and (2) the principles of increasingly unfavorable environment and increasingly unfavorable internal structure. The difference between the two entities is mainly the fact that certain rewards, threats, and controls available to organizational leaders are unavailable to movement leaders.

Reforms and revolutions differ because the former seek partial solutions while the latter seek total solutions. Revolutionary movements are more likely than reform movements to resort to violence and secrecy.

A dramatistic theory of movements sees movements in terms of three periods: inception, crisis, and consummation. This model can serve as a common denominator in studying the life cycle of movements.

The concepts of presumption and burden of proof have been brought forward from earlier chapters to show that movements must convince people the existing order is faulty and must recommend a new order. The establishment, on the other hand, need not prove anything to endure, unless the movements attain some degree of success.

The establishment tends to discredit a movement by such devices as ridicule, crying anarchy, setting impossible standards, and co-optation.

According to Talcott Parsons, the necessary and sufficient conditions for a successful revolution include alienation, an organized movement, symbolic legitimacy, and instability. A mere counter-culture is unlikely to produce a revolution or even much reform.

Finally, Lenin's principles for revolutionary organizing and communicating were presented, illustrating the secrecy and violence often associated with revolutionary, as opposed to reform, movements.

In the final chapter, we shall consider mass communication, which differs from other forms of communication in many ways.

Questions for Essays, Speeches, and Group Discussions

1. By using the files of your student newspaper for the late 1960s and early 1970s, chart the dramatistic life cycle of the student movements on your campus.

2. Without intending to be sacrilegious, Talcott Parsons saw a parallel between Marx and Jesus, Lenin and Saint Paul, Stalin and Constantine. Do research on these figures, and show the differences and the similarities between each pair.

3. Attack or defend this statement: Opposition to nuclear energy will be the most salient social and political movement of the 1980s and 1990s.

Additional Readings

Auer, J. Jeffery, ed. *The Rhetoric of Our Times*. New York: Appleton-Century-Crofts, 1969.

Bowers, John W., and Donovan J. Ochs. *The Rhetoric of Agitation and Control*. Reading, Mass.: Addison-Wesley Publishing Co., 1971.

Griffin, Leland M. "A Dramatistic Theory of the Rhetoric of Movements." In *Critical Responses to Kenneth Burke*, edited by William Rueckert. Minneapolis: University of Minnesota Press, 1969.

Simons, Herbert W. "Requirements, Problems, and Strategies: A Theory of Persuasion for Social Movements." *Quarterly Journal of Speech* 56(1970): 1–11.

Wilson, Edmund. *To the Finland Station: A Study in the Writing and Acting of History*. New York: Doubleday and Co., 1953.

Notes

1. Chester I. Barnard, *The Functions of the Executive* (Cambridge, Mass.: Harvard University Press, 1968), pp. 215–34.

2. Kenneth Boulding, *The Organizational Revolution* (Chicago: Quadrangle Paperbacks, 1968), pp. 22–23. Italics in original.

3. Herbert W. Simons, "Requirements, Problems, and Strategies: A Theory of Persuasion for Social Movements," *Quarterly Journal of Speech* 56(1970): 1–11. The quotation is from p. 4. Italics in original.

4. Ibid., p. 3.

5. Leland M. Griffin, "A Dramatistic Theory of the Rhetoric of Movements," in *Critical Responses to Kenneth Burke*, ed. William H. Rueckert (Minneapolis: University of Minnesota Press, 1969), pp. 456–77.

6. Ibid., p. 463.

7. Ibid., p. 464.

8. Ibid., p. 467.

9. Ibid., p. 468.

10. Andrew A. King, "The Rhetoric of Power Maintenance: Elites at the Precipice," *Quarterly Journal of Speech* 62(1976): 128.

11. Ibid.

12. Ibid., p. 130.

13. Ibid., p. 131.

14. Ibid.

15. Talcott Parsons, *The Social System*. Copyright 1951 by Talcott Parsons. Published by The Free Press, a Division of Macmillan Publishing Co., Inc. Reprinted by permission.

16. Ibid. Reprinted by permission.

17. Ibid., pp. 521–22. Reprinted by permission.

18. Ibid., p. 522. Reprinted by permission.

19. See Theodore Roszak, *The Making of a Counter Culture: Reflections on the Technocratic Society and its Youthful Opposition* (Garden City, N.J.: Doubleday and Co., 1969), p. xiii.

20. Parsons, p. 522. This book first appeared in 1951. Reprinted by permission.

21. Ibid., p. 523. Reprinted by permission.

22. Edmund Wilson, *To the Finland Station: A Study in the Writing and Acting of History*. Copyright © 1940, 1972 by Edmund Wilson, renewed 1968 by Edmund Wilson. Reprinted by permission of Farrar, Straus and Giroux, Inc., and Macmillan London Ltd.

CHAPTER

9

Mass Communication

The mind industry's main business and concern is not to sell its product: it is to "sell" the existing order, to perpetuate the prevailing pattern of man's domination by man, no matter who runs the society, and by what means. Its main task is to expand and train our consciousness – in order to exploit it.

The Industrialization of the Mind
Hans Magnus Enzensberger

But television has projected a walking replay of itself on United States streets.

Interfaces of the Word
Walter J. Ong, S.J.

Mass communication, by definition, is ubiquitous in our culture. It is everywhere. It's a handy term, but we forget the almost bewildering diversity of forms that are included under that heading. Television, radio, motion pictures, newspapers, and magazines are the predominant forms, but the concept also includes phonograph records, tapes, comic books, disco music, and direct mail advertising. Mass communication is the transmission of messages to be consumed by large audiences, sometimes measured in the millions. In recent years one of the most frequently analyzed forms of mass communication has been that of nationally broadcast presidential addresses (see Figure 9–1).

We shall begin by looking at the characteristics of mass communication that distinguish it from the other communicative forms covered thus far. Next, we shall examine three theories that describe the nature of mass communication and its role in society. Numerous scientific studies have been made to measure the media's impact on us. In this respect we shall explore the effect of media on society's leisure, attitudes, and violence. Finally, we shall review the humanistic theories of three leading thinkers on the subject of mass media: Hans M. Enzenberger, Marshall McLuhan, and Walter J. Ong, S.J.

Characteristics of Mass Communication

Mass communication differs from other forms of communication discussed in this book in several important ways. First, the messages are prepared not by individual persons but by organizations. As we have seen in the earlier chapter on organizations, communication is the internal means by which organizations produce goods and services. In the case of the *New York Times*, the Columbia Broadcasting System (CBS), and the Wadsworth Publishing Company, the very product is communication. The implications of this fact should be clear. For example, communication is both the means and end of such organizations.

A second difference is that the goal of mass media organizations (with few exceptions) is to make money. Television programing, in large, is an attempt to gain the attention of large audiences. Once that attention is secured, the products of other large business organizations are sold via commercial messages. We should not be surprised, then, if the content of such programing is often less than uplifting. To cite another medium, most magazines are sold for *less* than they cost to produce. An underpriced product is used to gain the attention of a large readership who cannot avoid the advertisements for products and services contained within the product. (It is an irony of broadcasting that advertising firms tend to overestimate their ability to influence the audience, while the commercial networks want to underestimate the effects of their programing—for example, the effects of violence—on that same audience.)

A third difference is that mass media feedback mechanisms lack the simultaneity of face-to-face communication. Feedback is delayed. Magazine circulation figures and the Nielsen ratings are two examples of such delayed feedback mechanisms. Mass communication is therefore less flexible and responsive than interpersonal communication.

A fourth difference is the diversity or heterogeneity of the audience. Mass audience analysis is carried out in detail. Surveys determine the demographic (characteristics such as age and income) attributes of intended and affected audiences. In some cases, a small audience of young affluent persons willing and able to buy products is preferred to a larger one lacking those characteristics. There is a kind of "feedforward," as the producers of mass communication try to analyze their audience to guess how audiences will

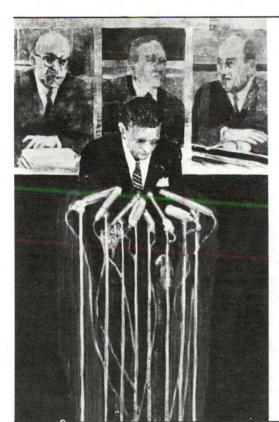

Figure 9-1. American presidents today rely heavily on mass media to garner support for their policies. Ironically, while mass media instantly takes a president's message to millions of listeners or viewers, the media's technology also distances him from his audience. The audience attends to an audio signal or video image, and the president receives delayed feedback in the form of polls and editorials. (James Gill: *In His Image,* 1965. Photo by Frank H. Thomas.)

respond to articles, films, and television shows. Actual responses of mass audiences prompt imitative behaviors. A successful disaster film begets other disaster films. A successful situation comedy begets spinoffs and imitations.

Theories of Mass Communication

Many different theories of mass communication have been developed, but no single theory has given us a complete understanding of the phenomenon. Let's look at three theories: the magic bullet, the two-step flow, and uses and gratifications.

The Magic Bullet

According to Wilbur Schramm, the prevailing theory of mass communication prior to World War II was the *magic bullet* approach. It was mechanistic in nature, assuming that messages were stimuli that could produce invariant responses from the target or receiver. The target was thought to be a passive listener; he or she reacted to the bulletlike message. As Schramm put it, "Communication was seen as a magic bullet that transferred ideas or feelings or knowledge from one mind to another."[1]

Since World War II and the advent of the electronic media (radio and television), the magic bullet theory has proved to be hopelessly simple and inadequate. Not everyone rushes out to buy toothpaste after being exposed to a commercial promising sex appeal. Audiences have proved to be more active than previously assumed. Different people "construct" the content of the mass media in different ways. Some viewers construed Archie Bunker of the recent television series "All in the Family" to be a desirable character, a hard worker, and good family man. Some construed him to be a bigot. Some construed him to be an accurate depiction of the American working class; others regarded him as a disfigured stereotype and atypical of the American worker. The "bullet," or message, was construed differently by different people.

Liberal intellectuals tend to view the content of television as an intellectual wasteland. Conservatives regard the media in general as tools of the liberal Eastern establishment. Radicals view the media as conservative in nature, serving the establishment and the status quo. We seem to be able to construe television to be whatever kind of scapegoat we want.

After World War II a series of research studies led to a new theory of mass communication. The "magic bullet" theory had regarded the media as powerful, perhaps all-powerful, in shaping the attitudes, values, and "consciousness" of audiences; the new theory did not posit such powerful media.

The Two-Step Flow

A study of the 1940 presidential election found that few of the voters in Erie County, Ohio, had been influenced by the media. Those who acknowledged that they had been influenced in their decisions identified the medium as an interpersonal one. They were influenced by "opinion leaders" during interpersonal communication. Thus, the theory was called the *two-step flow*: Messages transmitted via the media were received by opinion leaders or "local influentials," who, in turn, influenced other persons through interpersonal communication (see Figure 9–2).

Later studies seemed to support this hypothesis. For example, researchers tried to discover the process by which doctors were influenced to

Figure 9-2   "Local influentials" are the opinion leaders in a community who receive information via the media and then influence others around them in subsequent conversation. These Parisians, who are clustered around a TV to watch the 1981 installation of President François Mitterand, are all potential "local influentials." (©Guy Le Querrec/Magnum Photos Inc.)

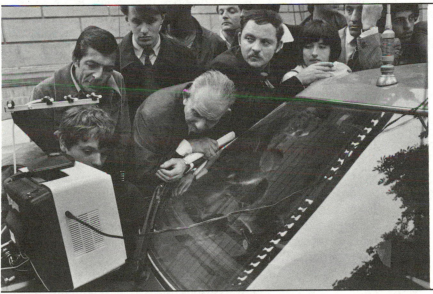

prescribe new drugs. The mass media in this case would be printed materials produced by drug companies and research published in scientific journals. Researchers found that doctors tended to be influenced by other doctors who had been exposed to the media and had tried the drugs. These doctors were the opinion makers or local influentials. Similar results were discovered in studies of how farmers came to plant a new hybrid seed corn.[2]

This theory enjoyed a widespread acceptance in the academic world. Let's look more closely at the idea. Several points should be emphasized. First, and this is sometimes used incorrectly as a criticism, the two-step flow is a theory of influence, persuasion, and rhetoric; it is not limited to the dissemination of information. (Communication is often defined in such a way as to exclude persuasion, influence, or rhetoric.)

Second, when examined closely, the "local influential" seems to project an "image" similar to that of ethos or credibility. The local influential is more knowledgeable than the follower by virtue of being exposed to the media, by personal contacts with experts, and so on. The opinion leader is often an acquaintance or friend judged to be trustworthy. The opinion leader is seen to have goodwill or good intentions toward the follower. In contrast, the politician seeking one's vote, the drug company trying to gain acceptance for a new product, the seed corn salesmen also pushing a new product — all have something material to gain from the target.

Third, most opinion leaders have opinion leaders. The doctor who is a local influential may know a researcher at a medical school in his state. That researcher may have a colleague, perhaps a former mentor, who serves as his or her opinion leader. Thus, one can theorize that society is a network of followers, leaders, leaders' leaders, and so on; the rhetorical constituents of ethos or credibility are the dimensions that define in a relative way the role to be played. One person's leader is another's follower; one person's follower is another's leader. We constantly measure ourselves against others in seeking the best advice before making a decision.

Fourth, the two-step flow revised the estimate of the media's power to influence the members of a society. The once powerful media were seen as relatively weak, at best supplying data to be used by opinion leaders in exercising interpersonal persuasion. As a result media research declined.

Then came the 1960s. In the words of Elihu Katz, perhaps the chief advocate of the two-step flow and the concept of weak mass media, "The first signs of revival of media research came in America in the 1960's, when the assassinations, the black revolt, the youth revolt, women's liberation, the Vietnam War, and, ultimately, Watergate, led to second thoughts about television."[3] Senior researchers in Germany and the United States were arguing for a "return to the concept of powerful mass media."[4]

In addition to the events of the 1960s there was another stimulus to the "new" view of the media — again according to Katz. This stimulus was the popular writings of Marshall McLuhan. We shall return to McLuhan in a later section of this chapter, but I can say at this point that McLuhan did persuade many theorists to consider that the power of the media is expressed not only in changed attitudes and behaviors but also as changes in modes of perception and cognition and in new patterns of seeing, hearing, and thinking.

Uses and Gratifications

The magic bullet theory emphasized reaction on the part of the mass media consumer. The two-step flow stressed interaction among consumers of mass media. The *uses and gratifications theory* gives a greater accent to action on the part of the consumer.

The other theories began by asking, What are the mass media doing to people? The uses and gratifications approach turns this around by asking, What are people doing with what they receive via the mass media? This approach is appropriate to the action orientation of this book because it supposes that both the producer and consumer act on the messages of mass communication.

If people are devoting a greater proportion of their time to mass media, they must be deriving a correspondingly greater proportion of their gratifications from the media. In discussing research on radio soap operas, Norman Felsenthal enumerated three main gratifications for the listeners:

> (1) They provided an emotional release for listeners; (2) they provided an opportunity for fantasy escape as audience members exchanged the dull routine of their own lives for a more exciting imaginary environment; and (3) listeners believed that the advice they obtained from fictional characters could be applied to help them deal with their own problems. It is very probable that these same three attractions are as valid for television viewers of daytime serials in the 1970s as they were for radio listeners in the 1940s.[5]

During the summer of 1981 there was a major league baseball strike. What did habitual baseball viewers do without major league games on the tube? As one of them, I watched videotapes of old games whose outcomes I knew. I watched baseball games telecast from Japan. I watched minor league games on television. I even watched part of a hypothetical all-star game that used videotapes of all-star players in regular games. In short, I sought a substitute gratification and can testify that it doesn't produce quite the same effect.

Felsenthal has divided media content into *fantasist-escapist* and *informational-educational*. The distinction is self-explanatory, but there seems to be a correlation between these categories and another pair—short-term versus long-term gratification. The fantasist-escapist gratification from a popular movie or television show would tend to be short term. The informational-educational gratification from your college textbooks would tend toward the long term because of the assumption that a college education will help you prepare for a better career and private life in the future.

In the rest of this chapter we'll attempt to assess the degree of the impact of mass media in a single case, television, by surveying scientific studies and the arguments of humanistic theorists and critics.

Scientific Studies of the Impact of Media

Effect of Media on Leisure

Probably the least controversial finding about television, and in some ways the most important, is that the tube determines what we do *not* do. Or, to put it more academically, "Television has revolutionized the leisure environment of Americans by not only affecting their allocation of time, but the options for the disposal of time."[6]

In the past two decades the amount of time devoted to televiewing has increased steadily. Citing studies of time allocation, George Comstock made the following generalizations: "Television has increased the time Americans spend on the mass media by 40 percent. Three-fourths of the time spent on the mass media is devoted to television. A third of leisure is devoted to viewing as the primary activity. Television ranks third behind sleep and work as a consumer of time."[7]

The increase in time devoted to televiewing during the past twenty years has left less time available for other activities. People today spend less time attending to other mass media such as radio and films. Interpersonal communication, both between and within families, has apparently declined (see Figure 9–3). A blaring, glowing television set also structures interpersonal communication. Conversations (and even arguments) center around program selection; programs punctuate the conversation, which tends to take place during the commercials. College-age readers of this book who find it difficult to conceive of life without television might well question their grandparents and others who lived before TV about their activities during that period — just to find out what the young today are missing.

Some evidence suggests that this increased viewing time is the result of *video addiction*, or a narcotizing effect of the medium. For example, consider this quotation from George Comstock:

Television is primarily approached as a medium rather than as a supplier of specific programs. People almost never include the desire to see a particular program when asked about their reasons for viewing, although three-fourths will affirm that the desire to see a particular program was a motive when the question is phrased that way. About a third acknowledged that what they view is determined by the channel that happens to be on or what someone else is watching. The concept of viewing for a particular program is not predominant.[8]

Additional evidence to support this time-consuming, addictive hypothesis is the remarkable stability in viewing habits. Sunday night is the peak viewing time; Friday night is the valley. Otherwise the television audience is stable at about eighty-three million individuals. This fact prompted a former National Broadcasting Corporation (NBC) audience researcher, Paul Klein, to develop a theory called "The Theory of the Least Objectionable Program." Inasmuch as over 90 percent of all viewing is attracted by the three commercial networks, Klein's theory asserts that TV addicts turn on the set, spin the dial to consider the three possible offerings and settle for a compromise — the least objectionable offering.[9] (Newspapers seem to create a similar addiction among regular readers. During a New York newspaper strike in 1949, Bernard Berelson sought to discover how readers coped with

Figure 9-3   One recognized effect of television on families is a reduction in communication between members. In this scene the children appear to be engaged in card playing, while the adults are silently transfixed by the television program. (Owen Francken/Stock, Boston.)

the absence of newspapers. The answer: They reread old newspapers until the strike ended.[10]) In summary, television has increasingly devoured the time of Americans (although we may have reached the saturation point), leaving less time for intra- and interfamily communication; this increased viewing period is stable, indicating an addiction that is relatively indiscriminate to content.

Effect of Media on Attitudes

Another question that has been pursued by scientific methods is, What effect does mass communication have on the attitudes of consumers? After surveying this research (up to 1967), Joseph T. Klapper gave testimony to a congressional committee. He made three main points. First, the persuasive effects of mass communication in the United States were found to be mainly reinforcing; that is, the views already held by the audience were buttressed or reinforced. Conversions were rare, and many of the converts admitted to being dissatisfied with the previous opinion *before* being exposed to the persuasive message. There are at least two reasons for this conservative finding: People tend to expose themselves to communication consistent with their own attitudes, and peer groups exert strong pressure to protect their norms from the threat of mass communication.

Klapper's second point is the exception to the first. Mass communication is extremely effective in *creating* opinion on "new" issues, or issues on which neither the individual nor the group has an opinion. An example of this (although not cited by Klapper) is the emergence of the ecological or environmental issue in the 1960s.[11]

On June 16, 1962, the *New Yorker* published the first of three installments of a condensed version of Rachel Carson's *Silent Spring*. The result was an uproar. The book was published in late September of the same year and quickly became a best-seller. Carson's attack on the uncontrolled use of pesticides and other chemicals brought praise from scientists and some counterattacks from pesticide manufacturers (a provoked countermovement). "CBS Reports" produced a documentary, "The Silent Spring of Rachel Carson," which was aired on April 3, 1963. The mass media of European countries repeated the book's warning that we were drenching the earth with DDT even though we had little knowledge of the ecological consequences, and what knowledge we did have was frightening. Attempts were made to block publication of the book, but these attempts were unsuccessful; in fact, the pesticide industry's counterattack brought about more publicity for the book. In the end, legislation was passed in the United States and other countries controlling, and in some cases totally banning, the use of DDT. It seems clear that most people in these countries had no position on the issue of DDT until Carson's remarkable magazine articles and book commanded the attention of television and other mass media.[12]

Klapper's third point was that people in the developing countries of the world, because of illiteracy and lack of technology, were unaware of many issues and therefore had no opinions about them. Such people are susceptible to the influence of mass media as filtered through opinion leaders.

Effect of Media on Violence

The third area of impact studies has to do with media violence. In 1969 Congress authorized the surgeon general to distribute one million dollars in support of studies of the effects of media violence. The studies were published three years later in five volumes. The findings were equivocal. One could argue from the findings that the media *do* and *do not* create violent behavior in consumers. One generalization, however, seems to be accepted by experts. According to Comstock, "the evidence supports the proposition that violence viewing increases the likelihood of subsequent aggressiveness on the part of the young."[13]

In reviewing the extensive literature on media violence, Felsenthal has identified three distinct hypotheses: the catharsis hypothesis, the imitative or modeling hypothesis, and the catalytic hypothesis.[14]

Catharsis Hypothesis. Catharsis is the act of purging emotions by observing the behavior of others. Thus, the catharsis hypothesis would hold that by watching violent behavior on television, we vicariously experience the act and are less likely to perform violent acts ourselves. According to this theory, a high content of violence in films and television should reduce the number of violent acts committed by the consumers. The research evidence gathered to test this theory is, at best, contradictory.

Modeling Hypothesis. This theory argues that children, and to a lesser degree adults, will imitate violent and aggressive behavior observed in films and television. Some evidence supports this hypothesis, but the methods used in the research are suspect. For example, children were shown films of adults beating an inflated Bobo doll. Then the children were taken to a room full of toys. After taking away all toys but the Bobo doll, the children were observed. Frustrated and limited by the removal of the other toys, the children did strike the Bobo doll. A criticism of this study is that an attack on a Bobo doll is not the same as a violent assault on human beings. Indeed, many parents encourage their children to purge their anger and frustration by hitting a Bobo doll.

Catalytic Hypothesis. According to this view, stable human beings do not imitate violent behavior depicted in the media. However, for some unstable persons predisposed to violent behavior, the media may be a catalyst and may even demonstrate new ways of expressing violence. For example, a film shown on television in 1974 depicted a gang of youths who burned to death a derelict with gasoline. Shortly thereafter a gang in Boston killed a woman in the same manner.

Each of these three hypotheses has some merit and probably explains some violence. Felsenthal feels that the "catalytic hypothesis seems to have the greatest validity."[15] I agree. The catalytic hypothesis is consistent with the truism about communication previously mentioned: People react to the same message in different ways; that is, some react violently, some nonviolently. The catalytic hypothesis is also consistent with the findings discussed earlier about the effect of the media in changing attitudes. Conversions are made when people are predisposed to change. Similarly, the catalytic hypothesis assumes that some people—the minority, fortunately—are more predisposed to violence than others.

Humanistic Theories of Mass Communication Impact

Some of the most interesting insights and theories of the mass media are generated not by scientific research but by the speculations of philosophers and rhetoricians. We shall consider the ideas of three such thinkers: Hans M. Enzensberger; Marshall McLuhan; and Walter J. Ong, S.J.

Hans M. Enzensberger

Hans M. Enzensberger, a German poet and philosopher of the "Frankfurt School," has formulated a radical criticism of the mass media and their effects on us. This effect he calls the "industrialization of the mind." Enzensberger attempts to shatter the illusion of the sovereignty of the mind. Most of us like to believe that the mind is a citadel or fortress, and that we are capable of making up our own minds. Enzensberger argues that the citadel has been invaded. Quoting Karl Marx, Enzensberger argues that what goes on in the mind has always been, and will be in the future, a product of society. In an oral society a well-established tradition determined that a few did the thinking for the many; the dependence of the flock on the priest, the pupil on the teacher, and the disciple on the master was taken for granted, straightforward, and visible.

Over the past hundred years, according to Enzensberger, this process has become cloudy and mysterious to the common man. The "mind-making" industry — the corporate worlds of television, newspapers, books, magazines, and advertising — is the culprit. This industry has grown so rapidly and in such diverse forms that the media of films, print, television, and public relations are conceived and analyzed separately and in terms of specific technologies and possibilities. "Hardly anyone," writes Enzensberger, "seems to be aware of the phenomenon as a whole: the industrialization of the human mind. This is a process which cannot be understood by a mere examination of its machinery."[16]

According to Enzensberger, the mind industry is the fastest growing of all industries, even including armaments. Therefore, the full deployment of the mind industry lies ahead of us in time; at this point it does not have full control of an essential sphere: education. The industrialization of instruction has barely begun; however, when completed, says Enzensberger, the mind industry will have total control. The purpose of the mind industry is to "sell" the existing order and to perpetuate in power those at the top. Four conditions are necessary to the existence of the mind industry:

1. *Enlightenment*. The mind industry cannot develop until the rule of theocracy, the people's faith in revelation and inspiration, is eradicated. The mind industry assumes independent minds, even when it attempts to eliminate that independence. The last theocracy in the world (Tibet) has vanished from the world; the first condition has been met.

2. *Human Rights, Equality, and Liberty*. This condition has been met in Europe by the French and Russian Revolutions and in America, Africa, and Asia by wars of liberation from colonial rule. These conditions need not be completely met; it is enough for people to understand the promise of human rights and to believe that it is desirable for each person to have a voice in the destiny of the social system. The discrepancy between the promise and the reality provides the mind industry with its "theater of operations." All authority seeks legitimacy and the consent of the governed. Coercion alone will not suffice. People must be persuaded, and in an industrial age all means at hand will be used to industrialize the mind.

3. *Economic Surplus Capital*. The society that cannot provide the necessary surplus capital for the buildup of the mind industry "neither needs it, nor can afford it."[17] Industrialization demands a constantly rising standard of education for the masses. With education people can achieve a mind of their own. The surplus capital generated by industrialization is plowed into the mind industry.

4. *Technology*. Given the kind of economic development discussed in point three, industrialization develops the last condition for the rise of a mind industry: the specific technologies upon which it is based. Note that we did not in the United States develop television sets and radio simultaneously with the discovery of electricity. Electricity was first harnessed to power, not communication. The dynamo and electrical motor preceded radio and television.

The technological conditions for the industrialization of the mind, says Enzensberger, exist everywhere on the planet; where the political and economic conditions have not been met in some parts of the world, it is only a matter of time before all four conditions will prevail. Enzensberger believes that the global mind industry will not be significantly different in capitalist as opposed to socialist systems. The reason lies in the service or function the mind industry provides.

> If you buy, you pay for [what you buy] in terms of its real cost of production; if you pick up a magazine, you pay only a fraction thereof; if you tune in on a radio or television program, you get it virtually free; direct advertising and political propaganda is something nobody buys — on the contrary, it is crammed down our throats. The products of the mind industry can no longer be understood in terms of a sellers' and buyers' market, or in terms of production costs: they are, as it were, priceless. The capitalist exploitation of the media is accidental and not intrinsic; to concentrate on their commercialization is to miss the point and to overlook the specific service which the mind industry performs for modern societies. This service is essentially the same all over the world, no matter how the industry is operated: under state, public or private management, with a capitalist or a socialist economy, on a profit or non profit basis. The mind industry's main business and concern is not to sell its product: *it is to "sell" the existing order, to perpetuate the prevailing pattern of man's domination by man, no matter who runs the society, and by what means. Its main task is to expand and train our consciousness — in order to exploit it.*[18]

If this seems to be a pessimistic view of the impact of the media, the reader should know that "contradictions" exist (according to Enzensberger) within the mind industry. First, in order for our leaders to gain our consent, they must grant us a choice, however small and deceiving it may be. Second, to harness the faculties of the human mind, those faculties must be developed. Third, the mind industry is so diverse and fragmented that it is probably not controllable. Fourth, the mind industry cannot function without enlisting the services of creative people. The media devour ideas and talent at a furious rate, and innovation and change preserve novelty. As we know, creative and innovative people can be troublemakers. Such people may from time to time be motivated to change the industry and the social system.

If Enzensberger is wrong, no harm has been done; he has simply forced us to consider important questions. If he is right, we learn that we are being exploited and can try to resist it. There is a liberating effect in reaching an understanding of how dependent we are.

Marshall McLuhan

I trust that my readers will give me high marks for courage (if not for clarity) for trying to summarize the thoughts of a writer who has been called by various commentators:

— a metaphysical wizard possessed by a spatial sense of madness;

— a Canadian Nkrumah who has joined the assault on reason;

— a distorter of immature minds and the sensibilities of the young;

— the highpriest of Popthink who conducts a Black Mass (for Dilettantes) before the altar of historical determinism;

— a writer who has looted all culture, from cave painting to *Mad Magazine*, for fragments to shore up against the ruin of his system;

— a very creative man who hits very large nails not quite on the head;

— the most important thinker since Newton, Darwin, Freud, Einstein and Pavlov.[19]

One way to an understanding of what Marshall McLuhan is saying is to know what he is doing. Few realize that McLuhan began his career as a rhetorical critic of literature (see Figure 9–4). McLuhan studied literature (and such authors as I. A. Richards, F. R. Leavis, T. S. Eliot, Ezra Pound, and James Joyce) at Cambridge University in England. Looking back on that experience, McLuhan reflected as follows:

> My study of media began and remains rooted in the work of these men. Thomas Nashe was a Cambridge pet in my terms there. I did my doctoral study on him, approaching him via the process of verbal training from the Sophists through Cicero and Augustine and Dante to the renaissance.[20]

Some of those writers, mainly James Joyce, were sensitive to human communication and the media, and McLuhan learned much from them. Then, and only then, did McLuhan turn his attention to the media. Whereas the rhetorical critics before him were concerned with the effect of rhetorical content on audiences, McLuhan sought to analyze the effect of media themselves, regardless of content, on human audiences.

McLuhan's basic idea is that "the medium is the message." McLuhan seems to mean that what the prevailing medium of an age does to its users is more important than what the content does. He has said that his point would have been easier to understand had he phrased it as "the medium is the massage"; thus, our brains and nervous systems are "massaged" by the media.

In the beginning was the word, and it was oral. Speech made for a certain kind of social system, the tribal village. This was a tightly knit system because oral communication requires the participants to be in proximity to each other. Because information could not be stored, people developed their memories to a far greater capacity than we do. Literature and history assumed the shape of tales that were told and retold.

When print technology became available, it changed the nature of people. Print proceeds a line at a time, left to right, with one line piled on top of another. Therefore, McLuhan claims, it created a kind of *linear logic*. Written communication could be conducted over long distances. From James Joyce, McLuhan learned that oral communication exists in time and that written communication exists in space. Oral communication is by nature "public," while reading and writing are "private" activities. Thus, print technology "detribalized" humans, allowing for the development of nation-states instead of villages.

Electronic media have "retribalized" humans. Radio and television allow us to know almost instantaneously the significant happenings in Uganda, Israel, Germany, New York, and Grand Rapids. We now inhabit a

Figure 9-4   Probably the most well-known and outspoken analyst of mass media in recent years has been Marshall McLuhan. A Canadian literary critic and professor of English, McLuhan wrote several popular books on the techniques and effects of media and coined the phrase "the medium is the message." (©Henri Dauman/Magnum Photos Inc.)

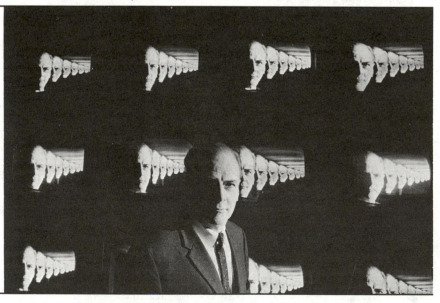

"global village" of interdependence. Television exists in time; it serves up a more "mosaic" fare than the linear mode of newspaper.

McLuhan became something of a media celebrity, particularly after the publication in 1964 of his book, *Understanding Media: The Extensions of Man*. He has also been the subject of fierce criticism. Some of it was directed at his use of "probes," or unreflected and incomplete forays into areas that he had not thought about systematically. Other criticism expressed the charge that he was an inexact, careless writer with concepts (such as "hot" and "cool" media) that are fuzzy at best and contradictory at their worst.

Two things must be said in his defense. First, as noted earlier, Elihu Katz credits him with creating a resurgence of the powerful media approach, and, thereby, being the stimulator of a new wave of research into media effects. Second, professional historians have acknowledged that from now on their accounts of the past will have to pay more attention to the roles of media specifically and of communication in general.

Walter J. Ong, S.J.

Although less popular with a mass audience than McLuhan, Father Walter J. Ong has also illuminated the media of the past and present with a humanistic approach. His writings are more precise and scholarly than McLuhan's.

In a series of books — *The Presence of the Word* (1967), *Rhetoric, Romance and Technology* (1971), and *Interfaces of the Word* (1977)[21] — Ong has delineated three main eras in human history. The first is called the period of "primary orality." Unlike writing, speech comes naturally to people, and it has an integrative effect. What anthropologists call the "savage mind" is simply called the "radically oral mind" by Father Ong. In most of the world this era has ended with the advent of writing and print. The second era, the "typographic age," has produced a deep alienation in modern societies because print technologies "separate the word from man and man from the word."[22] However, alienation has advantages as well as disadvantages. It does allow for progress. Consider Aristotle without writing. It seems inconceivable that he could have composed the *Rhetoric* or any of his books orally. Writing down thoughts a-line-at-a-time allowed for more systematic thinking.

Writing also encouraged the learning of a second language. The "mother tongue" is always learned orally (and is "feminine"); learning a second language, such as learned Latin, which is not spoken, requires that it be written down. Learned Latin was historically taught by men to boys (hence, "masculine") for the purposes of scholarship. Learned Latin held the real world, "with its passionate, rhetorical, practical concerns" at arm's length.[23] This detachment further encouraged analytic thinking. Thus emerged science. For centuries science was conducted, at least written, in Latin. (Although

Ong does not say so, this may have made science inaccessible to women in the past.) Only recently, that is, during about the past century, has science been conducted in vernacular languages such as English, and even that change was accomplished by injecting the vernacular with Latin terms and forms of thought.

Writing and print did have an alienating effect, but they also promoted science and analytic thinking. Indeed, the book index, first invented in the sixteenth century, was not practical with script. Two hundred handwritten manuscripts would need two hundred indexes because concepts would appear on different pages of the various scripts. These indexes would have to be prepared for each copy of the book. A printed edition of five thousand books needs only one index. The first visual information retrieval system was born in this way. The point of all of this is that writing and print changed our intellectual processes in dramatic ways.

Ong says that we have recently made another transition; we are now in the third era, "secondary orality." This period both resembles, and differs from, the period of primary orality. Radio and television have an oral, integrative function, but they depend on writers and scripts for their production. Closer to primary orality is the radio "talk show" in which listeners call a radio announcer and engage in a broadcast dialogue; the audience members become the "performers," and a kind of social integration is achieved.

We are being changed. As Ong puts it in an engaging line, "television has projected a walking replay of itself on United States streets."[24] The visually oriented intellect of the typographic era is being changed into a more open and oral mind. I am sure that some college students of today who have been raised with the electronic media as friends and babysitters find some college professors baffling. These professors constantly lament the deterioration of the visual skills (reading and writing) of their students without recognizing the value of oral-aural abilities.

Although we are changing, we are still caught in transition. The typographical era affected us in ways we are only beginning to perceive. Our *epistemology*, or our ways of knowing that something is true, is still visually oriented. In a culture of primary orality, hearing is believing. We, however, still cling to the typographical cliché that "seeing is believing." In an essay with the delightful title "I See What You Say," Ong catalogues (I almost wrote *shows!*) the visual terms we use in thinking about the intellect and knowing: *insight, vision, illuminate, clear, observe, demonstrate,* and *show* are but a few. According to Ong, "sight gives precision, but lacks intimacy: it operates only at a distance — eyeball-to-eyeball vision is impossible."[25]

This visual orientation may pass, but I doubt it. Although I generally agree with Ong, I differ with him on the following point. In describing the era of secondary orality he speaks of television as one medium that is basically oral. But for me, television's visual aspect is crucial. When the tape and film of the Vietnam War were brought into my living room, I was as much, if not more, affected by the pictures as by the words. The visual dimension of television seems to reinforce an oral orientation to knowing. Nonetheless, this is a relatively minor quibble with an *illuminating* and *insightful* analysis of modern communication.

Summary

Mass communication differs from other forms of communication in the following ways: (1) Messages are often produced by groups, even organizations; (2) the goal of mass media in our society is to make money by getting the attention of a large audience; (3) mass media mainly receive delayed feedback; and (4) mass media deal either with diverse audiences or carefully defined subaudiences.

Historically, the media have been considered powerful (the "magic bullet"); weak (the two-step flow); and again strong, particularly in shaping perception and cognition.

Scientific studies have led to the following tentative generalizations about television: (1) Increased televiewing has determined what Americans do *not* do with much of their leisure time; (2) the media are more likely to change attitudes on new issues or attitudes rather distant from direct experience; (3) some evidence (for example, the theory of the least objectionable program) suggests that Americans suffer from video addiction; and (4) the effect of television violence on viewers is probably best explained by the catalytic hypothesis, which says that unstable persons predisposed to violent behavior may respond to television violence as a catalyst.

Three humanistic approaches to mass media were considered. Hans M. Enzensberger has argued that mass media have the effect of creating the "industrialization of the mind." The four necessary conditions that allow the existence and the development of the mind industry exist everywhere on the earth; the mind industry's purpose is to "sell" and perpetuate the existing order and the existing patterns of domination, and to train our consciousness in order to exploit it. Marshall McLuhan, a rhetorical critic, has sought to analyze the effect of media themselves on audiences rather than the effect of the rhetorical content. He argues that the effect of the prevailing medium of the age is more important than the effect of the content. Walter J. Ong, S.J. has delineated three main eras in human history: primary orality, typographic, and secondary orality eras. Each of these eras, with its dependence upon written and/or oral messages, dramatically affects the intellectual processes of the culture.

Questions for Essays, Speeches, and Group Discussions

1. Monitor your local media, and make cross-comparisons of coverage given to an event by several media. Compare the coverage given by radio, television, and newspapers. Are there differences? If so, how can you explain them? If possible, talk to people involved in the events covered by the media for their reactions to the coverage.

2. What strategies should the leaders of reformist and revolutionary movements adopt in regard to mass media? Would these be the same for countermovements?

3. Attack or defend this statement: Hostile media coverage that leads to the ouster of political incumbents changes merely the cast, not the play.

Additional Readings

Comstock, George. "The Impact of Television on American Institutions." *Journal of Communication* 28(1978): 17–25.

Enzensberger, Hans M. "The Industrialization of the Mind." *Partisan Review* 36(1969): 100–111.

McLuhan, Marshall. *Understanding Media: The Extensions of Man*. New York: Signet Books, 1964.

Ong, Walter J., S.J. *Interfaces of the Word: Studies in the Evolution of Consciousness and Culture*. Ithaca, N.Y.: Cornell University Press, 1977.

Notes

1. Wilbur Schramm, "The Nature of Communication Between Humans," in *The Process and Effects of Mass Communication*, rev. ed., ed. Wilbur Schramm and Donald F. Roberts (Urbana, Ill.: University of Illinois Press, 1971), p. 8.

2. Elihu Katz, "The Two-Step Flow of Communication: An Up-to-Date Report on an Hypothesis," *Public Opinion Quarterly* 21(1957): 61–78.

3. Elihu Katz, "Looking for Trouble," *Journal of Communication* 28 (1978): 92.

4. Ibid.

5. Norman Felsenthal, *Orientations to Mass Communication* (Chicago: Science Research Associates, 1976), p. 32.

6. George Comstock, "The Impact of Television on American Institutions," *Journal of Communication* 28(1978): 20. Reprinted by permission.

7. Ibid. Reprinted by permission.

8. Ibid., p. 21. Reprinted by permission.

9. For a discussion of this theory, see Felsenthal, p. 12.

10. Bernard Berelson, "What 'Missing the Newspaper' Means," in *Communication Research, 1948 – 49*, ed. Paul Lazarsfeld and Frank Stanton (New York: Duell, Sloan & Pearce, 1949).

11. Joseph T. Klapper, *Basic Research in Persuasion and Motivation: The Capability of Communications Media to Influence Opinions on New Issues*. Testimony given at the Hearings before the Subcommittee on International Organizations and Movements of the Committee on Foreign Affairs, House of Representatives, 90th Congress (Washington, D.C.: U.S. Government Printing Office, 1967).

12. See Frank Graham, Jr., *Since Silent Spring* (Boston: Houghton Mifflin Company, 1970), p. x.

13. Comstock, p. 18. Reprinted by permission.

14. For a more complete discussion, see Felsenthal, pp. 35 – 37.

15. Felsenthal, p. 37.

16. Hans M. Enzensberger, "The Industrialization of the Mind," from the Consciousness Industry by Hans Magnus Enzensberger. English translation copyright © 1974 by the Seabury Press Inc. Used by permission of the publisher, The Continuum Publishing Corporation.

17. Ibid., p. 104. Reprinted by permission.

18. Ibid., p. 106. Italics added. Reprinted by permission.

19. Gerald E. Stearn, ed., *McLuhan: Hot and Cool* (New York: Signet Books, 1969), p. xiii.

20. Marshall McLuhan, Foreword, *The Interior Landscape: The Literary Criticism of Marshall McLuhan 1943 – 62*, ed. Eugene McNamara (New York: McGraw-Hill Book Co., 1969), p. xiv.

21. See my essay review of this third book in *Philosophy and Rhetoric* 11(1978): 282 – 89.

22. Walter J. Ong, S.J., *Interfaces of the Word: Studies in the Evolution of Consciousness and Culture* (Ithaca, N.Y.: Cornell University Press, 1977), p. 22.

23. Ibid., p. 35.

24. Ibid., p. 321.

25. Ibid., p. 135.

INDEX OF NAMES

INDEX OF SUBJECTS